The Chemistry of Breadmaking

You are holding a reproduction of an original work that is in the public domain in the United States of America, and possibly other countries. You may freely copy and distribute this work as no entity (individual or corporate) has a copyright on the body of the work. This book may contain prior copyright references, and library stamps (as most of these works were scanned from library copies). These have been scanned and retained as part of the historical artifact.

This book may have occasional imperfections such as missing or blurred pages, poor pictures, errant marks, etc. that were either part of the original artifact, or were introduced by the scanning process. We believe this work is culturally important, and despite the imperfections, have elected to bring it back into print as part of our continuing commitment to the preservation of printed works worldwide. We appreciate your understanding of the imperfections in the preservation process, and hope you enjoy this valuable book.

CHEM.
TX
769
G762c

PREFACE

THIS volume, on the application of science to the very important industry of Breadmaking, is put forward in the hope that it may fill in a gap which undoubtedly exists in the literature and text-books on this subject. It does not lay claim to any literary merit, but should rather be looked upon as an honest endeavour to assist learners who are groping in some amount of obscurity or darkness, with the dawn only just beginning to break. The majority of earnest students in breadmaking—and there are many—have not the same opportunities that are enjoyed by their fellows in other industries, in most of which there is a plethora of books, many of a very excellent character. For books the breadmaking industry at the moment is dependent upon the efforts of Mr. William Jago of Brighton, and Mr. John Kirkland of the School of Baking and Confectionery in the London Borough Polytechnic, in addition, of course, to several useful trade papers. This book is not intended to be a text-book on either chemistry or physics, but rather on the application of these and the kindred science of technical mycology to the subject of Breadmaking. It is advised that all who study its contents should do so in conjunction with some simple text-books on chemistry, physics, mechanics, and the elements of biology and botany.

Recourse has been had in a few instances to chemical equations, and whenever they have been used, the names of all substances taking part in the reactions have been inserted immediately below. As years advance, and a scientific education is given to the members of the trade generally, such an arrangement will become as unnecessary as it is in many other technical sciences dependent on a working knowledge of chemistry.

A large number of analytical figures are included in the little volume, which are quite original, and have not before been published. In other instances the sources of the information have been acknowledged. This has been considered advisable for reference sake, as very few of such exist to assist the student in his analytical studies.

If the book merits and receives the favourable consideration of the trade and allied industries, it is hoped that in future editions any imperfections may be eradicated, whilst its scope and usefulness may be greatly enlarged.

The author's thanks are due to his colleagues, Messrs. F. G. Richards, F.C.S., and Abraham Flatters, F.R.M.S., to the former for assistance in analytical work and proof-reading, and to the latter for kindly help in preparing many of the illustrations; also to his student, Mr. F. Robinson, B.Sc. Tech., for aid in the illustrations for the technical mycology portion of the work.

J. G.

MANCHESTER.

CONTENTS

CHAP.		PAGE
I.	INTRODUCTORY	1
II.	THE ATMOSPHERE. WATER	10
III.	ACIDS, ALKALIES AND SALTS	22
IV.	BAKERY PHYSICS: THERMOMETERS, BAROMETERS, AND CALCULATIONS	30
V.	HEAT AND PHYSICAL PROBLEMS	42
VI.	THE ORGANIC CONSTITUENTS OF THE CEREALS	55
VII.	THE CEREALS AND THEIR COMPOSITION	91
VIII.	MILLING, MEALS, FLOURS, MALTS AND EXTRACTS	102
IX.	FERMENTS, YEASTS, MOULDS, BACTERIA AND BARMS	125
X.	BREADMAKING PROCESSES AND BREADS	153
XI.	ANTISEPTICS AND BAKEHOUSE HYGIENE	172
XII.	FUELS AND OVENS	178
XIII.	THE ANALYSIS OF CEREAL FOODS	186
	BIBLIOGRAPHY	217
	INDEX	219

LIST OF PLATES

I. STARCHES . . . . *at page* 72

II. STARCHES . . . . ,, 73

III. (i.) WHEAT FLOWER. (ii.) SECTION OF WHEAT BERRY ,, 92

IV. (i.) SECTION OF A WHEAT ENDOSPERM. (ii.) SECTION THROUGH ALEURONE CELLS. (iii.) SECTION OF WHEAT GERM . . . . ,, 98

CHEMISTRY OF BREADMAKING

CHAPTER I

INTRODUCTORY

BREADMAKING and the kindred fermentation industry of brewing have been known and practised from the remotest ages of mankind. Long ages before the Christian era, the growing of wheat and other cereals, the preparation of the grain for the mill, the milling of the cleaned and prepared grain, and the conversion of the meal into cakes or bread both leavened and unleavened, have occupied the attention of mankind. To the German, French, and English explorers of the ruins of ancient Troy we are indebted for accounts of the wheat and barley growing in those early times and the certain knowledge that these cereals were used for the preparation of foods. The pyramids of Egypt, the mound tombs in North Africa and Asia, and the lake dwellings of Switzerland have all furnished evidence of the uses of wheat and barley, as the starting points for making bread and fermented liquids for the inhabitants of those ancient places. In the early chapters of the book of Genesis, an interesting account is given of the proclivities of one of the earliest Hebrews in making a corner in corn, and afterwards in selling the corn from his granaries to the famine-stricken nations around Egypt at enhanced prices.

Early Greek and Roman writers appear to have been intimately acquainted with both breadmaking and brewing. For example, the elder Pliny in his writings makes a statement to the effect that flour yielded one and a third times its weight of bread.

In our own country, the Anglo-Saxons were adepts in the art of making cakes and mead. In all cases, in these early times, the word 'flour' refers to meal, and this was produced by crushing the wheat in hand-stone mills or 'querns.'

The evolution of the present-day white loaf has been a question of time like that of any other important industry, and to trace it step by step would be a study of considerable interest, but entirely outside the scope of this work.

In order to produce bread of great food value, a loaf pleasing to the sight, palatable, easy of digestion and assimilation, and, above all, composed of three out of the four proximate principles of foods, is a work requiring much skill and manipulative power in addition to a general knowledge of flours and other raw materials. This implies that the modern, scientific baker should possess a working knowledge of such sciences as those of chemistry, physics, biology, botany, mechanics, and mathematics.

Chemistry is that branch of physical science which has for its chief object the study of the composition of matter. For convenience sake the study of chemistry is divided into two parts—*inorganic* and *organic*. The former deals with the forms of matter known as the non-metals or metalloids and the metallic bodies, together with the derivatives of both; organic chemistry has for its object the consideration of the carbon compounds and their derivatives. The same laws of combination, the same forces and all other influences affect the compounds of both groups equally, but as there are so many thousands of the carbon bodies it is better to consider them separately.

Matter is made up of almost infinitely small particles, the atoms and molecules. An *atom* is generally defined to be the smallest quantity of matter that can enter into chemical combination and can rarely exist in the free state; whilst a *molecule* is composed of two or more atoms and is the smallest quantity of matter that can exist in the free state. Matter under different conditions of temperature and pressure exists in three states: gaseous, liquid, and solid. Each of these three may be either elementary or compound matter.

An *element* or elementary matter is that which is composed of particles all of the same kind, as, for example, sulphur, iron, oxygen, etc., while a *compound* or chemical compound is composed of two or more elements in a state of chemical combination, as, for example, water, sugar, butyrin, gypsum, etc.

At the present time there are about eighty so-called elements recognised, but this number is not by any means a fixed one, for almost every year fresh additions are made to the list. The elements are divided into two groups: the non-metals or metalloids, and the metals.

The *metals* are characterised by possessing some of the following properties :—

They possess a bright shining surface or lustre when seen in the lump; they are of high specific gravity or are said to be dense compared with the non-metals; are good conductors of heat and electricity; possess ductility, malleability and tenacity; form alloys or mixtures of metals which contain not only the properties of the constituent metals as enumerated above, but in addition certain special ones; and in most cases they have a characteristic appearance or fracture when broken across or torn apart. All the known metals, with the single exception of mercury—a bright, very heavy, shining liquid—exist in the solid state.

Non-metals rarely possess any of the above properties, except a few of the solid ones such as sulphur, phosphorus, silicon, and arsenic, which approximate somewhat closely to the metals in a few of their properties. The metalloids, with the exception of bromine—a dark, heavy, reddish-brown, strongly smelling liquid—exist either as gases like hydrogen, oxygen, nitrogen, chlorine, etc., or as solids, for example, as carbon, iodine, boron, selenium, tellurium, and the four previously mentioned non-metals.

All the gaseous bodies, whether elementary or compound, conform to all the laws affecting gases, viz., those concerning the relation between volume and pressure, those of combination, diffusion, and so forth.

The important *laws of chemical combination* are :—

(1) The law of combination in fixed and definite proportions by weight.

(2) The law of multiple proportions.

(3) The law of reciprocal proportions.

To these laws of combination is attached the name of the Manchester chemist—John Dalton—who attempted to explain them by his Theory of Atoms.

The law of the *Conservation of Matter*, allied to that of the conservation of energy, points out that the sum of matter in the universe is fixed and unalterable. Matter can neither be created nor destroyed; all that is possible is to change its form. Chemical force, or the force of chemical affinity, tends to produce a permanent change in the form of matter, while physical forces tend to produce only a temporary change. For example, if cream of tartar and bicarbonate of soda, both perfectly dry, are ground together in a mortar, there has been formed simply a mixture of the two compounds, just as when sand and sugar are intimately mixed; but if the molecules of the two compounds are by any means brought so close that they actually touch, as, for example, when water is brought into them, then chemical combination ensues forming the new compounds, Rochelle salt, and carbonic acid gas (CO_2).

A chemical equation is an expression of the law of conservation of matter, for the sum of the substances taking part in the reaction is equal to the sum of the products obtained. These equations are usually expressed by symbols, which will now be explained.

The names of all the elements are expressed by a letter or letters, something like a form of shorthand. Similarly, the compounds are represented by bringing the symbols standing for the constituent elements close together.

The symbols also represent the relative weights of the atoms, or the relative quantities by weight which enter into chemical combination.

INTRODUCTORY

The more common non-metals and metals, their symbols, atomic weights and states of matter, are given in the table:

Non-Metals.				Metals.			
Name.	Symbol.	At. Wt.	State.	Name.	Symbol.	At. Wt.	State.
Argon	A	39·88	Gas	Aluminium	Al	27·10	Solid
Arsenic	As	74·96	Solid	Calcium	Ca	40·09	,,
Bromine	Br	79·92	Liquid	Copper	Cu	63·57	,,
Carbon	C	12·00	Solid	Gold	Au	197·20	,,
Chlorine	Cl	35·46	Gas	Iron	Fe	55·85	,,
Fluorine	F	19·00	Gas	Lead	Pb	207·10	,,
Hydrogen	H	1·008	Gas	Magnesium	Mg	24·32	,,
Iodine	I	126·92	Solid	Mercury	Hg	200·00	Liquid
Nitrogen	N	14·01	Gas	Potassium	K	39·10	Solid
Oxygen	O	16·00	Gas	Sodium	Na	23·00	,,
Phosphorus	P	31·04	Solid	Tin	Sn	119·00	,,
Sulphur	S	32·07	Solid	Zinc	Zn	65·37	,,

All chemical reactions may be expressed by equations. The bodies taking part in the reaction are placed on the left-hand side of a sign of equality =, whilst the products formed go on the right side of the sign. *Example.*—When silver nitrate solution is brought into a sample of water containing common salt, silver chloride—a white curdy compound insoluble in the liquid—and sodium nitrate are formed.

This may be expressed in the following way :—

$$AgNO_3 + NaCl = AgCl + NaNO_3$$
$$\text{Silver Nitrate} \quad \text{Sodium Chloride} \quad \text{Silver Chloride} \quad \text{Sodium Nitrate}$$
$$(107\cdot88+14\cdot01+16\times3) + (23+35\cdot46) = (107\cdot88+35\cdot46) + (23+14\cdot01+48)$$
$$169\cdot89 + 58\cdot46 = 143\cdot34 + 85\cdot01$$
$$228\cdot35 = 228\cdot35$$

It is the usual custom to write down the symbols as shown without the figures, which are here used to prove that the compounds taking part in the reaction are equal in weight to the products obtained.

Another example is as follows :—

Carbon dioxide gas, employed in the aerated water

industry, is prepared by decomposing pieces of marble with sulphuric acid.

$$\underset{\substack{\text{Marble or}\\\text{Carbonate}\\\text{of lime}}}{CaCO_3} + \underset{\substack{\text{Sulphuric}\\\text{acid}}}{H_2SO_4} = \underset{\substack{\text{Carbon}\\\text{dioxide}}}{CO_2} + \underset{\substack{\text{Calcium}\\\text{sulphate}}}{CaSO_4} + \underset{\text{Water}}{H_2O}$$

The sources of the non-metals and metals.—Many of the non-metals exist in the free state in nature, *e.g.* argon, nitrogen, and oxygen in the atmosphere; most of the remainder, owing to their active chemical properties, are found in a state of combination with one or more elements in which combination they form the acidic group, as chlorides, bromides, sulphides, fluorides, phosphates, carbonates, sulphates, and others.

A number of the lighter metals exist wholly in the combined state with the acidic groups of the metalloids, the metals taking the part of the base. Many of the heavy metals exist in the free state.

The combinations of the metals with the non-metals as existent in the solid crust of the earth give rise to a large number of important industries.

Aluminium is a typical instance of this. It exists in combination with oxygen and with oxygen and water. The oxide, corundum or emery, is used in the grindery and polishing trades. The combination with oxygen and water is known as bauxite or the hydrated oxide of aluminium, a body largely employed in the extraction of the metal itself, in the preparation of alums, aluminium sulphate, alumino-ferric, and in the manufacture of the artificial ultramarines. The ultramarines are used for whitening low grades of sugars, as the blue bag in laundries and by confectioners, for staining paper, etc. The clays are double silicates of aluminium; these are the starting points of the china, earthenware goods, and coarse red pottery industries. Asbestos is another mineral of the double silicate aluminium group, giving rise to a wide range of employment.

Calcium is another metal which in its combinations as

existing in nature gives rise to a large number of industries. It is only necessary to call to mind marble, limestone, chalk, pearls (all various forms of carbonate of calcium), or the sulphate as gypsum and selenite, or the apatites and other phosphates of lime, to see in the mind's eye a wonderful vista of industries; but enough has been written to show the value of a good general knowledge of chemistry.

Physics is a branch of natural science which has for its consideration the effects of force on matter. Like the science of chemistry it is studied for the sake of convenience under a number of divisions, as pure and applied physics; also under the terms—light, sound, heat, magnetism and electricity. Of these, light, heat, and electricity are of much importance to the baker; for example, a knowledge of light and optics is helpful in microscopy and polarimetry; electricity is used as a motive power and for lighting purposes; heat is an all-important subject affecting practically every branch of a baker's work. Each of these three branches of physical science will be considered in its proper place.

At this point it is only necessary to draw attention to the part taken by *heat* in assisting to bring about and hasten chemical reactions. One of the chief effects of heat on the different forms of matter is to expand it in all its dimensions, and when the source of heat is withdrawn most bodies contract again to their original form and size, demonstrating that a physical force tends to produce a temporary change in the form of matter. But heat also causes the force, chemical affinity, to act; as previously pointed out, chemical action does not take place except when the reacting particles are in actual contact. Heat when applied expands the particles until they do actually touch, then the force of chemical affinity acts and causes a combination of the particles, thus forming a new compound or compounds. For instance, some powdered iron and flowers of sulphur are ground together in a mortar, yielding a greenish-yellow mechanical mixture, the component parts of which may be readily separated either by using a magnet to withdraw the iron powder, or by shaking up the mixture with water, in which case the iron particles owing to their greater density fall to the bottom of the water while the sulphur remains on the surface. If, however, a portion of the mixture is gently heated, the particles first expand, then the sulphur melts; actual contact now takes place, and a new body is formed which is of a permanent character. The equation representing this reaction is as follows:—

$$Fe + S = FeS$$
$$Iron + Sulphur = Sulphide\ of\ iron$$

That FeS is a different body from the mixture of iron and sulphur may be demonstrated by bringing a few drops of acid on each. With the iron sulphide the nauseous-smelling sulphuretted hydrogen and a salt of iron will be obtained;

$$FeS + H_2SO_4 = H_2S + FeSO_4$$
$$Iron\ sulphide + Vitriol = Sulphuretted\ hydrogen + Iron\ sulphate$$

In the case of the mixture:—

$$Fe + S + H_2SO_4 = H_2 + FeSO_4 + S$$
$$Iron + Sulphur + Vitriol = Hydrogen + Iron\ sulphate + Sulphur$$

Biology is another of the physical sciences, which, on the one hand, is closely associated with botany, or the science dealing with the members of the vegetable kingdom, and, on the other, with zoology, the science that treats of animal life. With this latter the baker is not directly concerned; but that portion of biology which has for its object the consideration of life-action is of especial importance to him as it helps him to understand the part played by vital functions in fermentation. Without yeasts and barms the baker would be unable to place before the general public the wholesome, palatable product that appears on the table at every meal; hence the baker is compelled to give some slight attention to biology.

Nor has he time to neglect **botany**, which takes into consideration all that concerns the wheat and other cereals from which the daily carbohydrate food of the people is prepared. Everything that tends to improve wheat, so that flours better in all their properties are milled from it, is of the utmost interest to the trade. Moreover, a baker must not forget that division of botany, known as the *Cryptogamia*, for it has the group of microscopic fungi as one part of its many members. Unless he knows something of moulds and bacteria, his bread, flour, and cakes may suffer from this lack of knowledge.

In the modern machine bakery the master or bakery manager must understand something of **mathematics** and the sister science of applied mathematics or **mechanics**. These sciences deal with the construction and arrangement of machines, their speeds of running, gearing, pulleys, and all else that affects the driving mechanism. Add to this a good general knowledge of steam, then the master baker and his manager are in some ways fitted to cope with the things that come into the daily life of a baker. There is scarcely an industry of any importance that requires so much general information on the part of those engaged in it as that of breadmaking.

The commercial side of the business does not come within the scope of this or any book. Book-learning may assist it in some slight degree, but there is nothing like being deeply engaged in it to stimulate one's energies to make an effort to grasp this part of the many-sidedness of a baker's life.

CHAPTER II

THE ATMOSPHERE. WATER

THE word 'atmosphere' is derived from two Greek ones, *atmos*, vapour, and *sphaira*, a sphere or globe. It is the name given to the gaseous elastic fluid which envelops the earth's globe to a depth of about two hundred miles and exerts a pressure of 14·73 lbs. on every square inch, or 1033 grams per square centimetre of surface. The temperature as well as the density of this envelope decreases with increase of height from the earth's surface, and therefore the pressure also diminishes. For example, one volume of air at the sea-level expands to two volumes at slightly over half a mile in height; at a height of a mile and three-quarters it has expanded to eight volumes; while at three and a half miles it has become sixty-four volumes.

Previous to the Christian era it was known that air possessed weight. This was confirmed by Galileo in A.D. 1640 and by Torricelli and Pascal in 1643. One litre (1·76 English pints) of dry air in the latitude of Paris weighs 1·2934 grams, in London 1·29318 grams, and in Manchester 1·293 grams.

In the seventeenth century Hooke and Mayow pointed out that the atmosphere contained at least two substances, one that aided combustion—now known as *oxygen*—while the other—*nitrogen*—did not. In its chemical composition the air is a mixture of gases which varies according to position and circumstances; thus, normally it contains 20·833 per cent. of oxygen and 79·167 per cent. of nitrogen, both by volume; or approximately every five volumes of air consist of one volume of oxygen and four of nitrogen. The composition by weight of pure, dry air is 23·005 per cent. of oxygen and 76·995 of nitrogen.

In addition to the foregoing elements, ordinary air contains carbon dioxide, water vapour, ammonia and its salts, traces of ozone, nitric acid and other bodies. Associated with the nitrogen are the so-called nitrogen gases—argon, helium, krypton, and neon.

The atmosphere of towns contains numbers of impurities which differ somewhat with the trades established in the area; thus, sulphur dioxide and trioxide, particles of sooty matter, white arsenic, hydrochloric acid, etc., may be found. A large number of researches show that the composition of ordinary pure air is not by any means constant; for example, in various parts of the northern hemisphere the quantity of oxygen by volume averages 20·95 per cent., on high mountains about 20·94 per cent., in the Polar regions 20·90 per cent., and in crowded rooms and buildings from 20·22 to 20·45 per cent. During the dense fogs which often prevail in large towns, it has frequently been demonstrated that the amount of oxygen is much below the normal, while that of the *carbon dioxide* is augmented.

This latter gaslike water vapour may be looked upon as a regular constituent of the atmosphere, and like water vapour its quantity is variable. Black of Edinburgh in the eighteenth century was the first to prove its presence in air, and he recognised it as being the same gas as that which is set free in the burning of limestone and chalk. He further showed that carbon dioxide gas converted caustic alkalies into mild alkalies or alkaline carbonates. The normal amount in the air is from three to four volumes per ten thousand. In thickly populous areas this quantity is often doubled and trebled; in crowded rooms or public conveyances the quantity rises to an objectionable amount, as, for example, was formerly the case in London Underground Tube stations. Mr. D. A. Sutherland in 1902 showed that the carbon dioxide during morning and evening heavy traffic was from 11·0 to 20·46 volumes per ten thousand of Tube air. Anything above eight parts per ten thousand of air should be looked upon as deleterious to animal life, especially when accompanied by the noxious exhalations from the lungs of persons suffering from consumption and other pulmonary diseases. A table of comparison between the composition of ordinary and respired air is added :—

Constituents.	Ordinary air.	Respired air.
Nitrogen, . .	79·03 per cent.	79·03 per cent.
Oxygen, . .	20·94 ,,	16·99 ,,
Carbon dioxide, .	0·03 ,,	3·98 ,,

Carbon dioxide passes into the atmosphere from the following and other sources :—

The respiration of animals and certain plants.

The decay of organic matter.

The combustion of coal, coke, wood, and other carbonaceous bodies.

From subterranean causes.

Its presence and approximately a rough idea of any excess may be shown by the rapidity with which a film of calcium carbonate forms on a surface of clear, fresh lime water exposed in a soup-plate to the atmosphere. The physical processes of diffusion distribute this gas through the constituents of the air, while its amount in country districts is kept normal by the action of vegetation in assimilating it with the help of moisture, chlorophyll and sunlight; and also by the rain in all districts, which dissolves it and carries it down into the earth or into the streams.

Ammonia and its compounds exist in air to the extent of less than one per cent. Ozone, hydrogen peroxide, and nitric acid occur only in mere traces or not at all. Hayhurst and others have proved by means of kites that in the upper atmosphere, from five to thirteen miles, none of the three last-mentioned compounds occur.

Aqueous or *water vapour* is the most variable constituent, as its quantity changes with the degree of saturation, temperature and character of the earth's surface. In the

British Isles, air at 32° F. (0° C.) contains less than one per cent. by volume, but at 60° Fah. rather more; while in tropical land areas it is fully four times as much. At ordinary temperatures in a room an adult person respires about two-thirds of an ounce of water per hour. Its presence may readily be detected by placing some ice in a glass of water and noting the condensation of moisture or dew on the outside of the glass; or it may be observed by exposing on a plate dry caustic soda, which quickly becomes moist in the air owing to the absorption of the water vapour. The relative humidity or degree of moisture for house temperatures should lie between 64 and 72 per cent.

It will be seen from the foregoing statements that the atmosphere is composed of a mixture of elementary and compound gases together with some solid floating particles, all of which vary slightly in amount according to the prevailing circumstances.

The atmosphere over thickly-populated land areas contains countless myriads of very minute forms of plant life known as the micro-organisms, the most important and widely distributed of which are the ubiquitous *bacteria*. Many groups of these exercise a beneficent influence over animal life, but others, especially the pathogenic or disease-producing groups, have a destructive effect.

In concluding this chapter on the air it is advisable to emphasise the important part played by oxygen in killing disease and filth germs, in oxidising poisonous organic matter from animal and vegetable sources, and in its purifying action on rivers, vegetable and animal life; it is also the chief agent in all combustions.

The average composition of a thousand volumes of air may be approximately summarised as under:—

Nitrogen and its gases,	779 volumes.
Oxygen,	207 ,,
Water vapour,	13 ,,
Carbon dioxide, ammonia and its compounds, sooty particles, etc.	1

During recent years the gases of the atmosphere have been liquefied by the compression, cooling, and expansion principle of Hampson and Lindé. The liquid air is homogeneous, of faint blue colour, and extremely cold. It may best be preserved for a short time in silver-coated, double flasks, the space between the two being rendered as vacuous as possible.

WATER

Pure water is a chemical compound formed by the combination of the two gases, hydrogen and oxygen, as, for example, when hydrogen is burned either in oxygen, or in air which contains the latter gas. The natural waters occur in the oceans, seas, lakes, rivers, streams, subterranean waters and springs, and in the clouds as aqueous vapour. All such natural waters contain gases, liquids, and solids dissolved in them. Some of these are looked upon as impurities, whilst others are necessary ingredients of a drinking water.

The chemical composition of water may be determined either volumetrically or gravimetrically, *i.e.* either by the relative volumes or relative weights of its constituents. The composition by volume was shown by Humboldt, Gay-Lussac, and others to be two volumes of hydrogen combined with one of oxygen to form water. The reverse reaction may be carried out by electrolysing water, in which case it is split up into two volumes of hydrogen and one of oxygen. A little later in the nineteenth century, Berzelius, Dulong, Dumas, and Stas, worked out the composition by weight, and established the fact that 11·136 parts by weight of hydrogen combine with 88·864 parts of oxygen to form a hundred parts of water; or, water contains one-ninth of its weight of hydrogen, and eight-ninths of oxygen.

Pure water is a clear, tasteless, odourless liquid, which, when seen in bulk, possesses a pale greenish-blue colour. It is a poor conductor of heat and electricity, and is almost incompressible. One cubic centimetre at 4° C. weighs one

WATER

gram, and one pint, which consists of twenty ounces, weighs one and a quarter pounds, so that a gallon weighs ten pounds avoirdupois.

Water, according to the temperature and pressure, exists in the three states of matter, solid, liquid, and gaseous. Thus, if the temperature is at 0° C. (32° F.) or lower, water exists in the forms of ice and snow. Between 0° and 100° C. (212° F.) it is a liquid. At temperatures above 100° C. it becomes a gas or vapour.

In order to change it from the solid to the liquid state, heat is required, and as this cannot be registered by a thermometer, it is spoken of as 'latent' or hidden heat. Similarly, in passing from the liquid to the gaseous state, about seven times as much heat is necessary. *Latent heat* is defined to be the quantity of heat required to bring about a change of state in the matter without a rise of its temperature. Thus, if it is desired to convert one pound of water at 212° Fah. into steam at the same temperature, 967 British heat units must be brought into the water. On the other hand, when steam is condensed to water, the same quantity of heat is evolved. Use is made of this property to raise quickly the temperature of cold water, other liquids, and mixtures of liquids and solids.

It is both useful and instructive to study the change of volume in water as it is gradually heated from 32° to 212° F. From 32° a given volume of water continuously contracts until it reaches 39·2° F. At this point it is denser than at any other temperature. One cubic centimetre (1 c.c.) at 32° weighs 0·99987 grams, while at 39·2° the same volume weighs exactly one gram. This is said to be 'the point of maximum density for water.' From 39·2° towards 212° the volume continuously expands, and consequently becomes less dense. One volume of water at 212° F. yields 1696 volumes of steam. The *specific gravity* (sp. gr.) of steam, or its density compared with hydrogen, is 9·0, but compared with air, it is $\frac{9\cdot00}{14\cdot45}=0\cdot622$. (Air is 14·45 times denser than hydrogen.)

When water is converted into ice an expansion takes place, 100 volumes of water becoming 107 volumes of ice. The sp. gr. of ice compared with water is $\frac{100}{107}=0.9436$, which accounts for ice floating on the surface of water. Pure distilled water at 39·2°, or more generally at 60° F., for the sake of convenience is taken as the standard of comparison for the relative density or sp. gr. of liquids and solids.

Among the more important properties of water is its great solvent power. It is spoken of as the almost universal solvent.

By solvent power is meant the property that water and other liquids possess of overcoming the force of cohesion which binds the particles of solids together, or of being miscible with other liquids. A very large number of substances when shaken up with water rapidly disappear or are said to be dissolved. Most of these are more readily soluble in hot than in cold water. For example, 100 parts by weight of water at 32° F. dissolve 13·3 parts of nitre or potassium saltpetre. At 122° F. 86 parts are soluble, while 247 parts dissolve at 212° F.

Gypsum or calcium sulphate is an exception. This salt is less soluble in boiling than in cold water. Sodium chloride or common salt is almost as soluble in cold as in hot water. Gases, on the other hand, are less soluble in hot than in cold liquids.

Owing to its solvent powers the water that exists in nature invariably contains substances in solution. It often also has floating particles or substances in suspension. These latter settle out or may be removed by filtration.

The substances in solution vary in different localities according to the rock formations, soils, manuring of the land, and other causes. The presence on the land of cattle and sheep, the manuring and the decaying of vegetable matters and other refuse are causes of organic impurities in a water supply. The weathering of rocks introduces mineral matters that are responsible for the hardness of a water.

WATER

Some of these mineral salts, such as common salt and gypsum, possess antiseptic properties. When present in excessive quantities these check the fermentative action of the yeast. This is noticeable in the waters of the great Cheshire plain which come from the New Red Sandstone rocks, and also in the Burton waters, which owe their origin to the Keuper beds in that district. Frequently the smaller towns and villages on the seacoast, in which the water supply is drawn from wells, are troubled by the brackish character of the water. Mablethorpe on the Lincolnshire coast is an interesting case in point.

Water fit for drinking and for the manufacture of foodstuffs like bread and confectionery goods should be free from organic impurities and at the same time not too hard. Organic impurity may be destroyed by exposing the water freely to the air, either by passing it down a series of stone steps, by filtering it through specially devised filter-beds, by running it in a shallow broad sheet over sills, or by a combination of these methods. This exposure to plenty of light and air has also the effect of considerably diminishing the bacterial content of a water. If a water is excessively hard, as, for example, the supplies from limestone and chalk areas, it may be softened by heating it so as to decompose the bicarbonates of lime and magnesia, then filtering or allowing to settle; or by mixing suitable chemicals with the water and then filtering, or settling. For example, a Derbyshire water may readily be softened by the addition of milk of lime in the proper proportions and allowing the treated water to settle. Another common reagent for the purpose, suitable for many waters, is ordinary soda-ash, a crude dry form of carbonate of soda. On a small scale for washing and domestic uses, except for cooking, both soap and borax will be found useful.

It should be remembered that very soft pure waters, as well as those of an acid character, readily attack and dissolve lead, and then become highly poisonous. Such waters must not be conveyed by means of leaden pipes. Other poisonous bodies liable to occur in the natural waters are salts of iron and copper.

The following is a useful classification of waters :—

(1) Alkaline waters, in which the chief salts in solution are the compounds of sodium and potassium.
(2) Calcareous waters, the chief salts present being bicarbonates of lime and magnesia.
(3) Saline waters. These are of two types : (a) brackish, (b) gypsum. The latter contain chiefly sulphates of lime and magnesia, while the brackish waters contain excessive quantities of common salt.
(4) Siliceous waters. These are generally very soft pure types of water, and hence eminently suitable for all domestic purposes.
(5) Waters of no special type, in which there are no predominating salts.

Examples of some typical waters.

(1) *Manchester tap water*.

Calcium sulphate ($CaSO_4$),	1·728	grains per gallon.
Magnesium sulphate ($MgSO_4$),	0·587	,, ,,
Magnesium chloride ($MgCl_2$),	0·513	,, ,,
Sodium chloride (NaCl),	0·491	,, ,,
Oxides of iron, alumina, silica,	0·252	,, ,,
Organic matter including traces of nitrites and nitrates,	0·774	,, ,,
Total solids,	4·345	,, ,,

Total hardness 2°, all of which is permanent.

The Manchester water supply is a good example of a

WATER

pure soft siliceous water suitable for domestic, breadmaking, and boiler-feed purposes.

(2) *A Burton brewing well water.*

Calcium sulphate ($CaSO_4$),	22·968	grains per gallon.
Magnesium sulphate ($MgSO_4$),	8·895	,, ,,
Potassium sulphate (K_2SO_4),	6·672	,, ,,
Calcium carbonate ($CaCO_3$),	11·065	,, ,,
Magnesium carbonate ($MgCO_3$),	2·757	,, ,,
Sodium chloride (NaCl),	9·094	,, ,,
Potassium chloride (KCl),	1·874	,, ,,
Iron carbonate ($FeCO_3$),	0·573	,, ,,
Silica (SiO_2),	0·691	,, ,,
Organic matter,	traces	
Total solids,	64·589	,, ,,

A typical hard water from the Keuper Marls, well suited for brewing pale ales, and malting purposes.

(3) *A calcareous water from a London chalk well* (Steel).

Calcium carbonate ($CaCO_3$),	18·88	grains per gallon.
Magnesium carbonate ($MgCO_3$),	0·28	,, ,,
Sodium chloride (NaCl),	1·94	,, ,,
Sodium sulphate (Na_2SO_4),	0·74	,, ,,
Potassium silicate (K_2SiO_3),	0·65	,, ,,
Potassium sulphate (K_2SO_4),	0·38	,, ,,
Potassium carbonate (K_2CO_3),	0·26	,, ,,
Silica (SiO_2),	0·69	,, ,,
Organic matter,	0·73	,, ,,
Total solids,	24·55	,, ,,

CHEMISTRY OF BREADMAKING

(4) *An Edinburgh water of no particular type* (Steel).

Calcium sulphate ($CaSO_4$),	11·69	grains per gallon.
Magnesium sulphate ($MgSO_4$),	10·90	,, ,,
Sodium sulphate (Na_2SO_4),	4·46	,, ,,
Calcium carbonate ($CaCO_3$),	19·86	,, ,,
Magnesium carbonate ($MgCO_3$),	5·48	,, ,,
Sodium chloride (NaCl),	11·71	,, ,,
Potassium chloride (KCl),	2·86	,, ,,
Silica (SiO_2),	0·68	,, ,,
Organic matter,	1·56	,, ,,
Total solids,	69·20	,, ,,

Both the above waters are suitable for brewing and malting, but not for other purposes without careful softening treatment.

Mineral waters are useless either for domestic or breadmaking purposes. Medicinally, however, they are of considerable value.

The more important English mineral springs are those of: Epsom, containing magnesium sulphate or Epsom salts; Tunbridge Wells, which are chalybeate or iron waters; Cheltenham, containing Glauber's salt or sodium sulphate; Droitwich and Nantwich, famous for their brine baths; Buxton, Bath, and Leamington, which are mixed mineral waters; Harrogate, where there are two classes, the one containing sulphuretted hydrogen gas and mixed mineral salts, and the other mixed mineral salts alone.

The effect of waters of different classes in baking.—This question must be considered from the hygienic point of view, and also from that of the action of the mineral salts existing in the waters.

Pure, wholesome bread cannot be made from water contaminated either with sewage or decomposing vegetable matter; hence water in a bakery must be free from all forms of organic impurity. Soft and alkaline waters possess great extractive properties ; in addition they affect the protein constituents as gluten and permit of its being more readily modified and degraded. Hard waters, especially of a gypsum type, have an entirely opposite or retarding effect. Moreover, very strongly impregnated gypsum waters check the action of yeast by the antiseptic properties of this salt. Gypsum has also a general binding influence on flour, following in this the action of sulphates generally, and further causes bread after cutting to quickly become dry. This is very noticeable in the case of prize loaves at exhibitions, in which sulphate of lime has been employed as an improver of the texture.

CHAPTER III

ACIDS, ALKALIES, AND SALTS

THESE three groups of substances exist in the three states of matter, viz., gaseous, liquid, and solid.

ACIDS

The word ' acid ' takes its origin from ' acetous,' the name primarily given to the sour-tasting liquid obtained by exposing weak alcoholic wines to the atmosphere.

Acids possess most of the following properties : A sour or acid taste, resembling that of vinegar. The power of changing the vegetable dye litmus from blue to a red shade of colour. The neutralising of alkalies with the formation of salts and water, and the power of dissolving some of the more common metals, metallic oxides, hydrates, and carbonates.

Acids are classified as :—

(1) Mineral acids, or those which are prepared from minerals, as

Hydrochloric acid or ' spirits of salt ' (HCl);
Nitric acid or ' aqua fortis ' (HNO_3):
Sulphuric acid or ' vitriol ' (H_2SO_4);
Sulphurous acid (H_2SO_3);
Carbonic acid (H_2CO_3);
Phosphoric acid (H_3PO_4); and
Boric or boracic acid (H_3BO_3).

(2) Vegetable or organic acids, those which contain carbon as an essential constituent, *e.g.*

Acetic or the acid of vinegar ($C_2H_4O_2$);
Oxalic acid ($C_2H_2O_4$);
Lactic acid ($C_3H_6O_3$);
Tartaric acids ($C_4H_6O_6$), etc.

ACIDS, ALKALIES, AND SALTS

Occasionally acids are classed as the hydracids or those containing no oxygen, *e.g.* HCl; and the oxyacids or those which contain that element, *e.g.* HNO_3, etc.

Hydrochloric acid (HCl) is a strongly fuming gas obtained by the action of vitriol on common salt. It is also collected as a by-product in the manufacture of salt-cake.

The gas is very soluble in water, yielding the solution in which form it is sent into commerce.

It yields the series of salts known as the chlorides, of which sodium chloride (NaCl) is the best-known member.

Sodium chloride occurs as rock-salt and brine, from which sources the butter salt and fisheries salt, as supplied to the baking trade, are prepared. Settled brine is run in a continuous stream into a long shallow iron pan heated from below. If the temperature of evaporation is near the boiling point of the brine, a fine, granular salt separates out which is raked to the side of the pan, drained, purified, and sent out as butter salt. Such a product as supplied by the Cheshire manufacturers often contains 99 per cent. of pure NaCl.

When the temperature of evaporation is somewhat below the boiling point, say about 200° F., larger crystals of a shell-like structure are formed. These are raked to the side, drained and dried. Such a salt is not quite so pure as the previously mentioned butter salt, but it has the advantages of being easily soluble in water and cheaper. Bay salt is prepared by allowing sea-water, such as the Mediterranean sea-water, which contains about four per cent. of NaCl besides other bodies, to evaporate under the sun's rays in shallow rock tanks that are filled at high tide. Bay salt, though very suitable for medicinal purposes, is not fit for breadmaking.

The uses of salt in a bakery.—The most important use is that of conferring flavour on bread and other goods. The quantities employed vary in different districts for the same type of bread, and for various types very considerably.

For straight doughs the quantities are from 2½ to 4 lbs. per sack of 280 lbs. of flour.

For ferment and dough, and sponge and dough processes, the salt used varies from 3 to 5 lbs. Where very slow processes of fermentation are common, the quantity of salt may go up to 7 lbs.

For English tin bread the average is 3 lbs. per sack. It should be remembered that any quantity above 3½ lbs. can readily be tasted, whilst at the same time it destroys the delicate flavour and aroma of high-class bread.

Salt is also a strong antiseptic and germicide; hence care must be taken not to use too much or it may check the fermentative action of the yeast. Again, salt exerts a considerable influence in toughening and strengthening the gluten in a dough, while it assists the outside colour and bloom of bread and smalls.

Where other antiseptics cannot be obtained, strong hot brine is an excellent remedy against lactic, butyric, and other bacteria which lurk in the cracks, crevices, and corners of bakery appliances and of the bakery itself.

Nitric acid (HNO_3) is a dense, heavy liquid, colourless when pure, but often of a yellowish shade owing to the presence of free oxides of nitrogen. This acid may be obtained by heating well-dried Chili saltpetre ($NaNO_3$) with strong vitriol. It is a strongly corrosive liquid that is used in the preparation of high explosives like gun-cotton, nitro-glycerine, and blasting gelatin. The ancients, who knew it as *aqua fortis*, prepared by its aid lunar caustic or silver nitrate ($AgNO_3$), a salt used in weak solution for detecting the presence of chlorides in drinking water. Potassium nitrate, nitre, or saltpetre (KNO_3), is a product of the action of nitrifying bacteria on nitrogenous matter in soils. Nitre is largely employed in preserving such flesh-foods as tongues and hams, and also in the manufacture of gunpowder.

Sulphuric acid or **vitriol** (H_2SO_4) when pure and strong, is a heavy, oily liquid, even more corrosive than nitric acid. It is manufactured by several different processes, but all

ACIDS, ALKALIES, AND SALTS

depend on the burning of sulphur or a sulphide in air to form sulphur dioxide, the oxidation of this to sulphur trioxide, and the absorption of this latter gas by water. The salts of this acid, which is dibasic, are the acid or bi-sulphates and the normal salts as sulphate of lime.

Sulphurous acid (H_2SO_3) is a solution of sulphur dioxide gas in water, which solution smells strongly of burning sulphur. Its salts, the bisulphites, like the acid, are powerful antiseptics, and for this reason are largely used in bakeries for sterilising the various parts of the plant. The gas (SO_2) is also employed in bleaching hops, grain, straw, and isinglass, etc. The normal sulphites are valueless as antiseptics.

Carbonic acid (H_2CO_3), a solution of carbon dioxide in water, although a weak acid, yields two series of well-known salts, the normal and bicarbonates. The bi- or acid-carbonate, may be prepared by passing CO_2 into a solution of caustic alkali, e.g. $NaOH + CO_2 = NaHCO_3$, bicarbonate of soda, a salt employed in conjunction with cream of tartar for aerating purposes. Both carbonates of the alkali metals are manufactured in alkali works in enormous quantities and thus give employment to thousands of persons.

Phosphoric acid (H_3PO_4) and its salts are prepared either from mineral phosphates, as apatite, coprolites, etc., or from animal bones, or from spent char materials.

The acid itself is sent into commerce as sticks of glacial phosphoric acid, in the powdered form, or in solution. A weak solution is largely employed by flour millers to steep a portion of the wheat of their grist, as it is said to improve the flour. The normal phosphate of lime and its acid salt are also used by both bakers and millers as bread improvers. The acid- or super-phosphate is a common constituent of cream powders, which are cheap substitutes for high-class aerating materials in confectionery goods.

Boric or **boracic acid** (H_3BO_3) occurs in nature in weak solution, but it is mainly prepared from the natural borates such as borax. This acid and the salt borax are powerful antiseptics, and as such are used in considerable quantities for the preservation of food-stuffs, especially milk, butter, bacon, broken eggs, vegetables, and fruits. They are also constituents of ointments, salves, and other preparations.

The vegetable acids will be considered in a later chapter.

ALKALIES

The name 'alkali' is given to substances, spoken of as bases, most of which are obtained from the lower oxides of a number of metals, and which in solution possess some of the following properties :—

A soapy taste and feel; they soften and dissolve the skin; change neutral or red litmus solution to blue; and neutralise acids, forming salts and water, whilst many of them attack and dissolve metals, such as zinc, aluminium, and others, evolving hydrogen gas.

Alkalies are either caustic, as caustic soda (NaOH) and caustic potash (KOH), or mild, the latter name being given to metallic carbonates which possess alkaline properties.

The more common are: certain compounds of sodium, potassium, ammonium, lithium, calcium, magnesium, etc., which possess the previously mentioned properties.

SALTS

Salts are compounds composed of a base or bases combined with an acid.

Those salts, the base of which is a metal, are known as metallic salts, e.g. NaCl, KNO_3, $CaSO_4$, etc. These may be normal, or acid, or basic salts. Such salts may be prepared in a variety of ways, of which the following are the more common :—

(1) By substitution of a metal for the hydrogen of an acid, as when zinc is dissolved in sulphuric acid:

$$\underset{\text{Zinc}}{\text{Zn}} + \underset{\text{Vitriol}}{H_2SO_4} = \underset{\text{Zinc sulphate}}{ZnSO_4} + \underset{\text{Hydrogen}}{H_2}$$

The salt is zinc sulphate.

(2) By the combination of an acid-forming oxide with a

ACIDS, ALKALIES, AND SALTS

base, as SO_3 (sulphur trioxide) with the base CaO (lime), forming $CaSO_4$ (calcium sulphate).

(3) By the exchange of hydrogen and metal between an acid and hydrate or hydroxide, as

$$HCl + NaOH = NaCl + H_2O$$
Hydrochloric acid + Caustic soda   Sodium chloride + Water

This illustrates the neutralising of an acid with an alkali, forming a salt and water. When the whole of the hydrogen of an acid is replaced by a metal, then the salts are said to be normal ones; but when only a portion of the hydrogen is replaced, one or more acid or bi-salts are obtained, as in the case of phosphoric acid and its salts. This acid forms a normal and two acid salts, viz., K_3PO_4, K_2HPO_4, KH_2PO_4. This latter salt exists as the potassium phosphate of wheat and flour, and is one of the causes of flour possessing an acid reaction.

(4) By the combination of a normal salt with an acid-forming oxide, e.g.

$$Na_2SO_4 + SO_3 = Na_2S_2O_7$$
Sodium sulphate + Sulphur trioxide   Pyrosulphate of soda

or,

$$K_2CrO_4 + CrO_3 = K_2Cr_2O_7$$
Potassium chromate + Chromium trioxide   Potassium dichromate

(5) Basic salts are those formed by the combination between a normal salt and a basic hydrate or hydroxide. *E.g.* if lead nitrate solution be boiled with lead hydrate, basic lead nitrate is formed:

$$Pb{<}^{NO_3}_{NO_3} + Pb{<}^{OH}_{OH} = 2Pb{<}^{NO_3}_{OH}$$
Lead nitrate + Lead hydrate   Basic lead nitrate

Similarly, the formation of the basic lead acetate, which is so largely used as a clarifying agent in the polarising of sugar solutions, is a combination of this character.

In addition to metallic salts in which the acid is a mineral one, there are many salts the base of which is a metal, but in which the acid is a vegetable or organic one.

E.g., the ordinary soaps are sodium and potassium salts of fatty acids; cream of tartar is the acid-potassium salt of tartaric acid.

Further, the hydrogen of an acid may be replaced by an alcoholic group, as in the case of many of the flavouring essences, fats, etc., used in the trade. Hence the fats, and many compound ethers or esters, are true salts. In the case of the fats, the base is the alcohol glycerin, and the acid is one of the many fatty acids; therefore the butyrin, olein, palmitin, and stearin of butter are salts.

The inorganic constituents of the cereals.—These bodies are intimately associated with the salts, of which they are almost wholly composed. A chemical analysis of the mineral matters or ash will show these to be made up of bases or oxides of metals, especially those of the alkalies and earthy metals, combined with acid-forming oxides of the non-metals.

The quantities of the constituents differ considerably for each of the different cereals, as may be seen by noting the composition of the mineral constituents of the ash of wheat and barley given in Chap. VII., p. 100. There it will be seen that two salts in each stand out prominently, *the phosphates of potassium and magnesium*. The other salts are present only in much smaller proportions. These two phosphates form the chief salts in the ash of all cereals, as may be noticed in text-books on foods. The bases—oxides of potassium, magnesium, calcium, iron, and sodium—make up approximately 45 per cent. of the ash of wheat, while the acid-forming oxides of phosphorus, sulphur, and silicon, with minute quantities of chlorine, comprise the remaining 55 per cent. The only other inorganic constituent of wheat is water. The bases together with the phosphoric anhydride and water yield the phosphates.

The mineral phosphates are obtained by plants from the soil, whilst the soil gets its supply by the weathering or breaking up of the phosphatic rocks in the earth's crust by natural forces such as rain, frost, the sun's heat, and certain constituents of the atmosphere, especially oxygen and carbon dioxide gases. The element phosphorus, owing to its intense affinity for oxygen in the presence of moisture, never exists in the free state; but in the combined condition it becomes an important factor in all food substances, in the bones of animals and the embryos both of vegetable and animal life. The chief compounds of this element are the oxides and oxyacids and salts derived from these. Phosphates of calcium and magnesium exist in the bones of animals, and from this source many of the phosphorus compounds in common use are prepared. The soluble or super-phosphate of lime and free phosphoric acid are used in some of the so-called bread improvers, and also for sprinkling the semolinas during the milling of flour with the object of strengthening weak flours. The acid phosphate of potash is one of the causes of acidity in plant life and products derived therefrom.

CHAPTER IV

BAKERY PHYSICS

IN studying the subject of heat, two kinds of measurement are recognised : quantity of heat, and heat level or intensity of heat ; hence, two kinds of instruments are required in taking measurements.

Calorimeters are used in the first case, and thermometers for registering the intensity of heat and cold.

THERMOMETERS

Many different varieties of thermometers are in common use, but in the baking trade only three are of importance : the ordinary mercurial, the pyrometer, and the maximum and minimum instrument of the Sixe type. A wet and dry bulb psychrometer is also useful in determining the humidity or hygrometric conditions of the bakehouse.

The construction of a mercurial thermometer.—A piece of special glass tubing possessing a capillary bore, regular and even throughout its length, is first thoroughly cleaned, then a suitable bulb is blown at one end. The bulb and tube are filled with pure, clean, dry mercury, and the contents boiled, after which the tube is sealed off. It is allowed to rest for a short time and then graduated by bringing the lower portion of the instrument into melting ice ; the point at which the mercury column becomes constant being marked on the stem. Then the whole thermometer is immersed in steam at the pressure of the atmosphere and the position of the mercury column again marked on the stem. The first mark registers the freezing point, and the upper one the boiling point of water. The

THERMOMETERS, THERMOMETRIC SCALES 31

space between is divided evenly according to the scale to be used. Thus on the Fahrenheit it is divided into 180 divisions, and on the Centigrade into 100, each of which is a degree. The two thermometric scales in common use are the Fahrenheit and the Centigrade or Celsius.

Fahrenheit fixed his graduations as zero, the lowest temperature obtained by mixing together snow or ice and salt, the freezing point of water at 32°, and the boiling point at 212°. Thus between freezing and the boiling points of water there are 180°.

On the Centigrade instrument 0° is the freezing and 100° the boiling point of water.

Hence, F.° : C.° = 180 : 100, or 9 : 5.

The little diagram of Fig. 1 will serve to illustrate the relations between the two scales. These scales may easily be converted from the one into the other by observing that 9° F. = 5° C., and making the allowance of 32 in dealing with the Fahrenheit.

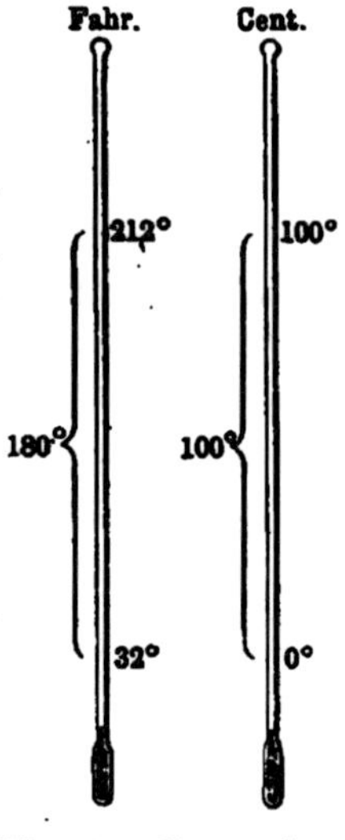

Thus to convert F.° to C.° :
$$(F.° - 32)\tfrac{5}{9} = C.°.$$

To convert C.° to F.° :
$$(C.° \times \tfrac{9}{5}) + 32 = F.°.$$

Three examples will make this quite clear :

It is required to convert 212° F. into C.°.

$$212° - 32° = 180, \text{ and } \frac{180 \times 5}{9} = 100° \text{ C.}$$

It is required to find the corresponding F. temperature to 360° C. :

$$\frac{360° \times 9}{5} = 648, \text{ and } 648 + 32 = 680° \text{ Fah.}$$

Prove that −40° C. corresponds with −40° F. :

$$\frac{-40° \times 9}{5} = -72, \text{ and } -72 + 32 = -40° \text{ F.}$$

Fig. 1.—Comparison of Thermometric Scales.

Or the converse:

$$-40° \text{ F.} - 32° = -72, \text{ and } \frac{-72 \times 5}{9} = -40° \text{ C.}$$

Fahrenheit thermometers bent at an angle of 90° are frequently used for registering oven temperatures. Provided that they are not required to indicate higher readings than about 650° F. (343·3° C.), they are sufficiently accurate. Above this temperature the readings approach the boiling point of mercury (678° F., 359° C.). In these and other cases, especially for cheapness, instruments known as **pyrometers** are commonly used. Of these there are many varieties. For example, Wedgwood, the famous potter, devised a pyrometer which depended on the contraction of a piece of baked clay ; Siemens invented an electrical one ; but for a baker's oven, two different metals or metallic alloys are soldered together to form a solid bar or ribbon. The differences in the expansion and contraction of the dissimilar metals is utilised to move an indicator arranged on a dial. Expansions move the indicator up towards the highest divisions, while contractions cause it to work in the opposite direction on the clock-face-like dial. Bakers' pyrometers generally range from 200° to 700° F.

Maximum and minimum thermometers are of use in the bakehouse to register the highest and lowest temperatures respectively. The wet and dry bulb thermometer, or Mason's hygrometer or **psychrometer**, is also a useful instrument in the bakery, since, as already mentioned, it gives the baker information regarding the amount of moisture present in the atmosphere of the bakery, and may thereby tend to prevent the ' skinning ' of surfaces of dough exposed.

BAROMETERS

Barometers are instruments employed for measuring the pressure of the atmosphere. They are of two types : the mercurial and the aneroid. The simplest form of barometer consists of a glass tube of regular and even bore throughout its length of about thirty-three inches. One end is sealed and the other left open. The tube is carefully filled with pure dry mercury, all the air bubbles removed by heating, and the tube then inverted in a cup or other reservoir containing mercury (Fig. 2). It should be so fixed as to allow the mercury to pass up and down the tube easily.

If the barometer is placed at the normal sea-level with a temperature of 60° F., the mercury column, when measured from the level in the reservoir, should stand at a height of 29·922 inches, or approximately 30 inches. If the bore is of one square inch section, the quantity of mercury in the column supported by the pressure of the air on the mercury in the reservoir is found to weigh 14·73 lbs., thus giving rise to the popular statement, 'The weight of an atmosphere is 15 lbs.' A water barometer would require a tube of about 35 feet in height, as the normal height of a water barometer is about 34 feet. A barometer, as its name indicates, is used for measuring the pressure of the atmosphere. Pascal, a celebrated French savant, demonstrated the value of a barometer for this purpose by carrying his mercurial instrument up the highest peak of the Puy-du-Dôme in France, and noting the gradual fall of the mercury until he reached the top, at which point the level became constant. His figures showed that for every ninety feet in height ascended the column dropped one-tenth of an inch.

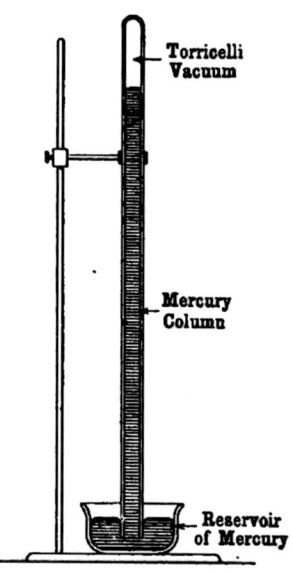

Fig. 2.—A Mercurial Barometer.

THE METRIC SYSTEM OF WEIGHTS AND MEASURES

In all scientific work the metric system of weights and measures is commonly used, therefore it is essential that students should possess a knowledge of the system. This decimal system owes its origin to the French philosopher, Gay-Lussac, who flourished about the end of the eighteenth century.

There are three chief units in the system, viz. :—

The **metre,** or unit of length, which equals 39·371 inches.

The **gram,** or unit of mass (weight), which equals 15·432 grains.

The **litre,** or unit of capacity, which equals 1·761 pints.

The subdivisions of the units are :—

deci—which equals 0·1, or $\frac{1}{10}$ of the unit.
centi— ,, ,, 0·01, or $\frac{1}{100}$,, ,,
milli— ,, ,, 0·001, or $\frac{1}{1000}$,, ,,

The multiples are :—

deka—which equals 10 times the unit.
hekto— ,, ,, 100 ,, ,,
kilo— ,, ,, 1000 ,, ,,

Thus in linear measure—

1 millimetre = 0·039371 or nearly $\frac{1}{25}$ of an inch.
1 centimetre = 0·39371 inch.
1 decimetre = 3·9371 inches.
1 metre = 39·371 inches.
1 dekametre = 393·71 inches.
1 hektometre = 3937·1 inches.
1 kilometre = 39,371 inches, or 1093·6 yards, or 0·621 miles.

In the measure of mass or weight—

1 milligram = 0·015432 English grains.
1 gram = 15·432 English grains.
1 kilogram = 15,432 English grains.

7000 grains = 1 lb. avoir., therefore a kilogram is equivalent to $2\frac{1}{5}$ lbs., and a demi-kilogram to $1\frac{1}{10}$ lbs., or approximately 1 lb.

A gram of pure water at 39·2° F. (4° C.) occupies a volume of one cubic centimetre (1 c.c.).

A kilogram of water occupies a volume of one litre, or 1·761 English pints (roughly $1\frac{3}{4}$ pints).

HEAT CALCULATIONS

In measures of capacity—

1 millilitre or c.c.   =   0·061027 cb. inches.
1 litre or cb. decimetre =   61·027 cb. inches, or 1·761 pints.
1 hektolitre or 100 litres = 6,102·7 cb. inches, or 176 pints, or 22 gals.
1 kilolitre or 1000 litres = 61,027 cb. inches, or 1,761 pints, or 220 gals.

A gallon of water weighs 10 lbs. or 160 oz. or 70,000 grains. One pint weighs 20 ozs., hence a fluid oz. = $\frac{1}{20}$ pint. One oz. equals 28·35 grams, occupying a volume of 28·35 c.c. One cubic inch equals 16·38 c.c., and a gallon equals 277·274 cubic inches. A litre is the cubical measure of 0·1 or $\frac{1}{10}$ metre in the side; hence a cubic vessel constructed on a square, the length of a side of which equals one decimetre, or 3·9371 inches, will contain exactly a litre of a liquid. In flour and bread analyses, measuring vessels, such as pipettes, flasks, and burettes, are invariably graduated in cubic centimetres.

Heat Calculations and Mechanics

A **calory** or heat unit is the quantity of heat required to raise unit weight of water through unit of temperature. In the British Isles this heat unit is the quantity of heat required to raise one pound of water through one degree Fahrenheit. In scientific circles, it is the quantity of heat required to raise one gram of water through one degree Centigrade or the gram-calory. Frequently, a unit one thousand times greater is taken as the standard for heat measurement.

In the bakehouse it is a regular occurrence to raise the temperature of a quantity of water. Instead of running heated water into cold water, by chance, the calculated quantity of hot water or steam is mixed with the cooler water, thus giving the mixture of water at the proper or required temperature. Several examples of useful heat calculations are here given to assist the beginner.

(1) How many heat or thermal units are there in five gallons of water at 85° F. ?

A gallon of water weighs 10 lbs.
Therefore 5 galls. weigh 10 × 5 = 50 lbs.

CHEMISTRY OF BREADMAKING

As each degree that 1 lb. rises corresponds to a thermal unit, then $50 \times 85 = 4250$ units of heat. More accurately an allowance should be made for the fact that water freezes or congeals at 32° F. But generally each degree is taken as a heat unit as shown in the example.

(2) Calculate the mean temperature of two different quantities of water when at different temperatures after thoroughly mixing together.

E.g. 28 galls. of water at 45° F. when mixed with 14 galls. at 180° F.

$28 \times 10 = 280$ lbs. and $280 \times 45 = 12,600$ thermal units.
$14 \times 10 = 140$ lbs. and $140 \times 180 = 25,200$,,
Total 420 lbs.   containing 37,800 ,,

$$\frac{37,800}{420} = 90° \text{ F. temperature of the mixture.}$$

(3) It is required to raise the temperature of 8 galls. of water from 55° F. to 102° F. How much water at 212° F. is necessary?

The difference between 102° and 55° is 47°.
8 galls. weigh $8 \times 10 = 80$ lbs.
The number of thermal units required will be
$$80 \times 47 = 3760.$$

Each pound of water in cooling from 212° to 102° gives up 110 thermal units;

therefore $\frac{3760}{110} = 34 \cdot 18$ lbs., or 3·418 galls. of water are required.

(4) Given 55 galls. of water at 62° F., how much boiling water at 212° and how much steam at 322° F. will be required separately to raise the temperature to 115° F.?

$55 \times 10 = 550$ lbs. of water at 62° F.
$115° - 62° = 53°$ of difference in temperature.
$550 \times 53 = 29,150$ thermal units required.

HEAT CALCULATIONS

Each pound of boiling water gives up 97° in cooling to 115°; therefore $\frac{29{,}150}{97} = 300\cdot52$ lbs., or 30·052 galls. of hot water are required.

Each pound of steam at 322° F. gives up in cooling to 115° the following :—

1 lb. of steam at 322° gives up   110 thermal units in cooling to 212°,
1 lb. of steam gives up   967 thermal units in changing to water,
1 lb. of boiling water gives up   97 thermal units in cooling to 115°,

∴ each lb. of steam gives up 1,174 thermal units in cooling to 115°,

hence $\frac{29{,}150}{1{,}174} = 24\cdot83$ lbs. of steam required.

Note.—In Chap. II., p. 15, the reader will see that the latent heat of steam was given as 967 British thermal units.

(5) How much cold water at 48° F. is required to cool down 5 galls. 2 qts. of water at 200° to 87° F. ?

5 galls. 2 qts. weigh 50+5=55 lbs.
In cooling from 200° to 87° each lb. loses 113°.
Therefore 55×113=6215 thermal units to remove.
Each lb. of water at 48° absorbs 87°—48°=39 thermal units, hence $\frac{6{,}215}{39} = 159\cdot359$ lbs. or 15·936 galls. of the cold water are required.

Specific heat (sp. ht.) has been defined to be the ratio of the quantity of heat required to raise unit weight of a substance through unit of temperature, compared with the quantity of heat required to raise unit weight of water through unit of temperature. The specific heat of water is taken as unity or 1, and that of all other bodies as decimals of this. Thus the sp. ht. of flour, malt, and cereals varies between 0·39 and 0·5. In the following problem showing the application of sp. ht., that of malt is taken as 0·42.

(6) A mash is to be made at 145° F. with 22 lbs. of malt and 80 lbs. of water. The temperature of the malt is 56°. Find the temperature of the water. Let x=the required temperature.

The number of thermal units in the malt will be
$22 \times 56 \times 0\cdot 42 = 517\cdot 44$ or say $517\cdot 5$.

$80 \times x \times 1 = 80x$ or number of heat units in the water before the mixing together or mashing;
and $80.x + 0\cdot 42 \times 22 \times 56° = 80 \times 145° + 0\cdot 42 \times 22 \times 145°$.
Therefore
$$x = \frac{80 \times 145 + 0\cdot 42 \times 22 \times 145° - 0\cdot 42 \times 22 \times 56°}{80}$$
$$= \frac{11600 + 1339\cdot 8 - 517\cdot 4}{80}$$
$$= \frac{12422\cdot 4}{80} = 155\cdot 28° \text{ F.}$$

Therefore the 22 lbs. of malt at 56° will require to be mixed with 80 lbs. of water at 155·28° F. in order to produce a mash at 145°, the best temperature for diastase.

Mechanics in a bakery.—In all machine bakeries a knowledge of mechanics is necessary. This branch of study can here only be considered in a very superficial manner, hence a good text-book on the subject should be consulted.

In connection with the transmission of motion by means of pulleys, it is essential to consider the mensuration of the circle very briefly, and more especially its circumference.

If D is the diameter, or twice the radius, of a circle, then πD is the circumference, where $\pi = \frac{22}{7}$ or 3·1416. If r is the radius in feet, then 2π times this radius equals the circumference in feet.

Example.—Find the circumference of a circle whose diameter is $3\frac{1}{2}$ feet?

The circumference $= \pi D = \frac{22}{7} \times 3\frac{1}{2} = \frac{22}{7} \times \frac{7}{2}$.
$$= \frac{22}{2} = 11 \text{ feet.}$$

Next, assume a disc to be rotating about a fixed axis, with a speed of 80 revolutions per minute.

Again, consider a point A (Fig. 3) at a distance r from the centre. Then from the above it is clear that the

MECHANICS

distance through which A moves in one revolution is
$$\pi D = \pi \times 2r,$$
i.e. the distance moved through in 80 revolutions per minute will therefore equal $80 \times 2\pi r$ or $80 \times \pi D$.

Thus take the case of a pulley of diameter D over which a strap is passing, the revolutions of the pulley being equal to N. Also assume that the belt is moving at the same speed as the rim of the pulley; it is evident from the above that the velocity of the belt in feet per minute will be

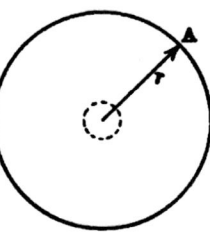

Fig. 3.

$$N \times \frac{22}{7} \times D = \frac{N.D.22}{7},$$

where D=diameter in feet, and N=revolutions per minute.

Example.—A pulley of 3 feet diameter is keyed on to a shaft which is running at 250 revolutions per minute. Power is transmitted from this pulley to a machine by a belt. Find the speed of the belt in feet per minute and also in feet per second.

The speed of strap in feet per minute

$$= \frac{N \times 22 \times D}{7}$$

$$= \frac{250 \times 22 \times 3}{7} = \frac{16500}{7} = 235 \cdot 7 \text{ feet per minute.}$$

$$\frac{235 \cdot 7}{60} = 3 \cdot 928 \text{ feet per second.}$$

If the above formula be examined it will be observed that if the diameter is doubled, then the speed is also doubled; similarly if it is increased in any proportion, then the speed is increased in a similar proportion; that is, the rim speed is accelerated directly as the diameter, for a constant number of revolutions per minute.

The ratio of the revolutions of two pulleys connected

by a belt may be considered. In this it is assumed that there is no slipping of the belt.

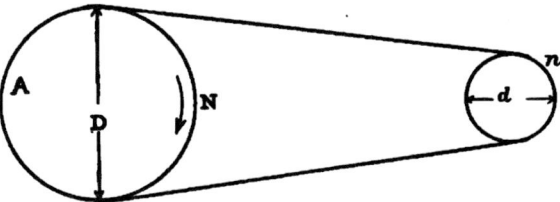

Fig. 4.—Driving by Belt.

The surface velocity of either pulley will be the same, because in each case it is equal to the velocity of the strap.

The surface velocity of the driver A (Fig. 4)
$$= N \times \frac{22}{7} \times D.$$

The surface velocity of the follower
$$= n \times \frac{22}{7} \times d.$$

But these are equal
$$\therefore \frac{N \times 22 \times D}{7} = n \times \frac{22}{7} \times d.$$

or $\quad N \times D = n \times d.$

$$\frac{N}{n} = \frac{d}{D} \text{ or } d = \frac{N.D}{n}$$

$$n = \frac{N.D}{d}$$

In exact work it is necessary to make corrections for the thickness of the belt.

From the formulae obtained it is possible to deduce the following self-evident rule for ascertaining an unknown term, thus:—

Multiply those two numbers which belong to the same pulley and divide the product by the third number; then the quotient is the term required.

The belt is not used where an exact velocity ratio is required.

MECHANICS

Given the HP. (horse-power) to be transmitted, the diameter of the pulley, and the number of revolutions per minute of the pulley. Find the width of the belt.

$$HP. = \frac{w.V}{600} = \frac{w}{600} \times \frac{22}{7} \times D.N,$$ where V is the velocity of the belt.

$$w = \text{width in inches} = \frac{HP. \times 4200}{22} \times \frac{1}{D.N}$$

$$w = \frac{HP. \times 192}{D.N}$$

where D = diameter in feet, N = revolutions per minute.

Example.—Assume that a dough mixer requires 4 HP. to drive it. Also that the pulley is 18 inches in diameter and that it makes 150 revolutions per minute. Then width of belt, $w = \frac{4 \times 192}{1 \cdot 5 \times 150} = 3\frac{1}{2}$ inches.

For very slow speeds, the values of w work out very high, in which case a double-ply belting would be used of half the width obtained by the above calculation. For example, if the speed were 75 revolutions instead of 150, then the width of the belt would be 7 inches, or a double ply of $3\frac{1}{2}$ inches.

Again if the width of belt, the HP, and the diameter of the pulley are fixed, then the number of revolutions per minute at which it would be safe to run can readily be found.

CHAPTER V

HEAT AND PHYSICAL PROBLEMS

HEAT is the name given to a very well-known sensation which the agent produces when in contact with the human body. Cold is the term applied to the opposite sensation, but experience shows that both terms are only relative, for what to one person would be termed hot, to another might produce the sensation of being cold. Two bodies may be said to be equally heated when in contact there is no interchange of heat between them.

A heated body gives off its heat in two ways : (1) By being in contact with a cooler body ; (2) By radiation through space.

Heat radiates through space in straight lines in all directions and at the rate of 186,000 miles per second.

Heat, like light, consists of vibrations of enormous velocity, and with increase in temperature there is a great increase in the rate of the vibrations and a corresponding decrease in the wave-length of the vibrations. A just perceptible red heat is about 400° C. (752° F.) ; a cherry-red heat is 900° C. (1652° F.) ; whilst a white heat is 1800° C. (3272° F.).

The sun is the great source of heat on the earth, and if a beam of the sun's light be passed through a glass prism the spectrum so obtained consists of a band of colours spoken of as the colours of the rainbow. These are red, orange, yellow, green, blue, indigo, and violet. Beyond the red at the one end and the violet at the other, there are bands of waves, not visible to the human eye, known as the ultra-red and ultra-violet respectively. If these are studied it will be found that the ultra-red rays produce the sensation

HEAT

of heat, and the ultra-violet intense chemical action. It has further been shown that the sensation produced by the ultra-red rays of the sunlight agrees with that obtained by heating a rod of metal such as a poker to such a temperature that when brought into a dark room the red heat is faintly perceptible.

Heat may be propagated in three ways :—
(1) through solids by conduction;
(2) through liquids and gases by convection currents;
(3) through space by radiation.

All these processes are involved in the baking industry; it is therefore desirable that the workers should possess some knowledge of them.

Conduction of heat.—Conduction is the name given to the process by which heat is propagated through solid matter. In this process there is no motion of progression of the particles of the solid themselves, but as particles of the solid which are in contact with those around them become heated or cooled, the sensation is conveyed by the contact to the other particles, consequently the whole of the solid will gradually become heated or cooled.

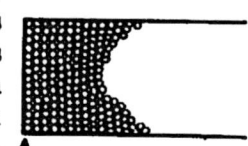

Fig. 5.—Conduction of Heat.

In the case of metals the process goes on fairly rapidly, whilst with non-metals, mixed materials as slate, wood, and many other solids, the heating or cooling is very slow. Metals are therefore termed good conductors, and the other bodies poor or even non-conductors. The heating or cooling proceeds until the whole of the solid is at the same temperature.

The process may be illustrated by the sketch of Fig. 5. Conceive of a bar of metal made up of an almost infinite number of particles represented by the circles. Heat is applied to the bar at the point A. The particle being in contact with particles on all its sides communicates the heat to them; they in turn communicate the heat to other particles until the whole bar becomes equally heated.

Conduction is evidently carried out in two stages. The first is the variable one, during which the heat is applied and the parts of the solid are increasing in temperature. The second stage is that in which all parts have become equally heated and every particle will give out as much as it receives, thus verifying Stewart's well-known Theory of Exchanges, and this stage itself is clearly the permanent one.

The following short table gives a comparison of the conducting power of metals, based on silver as possessing the highest conductivity.

Metal.	Conductivity.	Metal.	Conductivity.
Silver (Ag),	100·00	Zinc (Zn),	19·89
Copper (Cu),	77·63	Tin (Sn),	14·52
Gold (Au),	53·20	Iron (Fe),	11·94
Brass,	33·10	Bismuth (Bi),	1·92

The good conductivity of the metals and the poor conducting power of wood, slate, chalk, etc., explains the sensation of cold that a person experiences when touching a metal surface and the opposite sensation when in contact with wood, both materials being in the same room and at the same temperature. It also partly explains why a copper or brass cooking vessel is more efficient than an iron one for its purpose.

Convection.—Convection is the name given to the process by which heat is propagated through liquids and gases. In this process there is an actual movement of progression. For example, a liquid contained in a vessel is heated from below; the particles near to the source of heat expand and so become lighter or of less density than the particles above; they therefore rise and the cooler heavier particles flow downwards to take their place, in this way setting up convection currents. The same applies equally to gases; so in general, when different parts of a liquid or gas are heated to different temperatures, like differences of density are caused, leading to the formation of currents which are known as 'convection currents.'

Numbers of examples of this occur in the daily life of a baker, *e.g.* the pans and kettles that are heated over gas or other sources of heat; the filling of the attemperating tank in connection with the dough mixer, based on the principle that hot water is lighter than cold, therefore the hot water is run into the tank first, and the heavier cold water next which sets up convection and thus tends to equalise the temperature. The heating of buildings by hot water is similar; the water in the boiler becomes heated and lighter, consequently it rises to the highest point, whilst the cooler water flows by the return pipe to the boiler setting up a complete circulation. Even a steam-pipe oven is dependent partly on convection, partly on conduction, and very largely on radiation. Convection also plays a highly important part in meteorology. Moreover, the natural ventilation of our buildings is largely dependent on both convection currents and the diffusion of gases.

Radiation.—Radiation is a process for the dispersion and dissipation of heat. From its source radiant heat travels in straight lines and at the same velocity as light, viz., 186,000 miles per second. As the heat is propagated in straight lines, it does not warm the intervening space. Radiant heat is, in fact, not heat at all, but a form of energy that can be easily changed into heat. The fact that it travels at the same rate as light and conforms to the same laws as light rather points to such a conclusion.

Of the three processes by which heat is propagated, radiation is almost instantaneous; convection is slow; conduction very slow by comparison. It is important to remember that heated bodies radiate heat in straight lines in all directions; thus it is that the space of the baking

46 CHEMISTRY OF BREADMAKING

chamber becomes heated and is able to transmit its heat to the dough, which in this way is baked.

The Microscope and Polarimeter

Light, like heat, consists of vibrations in which the wave-length is very minute and the velocity enormous. Light vibrations require the presence of an extremely subtle fluid, of which our senses can take no cognizance, known as the ethereal medium. These vibrations are transverse to the direction in which the beam is being transmitted, while those of sound are longitudinal. The phenomenon of light is the cause of vision and enables us to see objects; it is also the all-important factor in the use of such optical instruments as are in part constructed of lenses, like the microscope and polariscope or polarimeter.

Lenses.—Before proceeding to discuss the microscope it is first necessary to understand the action of lenses. A lens is a piece of glass bounded by two surfaces which are portions of spheres. Of these there are two classes, the *converging* and *diverging* lenses. The converging are also known as *convex* lenses, while the diverging are *concave*. The former alone are used in microscopy, as they are the only magnifying ones. There are three different forms of convex lenses: the double convex, the plano-convex, and the concavo-convex. The double convex (Fig. 6) when placed in a frame forms the simple microscope or burning-glass. The plano-convex (Fig. 7) is generally used in combination with other lenses both in the microscope and optical lantern.

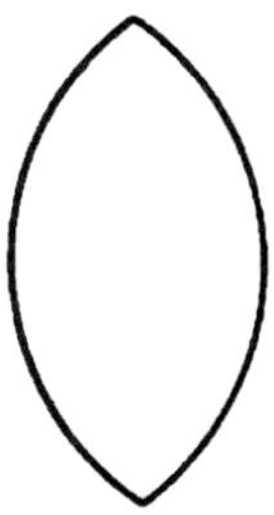

Fig. 6.—A Double-convex Lens.

Fig. 7.—A Plano-convex Lens.

When beams of light enter a lens they are bent out of their course or refracted on entering and again on leaving the lens. These beams all converge to a point, which lies on a straight line passing through the centre of the lens. This straight line is the *principal axis*, and the point on either side of the lens and at equal distances from it is the *principal focus* of the lens; while the distance between the lens and this point is its *focal length*.

The formation of images.—Images formed by lenses are either real or virtual. When an object is placed at a distance of less than twice the focal length of the lens, a real and magnified image is formed on the other side of the lens. If placed at exactly twice the focal length, a real image but not magnified is obtained, and if placed at a distance greater than twice the focal length, a real but diminished image is formed. When the object is placed between the principal focus and the lens, a magnified virtual image on the same side of the lens is formed. This latter is the construction in the case of a single microscope or simple magnifying glass. A convex lens of shorter focal length than the eye is placed at a distance rather less than the focal length of the lens from the object, whereby a virtual and magnified image is the result.

The compound microscope.—A simple form of compound microscope is composed of a stand carrying two lenses, the lower of the two being the objective and the upper one the ocular or eye-piece. The objective forms a real and magnified image on the other, that is the upper, side of the lens; this image is arranged to fall between the principal focus of and the upper lens, thus giving a virtual and magnified image, which may be observed by looking down through the eye-piece or ocular. Such an instrument was first devised by Hans and Zacharias Janssen, two Dutchmen—father and son—about the year 1590.

A modern compound microscope (Fig. 8) has the following parts: A firm stand with telescopic tube, a hinge, two motions—the rack and pinion or coarse adjustment, and the micrometer or fine adjustment—a stage with sub-stage fittings, viz., the Abbe condenser and reflector, an iris diaphragm, centering arrangement, and a plano-concave

48   CHEMISTRY OF BREADMAKING

mirror. At the upper end of the telescopic tube is the fitting T_1 to receive the ocular, at the lower end a double

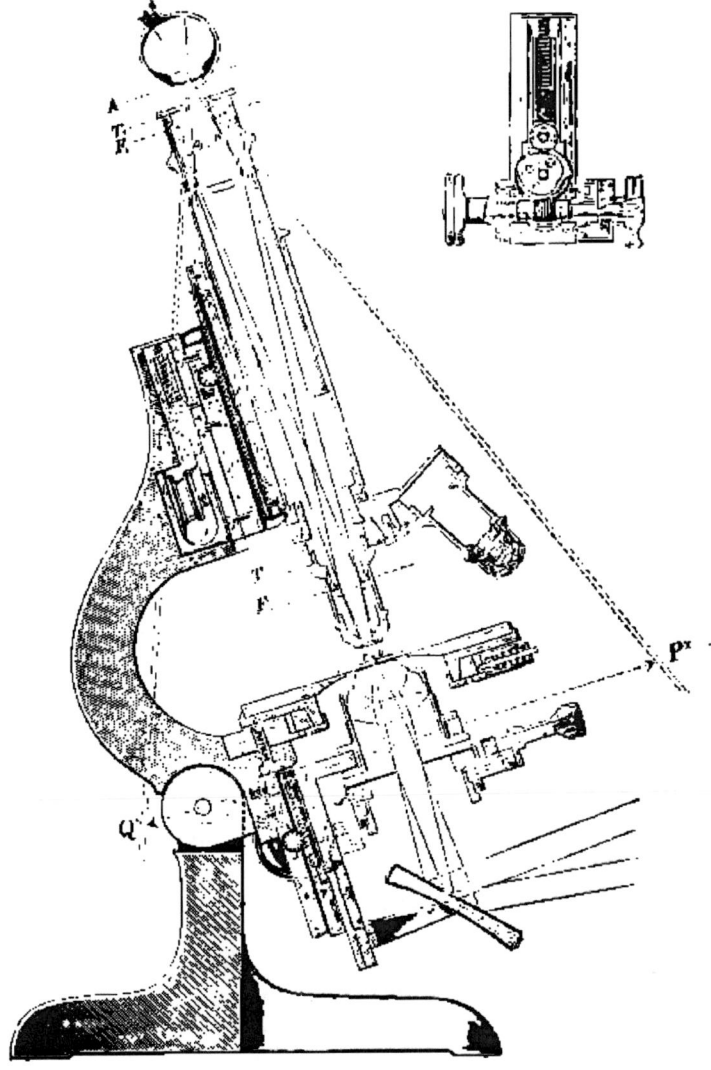

Fig. 8.—Longitudinal Section through Compound Microscope.
[*By permission of Messrs. E. Leitz, London.*]

THE MICROSCOPE

or triple nose-piece on which the objectives may be screwed as at T. An image of the object PQ is formed at Q_1P_1, and this is again multiplied by the ocular at T_1 to give the magnified image at $Q^\times P^\times$. The stage is frequently fitted with a mechanical arrangement to enable the observer to make accurate measurements. The loose fittings consist of a series of five Huyghenian oculars, various objectives both dry and oil-immersion, polariser and analyser for starch and other special work, together with micrometer scale attached to ocular No. three, and sundry micro-slips three inches long by one inch wide of white or colourless glass, cover glasses, etc. A small pamphlet on the microscope issued by Messrs. Reichert and Sons of Vienna (Wien) will prove of great use to beginners and others; or the large book by Dr. Carpenter on the microscope will be invaluable in aiding a worker to get the best out of a good instrument.

The Huyghenian oculars of themselves give the following magnifications :—

Number.	1	2	3	4	5
Focus in Millimetres	50	40	30	25	20
Magnification in Diameters	3	4	5·5	7	9

The magnification due to an objective may approximately be taken as follows :—

The one-inch gives 10 diameters,
The half-inch gives 20 ,,
The one-eighth of an inch gives 80 diameters,
The tenth of an inch gives 100 diameters, etc., when the draw tube is at its full length of ten inches, which is that of normal vision; hence the total magnification in diameters may be found by multiplying the magnification due to the

objective by that due to the ocular. *Example.*—A No. 4 ocular and an eighth of an inch objective.

⅛ inch gives 80 diameters.

$$80 \times 7 = 560 \text{ diameters.}$$

Or, more accurately,

$$\frac{\text{Magnification due to ocular} \times \text{Magnification due to objective} \times \text{Length of tube}}{10}$$

$$= \frac{7 \times 80 \times 10 \text{ inches}}{10} = 560 \text{ diameters.}$$

A good microscope ought to be capable of giving—
Power of penetration,
Brightness of field,
Flatness of field,
Sharp and clear definition,
Great resolving power,
Freedom from chromatic and spherical aberration.

As a good microscope is very delicate in its parts and easily injured, great care should be observed in its treatment. When not in actual use, it ought to be placed in its case or put under a glass shade to protect it from dust. The oculars and objectives should be cleaned with a piece of soft tissue paper or a fine chamois leather, both free from gritty particles which would scratch and spoil the lenses. Under no circumstances whatever should it be allowed to stand in the direct light from the sun.

Polarimeters (polariscopes).—A polarimeter is an instrument for measuring the amount of bending out of its course or refraction which a beam of plane polarised light suffers on passing through a column of liquid which possesses optical activity.

Polarised light, which to the naked eye resembles ordinary white light, consists of vibrations in one plane only. Light may be polarised by either reflection or refraction single or double. For the purposes of ordinary polarising instruments used in the analysis of sugar solutions or other liquids possessing optical properties, the process by double refraction alone is employed. All doubly refracting crystals

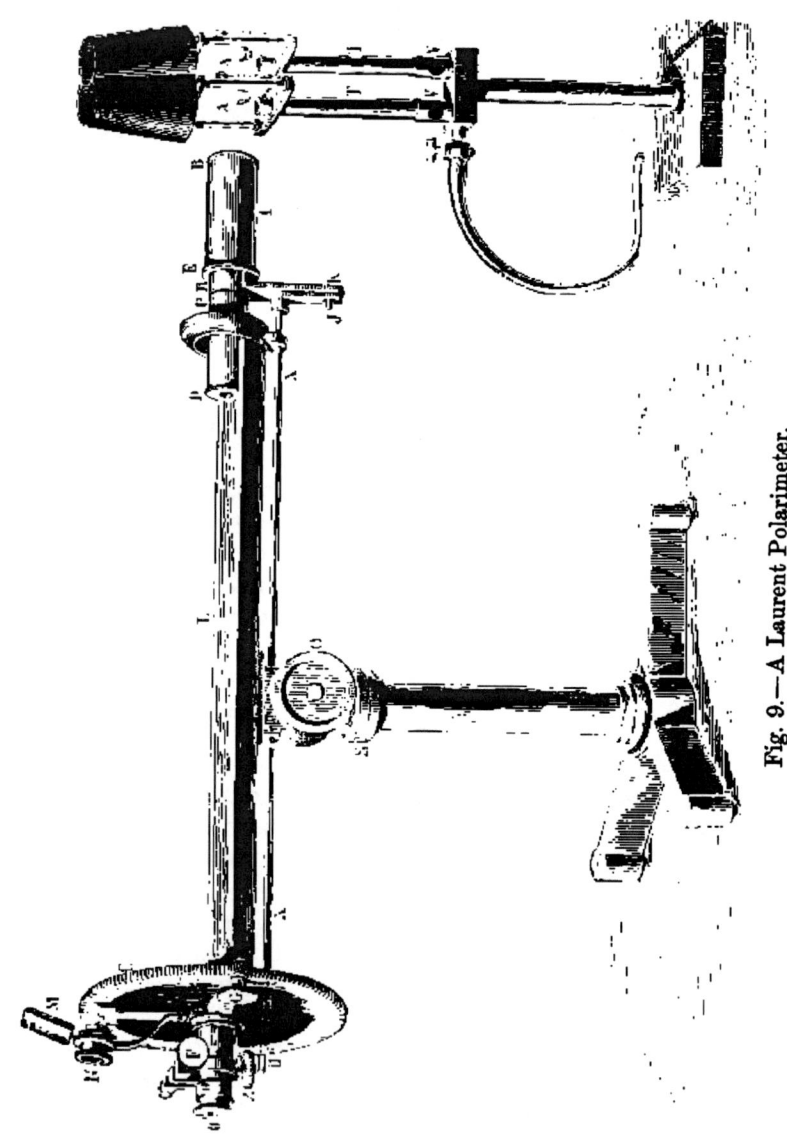

Fig. 9.—A Laurent Polarimeter.
[*By permission of Messrs. Baird and Tatlock (London), Ltd.*]

such as tourmaline and Iceland spar possess this power. When a beam of ordinary light passes through one of these crystals, except in its optical axis, the beam is resolved into the *ordinary* and *extraordinary* rays. This latter ray if passed through a second crystal behaves in a peculiar way and is said to be 'polarised.' The plane in which a ray of polarised light is reflected is known as the plane of polarisation. If the beam of polarised light vibrates in parallel straight lines, the beam is said to be plane polarised.

The most useful crystals for the purpose of producing polarised light are rhombs of calc or Iceland spar ($CaCO_3$). The Nicol prism is such a crystal split along its optical axis, that is, through its shorter diagonal, and then fixed together again with Canada balsam. Two such prisms are employed in the construction of polarimeters, one to act as the *polariser* and the other as the *analyser*, the space between them being occupied by the tube containing the optically active liquid. The theory of a polarimeter is fairly easy to understand : the beam of sodium (yellow) light or white light passes through the first Nicol or polariser ; emerging in a polarised condition it passes on through the liquid contained in the tube where its plane is bent to the right or left hand according as the opticity of the liquid is dextro- or lævo-rotatory ; it then enters the second Nicol or analyser, which must be rotated to the left or right until its principal section, which was parallel to that of the other prism, is in a position to allow the refracted beam to pass ; the amount of bending can then be read off on the scale of the instrument.

From the above, it follows that some substances turn the plane to the right hand or are dextro-rotatory, *e.g.* sucrose, maltose, dextrose, and dextrins ; others turn it to the left or are lævo-rotatory, as lævulose, invert sugar and many of the proteids. The dextro bodies are signified by the + and the lævo bodies by the − sign.

The construction of a Laurent polarimeter.—This instrument consists of a tube, in the centre of which is fixed the

THE POLARIMETER

polariser (Figs. 9 and 10). At the end of this tube near the sodium flame, in the better-class instruments, is fixed a

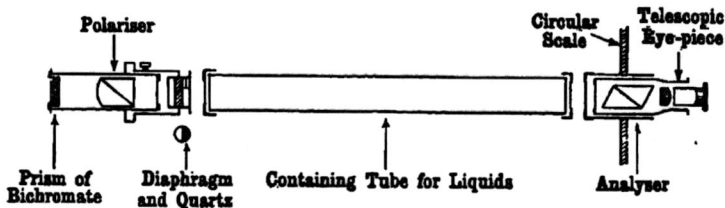

Fig. 10.—The arrangement of parts of a Laurent Polarimeter.

crystal of bichromate of potash to absorb all the beams of light with the exception of orange or yellowish coloured; hence yellowish light only passes through the polariser, and from the polariser the extraordinary ray comes out at the end of the tube. Here is placed a disc or plate of quartz exactly 3·75 millimetres in thickness, and agreeing with an angular rotation of 22°. This gives the half-tint, and these instruments are called *half-tint instruments*, because half of the quartz is dark, and the other half light. There is an open portion of the polarimeter so arranged that a tube of two decimetres in length containing a solution may be enclosed.

The remaining portion of the instrument is another tube. In the centre of this tube is placed the second Nicol or analyser, and exactly in the centre of this Nicol is arranged the stand on which the graduations and vernier are fixed. This Nicol is made to revolve in two directions, and the amount is shown by the circular plate.

There is further a telescopic arrangement for examining and magnifying the beam of light.

There are two general classes of polarimeters :
(1) The half-shadow instruments which require a monochromatic light, and
(2) Instruments which use white light.

The only difference of construction between these two is that compensation must be made where light is used of all degrees of refrangibility. Thus red rays give a rotation of 19°, orange gives 21°, and sodium light about 22°; at the far end of the spectrum, indigo gives 38° and violet 41°, so that between these numbers 19° and 41° come beams of all degrees of refrangibility, and hence compensation must be made. This is done by introducing lenses and crystals which have the effect of darkening the instrument. The most important of the half-shadow instruments are the Laurent and the instruments the modification of which led up to the Laurent.

In Fig. 9 AA are the spoons or cups of platinum gauze to hold the salt for giving a yellow monochromatic jet in the Bunsen burners, which have collars at V for opening or closing the air-holes. B is the lens screwed on to the tube I, which itself screws on to the barrel E. The latter carries a diaphragm with a small hole which receives a cap containing a crystal of potassium bichromate used when the liquids are colourless. The lever K, fixed on the polarising tube R, can be rotated by the crank J, and this is moved by the shaft X and lever U. The diaphragm D, one half of which is covered by a plate of quartz, is in line with the telescope O,H. The mirror M throws the light from the burners on to the divisions of the disc C, and N is the lens for reading the divisions of the scale.

Amongst white light polarimeters mention may be made of the Soleil-Duboscq-Ventski and the instruments coming previous to them. One of the best of these is that made by and known as the Schmidt-Haensch.

CHAPTER VI

THE ORGANIC CONSTITUENTS OF THE CEREALS

THE study of organic chemistry is of the utmost importance in connection with food-stuffs. It is therefore advisable to give a short introduction to this subject.

By organic chemistry is understood the chemistry of the carbon compounds, or better the chemistry of the hydrocarbons and their derivatives. As there are many thousands of these compounds, it is easy to perceive that the study of this subject must be thoroughly systematised or nothing but confusion would result. It includes all bodies of which carbon is an essential constituent; hence all the component parts of animal and vegetable life, with the exception of the mineral salts, are carbon compounds. To these must be added the many compounds which are built up by synthesis in the chemical laboratories, and the numerous substances obtained in the destructive distillation of coal, peat, wood, shale, the many tars, bones and petroleum oils.

All of them may be classified, according to the elements of which they are composed, and the relation they bear to one another. Those composed of carbon and hydrogen alone are the *hydrocarbons*, a numerous class of important and useful compounds, including the rock oils or paraffins, the terpenes and the aromatic or benzene derivatives.

The compounds composed of carbon, hydrogen, and oxygen form a still more numerous class. These include the *alcohols*, and also the *carbohydrates*, which latter are neutral compounds, neither salts nor oxides, composed of carbon and the elements of water. Closely related to the carbohydrates are the alcohol derivatives, the *aldehydes*, *ketones*, and *acids*. The *fats* also belong to this group, since, although not carbohydrates, they consist of the same three elements. In chemical composition, the fats are glycerides or compounds of glycerin with the fatty acids, and hence they are salts.

The next important class are those containing the elements carbon, hydrogen, nitrogen, oxygen, and sulphur. This class includes the *albumenoids* and *proteins*. Associated with them are the *nucleins*, still more complex bodies composed of the five elements of the proteins together with iron and phosphorus.

Other groups of organic bodies contain the halogen elements chlorine, bromine, and iodine ; or contain some metal such as do the metallo-organic compounds.

If some of the important members of each class be studied, then a fairly accurate idea of the whole is acquired. A few important and useful groups of compounds are considered in this chapter under the following heads :— alcohols, acids, fats, carbohydrates, and nitrogenous constituents of the cereals.

The organic constituents of the cereals may be divided into the nitrogenous and the non-nitrogenous bodies.

The *nitrogenous* include the proteins, nucleins, derivatives of these two groups or hydrolytic products, and the soluble ferments or enzymes.

The *non-nitrogenous* comprise the carbohydrates, organic or vegetable acids, and the fats or glycerides. Under the heading carbohydrates are included the sugars, cellulose or fibrous compounds, the starches, dextrins, gums, and other related bodies. Reference to Chap. VII., pp. 99-101, will give a fairly comprehensive idea of the quantities of these organic bodies present in the more common cereals.

The Alcohols

The word 'alcohol' is a generic term applied to a large number of organic compounds which are weak bases, and yield salts spoken of as 'esters' or ethereal salts. They may be classified according to their behaviour towards

ORGANIC CONSTITUENTS OF THE CEREALS 57

reagents, or to their formulae. Thus they are primary, secondary, or tertiary according to their behaviour towards oxidising reagents; or they are monohydric, dihydric, trihydric, or polyhydric alcohols, according to the number of hydroxyl or OH groups contained in their composition.

The most important monohydric alcohols to a baker and confectioner are wood-spirit or methyl alcohol ($CH_3.OH$), and spirits of wine or ethyl alcohol ($C_2H_5.OH$). Both of these are primary alcohols because when gently and partially oxidised they yield an aldehyde, and when completely oxidised an acid; thus, methyl alcohol yields first formaldehyde and then formic acid. Formaldehyde is sold commercially as formalin, a powerful antiseptic and germicide. It exists in nature in the bright green tips of growing grass and other vegetation. Ethyl alcohol when similarly treated yields acetaldehyde and then acetic acid, the acid of vinegar.

Glycerin is an example of a trihydric alcohol. It is at the same time both a primary and secondary alcohol. This body will be further mentioned in connection with the fats. The polyhydric alcohols are closely related to the sugars, and like glycerin may be both primary and secondary alcohols at the same time.

Wood-spirit or methyl alcohol ($CH_3.OH$).—Methyl alcohol is one of the products formed in the destructive distillation of wood in iron retorts. Gaseous bodies are given off and charcoal is left behind in the retort. Some of the gaseous compounds condense to a liquid, which contains crude acetic or pyroligneous acid, acetone, wood-spirit, etc., and wood-tar. The non-condensable gases are used up in heating the retorts or for lighting purposes. After settling so as to eliminate the tar, the acid liquors are distilled and the vapours passed through milk of lime. The acetic acid is neutralised, forming acetate of lime, whilst the neutral gases like acetone and wood-spirit which pass over are collected separately and subjected to fractional distillation in order to obtain the wood-spirit.

This is a liquid of low boiling point, 150° F. (66° C.) and sp. gr. 0·7963, which is largely employed as a solvent for lacs, varnishes, resins, etc., and for methylating silent spirit or spirit of wine, thus giving the ordinary methylated spirit. A further portion is used for the manufacture of formalin, a powerful antiseptic containing about forty per cent. of the active agent, formaldehyde.

Spirits of wine or ethyl alcohol ($C_2H_5.OH$).—Spirits of wine is a liquid which has been known to exist, and to give the special and peculiar properties to alcoholic beverages, from the earliest times. Even savage and barbaric peoples have known how to prepare both alcoholic liquors and ardent spirits. The body is always manufactured by the fermentation of sugar solutions and thus gives rise to some of the greatest industries on the earth's surface, these including brewing and distilling and the production of wines, cordials, and liqueurs.

The preparation of alcohol is conducted as follows: Raw grain, as oats, rye, wheat, or maize, is cleaned and crushed between heavy rolls, then mixed with about one-third its weight of crushed barley malt. The mixture is now made into a kind of thin porridge with water at 150° to 152° F. so as to obtain a mash of 142° to 145° F. After standing for three hours the liquid is run off and any sugars left in the grains are washed out with hot water.

The 'wort' or sweet liquor, consisting chiefly of a solution of maltose, is cooled rapidly to 68° or 72° F. and filtered to take out floating particles. It runs from the filter press into large fermenting vats where it is mixed with fresh, strong yeast. Fermentation proceeds rapidly for some hours, and when the sp. gr. of the wash or fermented liquor has gone down to nearly 1·000 the wash is freed from yeast and passed into a patent wash-still in which the alcohol is separated from the other products of fermentation by one distillation.

Such spirit is rarely of less than 84 per cent. strength, and is known as rectified spirit or silent spirit. By another

ORGANIC CONSTITUENTS OF THE CEREALS

distillation it may be brought up to nearly 95 per cent. strength. Beyond this it must be purified by chemical means, viz., by bringing into it quicklime which abstracts a quantity of the remaining water. It is again distilled to free it from the slaked lime. This final product, although not quite free from water, is the absolute alcohol of commerce.

Alcohol is a colourless mobile liquid possessing a pleasant, ethereal odour and burning taste. It has a sp. gr. of 0·7934 at 61° F., boils at 172·5 F., and does not solidify until cooled to $-267°$ F. ($-130·5°$ C.). Strong alcohol acts as a poison when taken internally, since it absorbs water from the system and coagulates albumen. When mixed with water a contraction in volume takes place; *e.g.* if 100 volumes of rectified spirit be mixed with 60 volumes of water, only 156 volumes of proof spirit are obtained.

Alcohol readily burns in air with a smokeless, almost colourless flame; owing to this it may be used in spirit lamps, as motor spirit and for specially constructed engines. It is the active constituent of all alcoholic beverages, and ardent spirits. One of its chief uses depends on its solvent properties.

THE CARBOHYDRATES

This is the name applied to a group of important food substances which are composed of carbon and the elements of water. They are neutral bodies, possessing neither an acid nor alkaline reaction, and at the same time although compounds are not salts.

Although carbohydrates are distributed through the animal and vegetable kingdoms, there is little doubt as to their being derived from vegetable sources. A large number of theories, some based on facts and others on supposition, have been put forward to explain the formation of these compounds, but so far none of the theories are quite satisfactory.

It is generally accepted that the carbon dioxide of the atmosphere and water in the presence of warmth, sunlight, and chlorophyll form the starting point; for Sachs, the celebrated botanist, was able to show that the green leaves with the above-mentioned materials formed a condensation product and gave out oxygen.

$$\underset{\text{Carbon dioxide}}{CO_2} + \underset{\text{Water}}{H_2O} = \underset{\text{Formaldehyde}}{H.CHO} + \underset{\text{Oxygen}}{O_2}$$

and $\underset{\text{Carbon dioxide}}{6\ CO_2} + \underset{\text{Water}}{5\ H_2O} = \underset{\text{α-acrose}}{C_6H_{10}O_5} + \underset{\text{Oxygen}}{6\ O_2}$

The processes of assimilation probably depend on :— the decomposition of carbon dioxide and formation of condensation products; the further breaking up of some of these latter and recombination to form other bodies; the formation of proteids and of the materials from which carbohydrates are obtained. The assumption that the carbon dioxide of the atmosphere is insufficient to supply all the carbon required, and that bicarbonates are taken up by plant roots and thus assist, is possibly correct.

When formed the carbohydrates are used to build up the cellulose structure of the plant, while the excess is stored in the seeds, tubers, bulbs, etc., as a reserve food supply, or to supply the first food to the young embryo when germination begins. The great family of the sugars, gums, starches, and cellulose, commonly known as the carbohydrates, constitutes a very important group of organic substances which plays a decisive part in the animal and vegetable organism, forming a large proportion of its foods and tissues.

Very closely related to the carbohydrates are the alcohols, many of the higher of which exist free in nature as such, while the lower ones are obtained by vegetative processes. Thus mannite, dulcite, and sorbite, white solid alcohols, exist widely distributed in plant life. If these are gently oxidised they yield sugars. For example, mannite so treated forms a glucose-like compound. Conversely, many of the sugars may readily be reduced back to the alcohol compound, showing how closely allied the two groups of bodies are to each other.

Many classifications of the carbohydrates have been put

ORGANIC CONSTITUENTS OF THE CEREALS

forward, but none of these are altogether satisfactory. For simplicity's sake the following will assist in their study :—

Group I.—The Monoses.

Group II.—The Bioses and higher sugars.

Group III.—The Polyoses, or those carbohydrates which may be converted by hydrolysis into sugars.

GROUP I.—THE MONOSES

General formula $C_6H_{12}O_6$

These include dextrose or grape sugar, lævulose or fruit sugar, galactose, and the mixture of dextrose and lævulose known as invert sugar. The term 'glucose' is also applied to dextrose, but it is more suitably given to the mixture of which dextrose is the chief constituent. Glucose is a commercial sugar which varies considerably in its composition.

The monoses possess the following properties :—

All are soluble in water, crystallisable and diffusible. They are powerful reducing agents, and consequently readily reduce Fehling's [1] solution and Trommer's reagent. They rotate a beam of plane polarised light, and may be said to possess optical properties. Chemically, they are either aldehydes or ketones. All but galactose easily ferment when brought into solution and mixed with distillers' or brewers' yeast.

Dextrose or grape sugar, and the glucoses.—As its second name indicates, dextrose is the chief sugar in grapes, raisins and currants; it occurs in many other fruits, especially sweet ones such as cherries, pears, bananas, generally mixed with an equal quantity of lævulose; also in leaves and roots of plants; in honey; in animal fluids as the chyle, allantoic fluid, blood and urine; in the liver, in eggs, etc. It is also obtained as a decomposition product of vegetable glucosides.

[1] Fehling's solution is composed of alkaline copper tartrate.

Dextrose may be prepared by the action of acids and soluble ferments or enzymes on the glucosides; by the continuous action of dilute acid on starches and dextrins; by separating out the dextrose from raisins or from invert sugar, or by hydrolysing maltose.

When pure it crystallises in fine, hard needles, which melt at 295° F. (146° C.). The specific gravity of the crystals is 1·386, whilst that of a saturated solution at 60° F. (15·6° C.) is 1·221. Dextrose is not charred by concentrated sulphuric acid except when strongly heated. It is only about two-thirds as sweet as cane sugar.

A solution of this sugar is, owing to its aldehyde formation, a powerful reducing agent, precipitating gold, silver, and platinum from their solutions of salts; and also reducing Fehling's and Trommer's reagents to red cuprous oxide. The solution is dextro-rotatory, that is, it bends or refracts a beam of plane polarised light to the right hand. When examined with the aid of a sodium flame, its rotation is stated thus: the specific rotatory power (see p. 196) is $(a)_{D_{3·86}} = +52·8$.

A solution not exceeding fifteen per cent. strength readily and directly ferments with yeast or yeast-juice.

The glucoses.—The name 'glucose' is applied to the commercial article which is sent into the trade either as a colourless, very viscid liquid used in the making of fondant, or as a white or amber to dark-coloured solid. The best qualities are manufactured from the cereals, especially maize, starches or from mixtures of these and cassava starch. Cheap, inferior glucose is prepared from potato starch. The moist starches are heated under pressure with dilute sulphuric acid in a converter, the syrup neutralised with chalk or whiting, then clarified through bone-chars, and evaporated to the proper consistency in vacuum pans. For confectionery and cotton-finishing purposes, the glucose must contain a considerable proportion of dextrin. This is regulated by the length of time the reactions in the converter are allowed to continue. For the brewer

ORGANIC CONSTITUENTS OF THE CEREALS

not more than about ten per cent. of dextrin is required; hence the time is rather longer.

A good glucose should give a clear solution in water; should contain no unconverted starch which would cause a turbidity; should leave no unpleasant after-taste in the mouth, and must contain no iron salts nor free acidity. The colourless variety is obtained by bleaching a syrup with sulphurous acid or a hydrosulphite solution.

The glucoses vary considerably in their chemical composition, as may be seen from the examples given below.

Constituents.	High Grade.	Medium Grade.	Low Grade.	Potato Glucose.
Dextrose,	71·58 %	54·56 %	42·28 %	53·56 %
Maltose,	7·26 ,,	8·42 ,,	11·47 ,,	7·72 ,,
Dextrine,	8·53 ,,	21·25 ,,	25·65 ,,	20·34 ,,
Nitrogenous,	0·86 ,,	1·66 ,,	1·52 ,,	1·84 ,,
Mineral Salts,	0·72 ,,	1·12 ,,	0·85 ,,	0·34 ,,
Water,	11·05 ,,	12·99 ,,	18·23 ,,	16·20 ,,

As mentioned above, the various forms of glucose are used in the preparation of beer worts and priming solutions; in manufacturing sweets, confectionery, and table syrups; in the adulteration of golden syrup, and in the finishing of cotton goods.

Lævulose or fruit sugar or fructose.—Lævulose was discovered by Dubrunfaut in 1847. It occurs in most sweet fruits together with an equal quantity of grape sugar.

Lævulose may be prepared by hydrolysing cane sugar with acid, and separating this sugar from the dextrose by the insolubility of its lime-compound; or, better, by boiling inulin, the starch from dahlia tubers, for about twenty-four hours with water.

When pure it separates from alcohol in small, hard yellowish nodules which are much sweeter than dextrose.

The crystals melt at 203° F. (95° C.). This sugar is more easily decomposed than dextrose by acids and other reagents. Its solution is a powerful reducing agent, and is lævo-rotatory. Its opticity is $(a)_{D_{3·86}} = -95·65$. The copper-reducing power (K) is rather less than that of dextrose. If the latter is taken as 100, then that of laevulose is 92·4.

Galactose.—This sugar is not known to exist free in nature, but it is a decomposition product of the group of gums known as the galactans, and also of lactose or milk sugar. It is best prepared from gum-arabic by the action of dilute sulphuric acid, or from the hydrolytic products of lactose. It crystallises in rhombic crystals which melt at 320° F. (160° C.). It is readily soluble in water, and the solution reduces Fehling's solution. This sugar is only slightly sweet to the taste. Its solutions turn the plane of polarisation to the right hand, the opticity being $(a)_{D_{3·86}} = +80·3$. Chemically it is the aldehyde of inactive dulcite, which under ordinary conditions does not ferment with yeast.

Invert sugar.—When pure, this body is a mixture of equal quantities of dextrose and lævulose, but owing to the ease with which the latter sugar decomposes, invert sugars invariably contain an excess of dextrose. Invert is a constituent of ripe sweet fruits, cane juices, and of honey, in which it is mixed up with sucroses, dextrins, nitrogenous matter, mineral salts, etc. It is used to a considerable extent as an adulterant of honey.

Inverts are prepared commercially by two processes. (1) By the action of invertase, one of the soluble ferments or enzymes in yeast, on a solution of cane sugar. The sugar solution of about ten to twelve per cent. strength is brought into a jacketed pan mixed with yeast and the temperature raised to 131°-133° F. (55°-56° C.). Yeast cannot ferment at temperatures much over 110° F.,

ORGANIC CONSTITUENTS OF THE CEREALS

but at 132° F. the inverting agent is most vigorous. In a short time the whole of the cane sugar is hydrolysed according to the equation—

$$C_{12}H_{22}O_{11} + H_2O = C_6H_{12}O_6 + C_6H_{12}O_6$$
$$\text{Cane sugar} \qquad\qquad \underbrace{\text{Dextrose} \quad \text{Lævulose}}_{\text{Invert sugar}}$$

(2) The more common process is by the action of dilute acid on the sucroses at a boiling temperature. The liquors are neutralised with carbonate of lime, filtered and clarified in bone-chars, then evaporated in vacuum pans.

Inverts as seen in commerce are light to dark coloured bright-looking syrups, or they may be solid. When pure and prepared from a good sugar, they dissolve to a clear solution in water, possess neither acidity nor iron salts, and do not leave an unpleasant after-taste in the mouth. They readily reduce Fehling's solution (K=96·6), and turn the plane of polarisation to the left hand. The opticity of pure invert is $(a)_{D_{3\cdot 86}} = -21\cdot 30$, but that of the commercial article varies from $-16°$ almost to $0°$.

Constituents.	High Grade Invert.	Medium Grade Invert.	Low Grade Invert.	Honey Pure.
Dextrose,	36·39 %	35·54 %	31·72 %	39·24 %
Lævulose,	35·46 ,,	34·12 ,,	23·94 ,,	35·71 ,,
Sucrose,	0·61 ,,	1·47 ,,	3·00 ,,	2·69 ,,
Intermediate bodies,	7·17 ,,	6·53 ,,	18·58 ,,	2·16 ,,
Nitrogenous,	0·52 ,,	1·39 ,,	0·69 ,,	1·28 ,,
Mineral salts,	2·29 ,,	2·76 ,,	2·21 ,,	0·34 ,,
Water,	17·56 ,,	18·19 ,,	19·86 ,,	18·58 ,,
				Traces of Formic Acid, etc.

Invert sugars are used chiefly in the brewing industry, and for the adulteration of honey, and to some extent in confectionery, but not in breadmaking.

None of the sugars, except the sucroses, and maltose

which is present in malt products, are available for bread as all others give the crust of the loaf a peculiar reddish appearance not unlike foxiness. Of the sugars glucose is the worst in this respect.

GROUP II.—THE BIOSES AND HIGHER SUGARS

The more important bioses are the sucroses, maltose, and lactose. The term 'sucrose' is used in preference to cane sugar, as it includes all the sugars possessing similar properties but derived from different sources, whereas cane sugar refers to the sugar extracted from the sugar cane only. The general formula $C_{12}H_{22}O_{11}$ is applied to each except when in the crystalline condition. The sucroses are anhydrous, but maltose and lactose each crystallise with one molecule of water, hence to them is given the formula $C_{12}H_{22}O_{11}.H_2O$. The only higher sugar of importance is raffinose ($C_{18}H_{32}O_6.5\ H_2O$). This occurs chiefly in such cereals as oats, and in beetroot juice.

The Sucroses ($C_{12}H_{22}O_{11}$).

The word 'sucroses' is intended to include the sugars from the sugar cane, sorghum cane, sugar maple, date and sago palms, sugar beet, chicory, the cereals, and other sources. The sugar cane contains about eighteen per cent. of this sugar in the ripe cane juices, while the juice of the sugar beet contains from fourteen to eighteen per cent.

Much of the sugar used in the bread and confectionery trade is obtained from these sources. Beet cultivation and the extraction of sugar therefrom is confined mainly to the countries occupying the centre of Europe, viz., Germany, France, Austria, and Belgium, and recently in England.

The growth of the sugar cane is only possible in tropical regions, especially the West Indies, Peru, Brazil, Central America, Mexico, Florida, Texas, the Eastern Sea Islands, as Sumatra, Java, Formosa, etc., Queensland, the Federated

ORGANIC CONSTITUENTS OF THE CEREALS 67

Malay States, and Egypt. The ripe canes possess the average composition :—

Sucrose,	18·0	per cent.
Fibre,	9·5	,,
Water,	71·0	,,
Ash, etc.,	1·5	,,
	100·0	

The ripe expressed juice has the following average composition :—

Sucrose,	19·2	,,
Other sugars,	0·3	,,
Gums, nitrogenous,	0·7	,,
Mineral salts,	0·3	,,
Water,	79·5	,,
	100·0	

The processes of obtaining the raw sugars may be summarised as follows :—

The extraction of the ripe juices by pressure and diffusion; the clarification or defecation; the evaporation of the juice; the obtaining of the ' strike ' and the separation of the sugar crystals from the molasses or uncrystallisable sugars. The firsts, seconds, and ' pieces ' sugars so obtained are then refined to produce the sugars seen on the market.

Sugar refining.—The raw sugars from the cane and beet are stored separately in a refinery, and when required are blended in the right proportions, washed somewhat, dissolved in hot water, boiled down at a high vacuum (temp. 145°-150° F.), crystallised, and passed into the centrifugals to be separated from the syrup. The sugars are again dissolved in hot water, and passed through the animal chars generally downwards; the clarified syrup is then boiled in vacuum pans and the various grades of refined sugars obtained, viz. :—

Firsts: in all forms including crystals, super-crystals,

granulated, and the cube sugars. Also the milled sugars as casters and icing, this latter being dressed with the silks. Most of the 'firsts' sugars contain over ninety-eight per cent. of real sucrose. Many of the granulated run from 99·2 to 99·8 per cent.

Seconds: in all the above forms, but not so pure.

Thirds, fourths, etc., are usually sent out as raw sugars.

The chars, or animal-charcoal filters, consist of iron cylinders fitted with a perforated false bottom and top. The whole of the space between is filled with granular animal charcoal. The active condition of the char is all-important in obtaining high-grade sugars of all kinds, including the sucroses, inverts, and glucoses. The action of the char is probably of a four-fold character: filtering, oxidising, deodorising, and decolorising.

The animal charcoal itself is prepared by cleansing bones of horses and cattle, and then destructively distilling them in iron retorts (just as coal or wood is distilled to yield coke, ordinary charcoal, and illuminating gas), after which the charcoal is crushed and graded to the right sizes. After being continuously in action for from twenty-five to thirty hours, the contents of the char must be revivified by heating in the absence of air. This may be repeated several times, after which the charcoal is useless for further char work. It is then burned in open grates and used as bone-ash either for the extraction of phosphorus or as an artificial manure. The following analysis gives some idea of the composition of char:—

Carbon,	10·91 per cent.
Phosphate of lime,	77·58 ,,
Phosphate of magnesia,	0·97 ,,
Calcium carbonate,	7·18 ,,
Calcium sulphate,	0·22 ,,
Oxide of iron, alumina, silica, etc.,	1·59 ,,
Sulphur and nitrogen compounds,	1·43 ,,
Undetermined,	0·12 ,,
	100·00

ORGANIC CONSTITUENTS OF THE CEREALS

Properties of the sucroses.—The sucroses crystallise from water in hard four-sided monoclinic prisms, which are soluble in half their weight of water, but only slightly soluble in spirits of wine. The crystals melt at 320° F. (160° C.). When heated to nearly 393° F. (200° C.) they lose water and caramel-like compounds are formed.

The solutions of sucrose are dextro-rotatory, the opticity being $(a)_{D_{3·86}} = +66·5$ or $(a)_{j_{3·86}} = +73·8$. Sodium flame readings $(a)_D \times 1·1084 =$ white light readings $(a)_j$.

The solutions do not reduce Fehling's reagent, nor do they directly ferment with yeast.

Dilute acid inverts this sugar, yielding invert sugar, as also does yeast at 133° F. (56° C.).

$$C_{12}H_{22}O_{11} + H_2O = C_6H_{12}O_6 + C_6H_{12}O_6.$$
Sucrose Water Dextrose Lævulose.

Strong sulphuric acid chars it by abstracting water. Oxidising agents like nitric acid convert it into saccharic and mucic acids.

This is the only sugar which can be used with advantage in breadmaking and confectionery.

Malt sugar, Maltose, Amylon, or Maltobiose

$$(C_{12}H_{22}O_{11} . H_2O)$$

Maltose was first prepared in the pure state by Dubrunfaut in 1847, and then forgotten until the late Cornelius O'Sullivan published his classical researches on starch transformations in 1872-76.

It occurs in the commercial glucoses, in worts, beers, bread, germinated cereals, in the intestinal canal, and reducing sugars of the blood. It is the important sugar in malt extracts and diastase pastes.

Maltose may be prepared by the action of diastase, and all substances containing it, on starch paste or soluble or malted starch at suitable temperatures, *i.e.* at about 145° F.

$$3\ C_{12}H_{20}O_{10} + 2\ H_2O = 2\ C_{12}H_{22}O_{11} + C_{12}H_{20}O_{10}.$$
Starch Water Maltose Dextrin

Also by the action of the enzymes of the saliva, and pancreas, on starch and glycogen (animal starch). Also by the action of dilute acids on starch, in which case maltose is an intermediate product.

When prepared pure, maltose exists in fine, white needle-shaped crystals which lose water when heated to 212° F. (100° C.) and become anhydrous. It is only moderately sweet but very soluble in water. The solution readily reduces Fehling's solution, $K=61\cdot07$. It turns the plane of polarisation to the right, its opticity being $(a)_{D_{3\cdot86}} = +138$. Dilute acids and the enzyme maltose hydrolyse it to two molecules of dextrose.

$$C_{12}H_{22}O_{11} + H_2O = 2\ C_6H_{12}O_6$$
$$\text{Maltose}\quad\text{Water}\quad\text{Dextrose}$$

Like the sucroses, maltose does not directly ferment. It is first hydrolysed to dextrose and then readily ferments with yeast and yeast-juice. The enzyme diastase has no action on it although it is the agent that produces it. Maltose is the anhydride of dextrose and probably contains an unchanged aldehyde group, hence its reducing action on Fehling's and Trommer's reagents. So far, it has not been prepared in the pure state on a commercial scale.

Milk sugar, lactose, or lactobiose ($C_{12}H_{22}O_{11}.H_2O$).—Lactose was discovered in 1615 by Fabriccio Bartoletti. It occurs in varying proportions in the milk of all mammals, in certain pathological secretions, and in the sap of several tropical trees, especially the West African cow tree.

Lactose is best prepared from whey in cheese-making after the separation of the casein.

It forms white, hard, rhombic crystals which melt and become anhydrous at 284° F. (140° C.). The crystals possess a faint sweet, gritty taste, and are only moderately soluble in water, but insoluble in alcohol. The solution reduces Fehling's reagent, and is dextro-rotatory, its opticity being $(a)_{D_{3\cdot86}} = +52\cdot53$, or nearly that of dextrose which is $+52\cdot8$.

When hydrolysed with dilute acid or the enzyme lactose, it yields dextrose and galactose:

$$C_{12}H_{22}O_{11} + H_2O = C_6H_{12}O_6 + C_6H_{12}O_6$$
$$\text{Lactose} \quad \text{Water} \quad \text{Dextrose} \quad \text{Galactose}$$

The trisaccharose, raffinose $(C_{18}H_{32}O_{16}.5\,H_2O)$. — This sugar occurs in several varieties of Australian eucalyptus, in the flour of cotton-seeds, in the sugar beet, in sugar molasses, in cereals, etc. From all these sources it may be prepared.

It crystallises in small needles or prisms possessing peculiar terminal points. The crystals have only a faint sweet taste; are soluble in water, but only slightly so in alcohol. The solution is strongly dextro-rotatory, its opticity being $(a)_{D_{3°86}} = +104.5$.

When hydrolysed with dilute acid it breaks down first into fructose (laevulose) and melibiose; then the melibiose hydrolyses into dextrose and galactose, thus by hydrolysis it yields the three common monoses, dextrose, laevulose, and galactose.

The detection of this sugar in a sample of so-called cane sugar rather points to the fact that the sample is a mixture of cane and beet sugars.

Group III,—The Polyoses or Polysaccharides

General formula $(C_{12}H_{20}O_{10})_n$

This group of carbohydrates comprises the starches, dextrins, celluloses, gums, pectans, amylans, galactans, etc. They cannot be called sugars although readily convertible into such. Not only do they differ from the sugars in their chemical and physical properties, but they are much more complex, and their general properties point to a very high molecular weight.

They are characterised as a rule by their insolubility in water, their non-crystalline structure, non-diffusibility, non-fermentability by yeast, and by their not reducing Fehling's reagent. Two of them, starch and cellulose, possess an organised structure.

The Starches or Amylans $(C_{12}H_{20}O_{10})_n$.

Starch is widely distributed throughout the vegetable kingdom, being found in all parts of the green plant; it occurs to some extent in animal life as glycogen, a body also shown to exist in the cells of micro-organisms.

In the growing plant it is formed in the protoplasm of the chlorophyll granules. From mere points the starch granules gradually increase in size, until ultimately they fill up the space and the chlorophyll nearly disappears. They only continue to grow so long as they are in contact with protoplasm under suitable conditions of warmth and light in the presence of carbon-dioxide and water; hence starch in leaves must be regarded as an assimilation product. As fast as this, the raw material of the plant, is formed it is carried off for various purposes by the plant, and amongst other things is stored as a reserve food supply, for example, in the tubers of the potato, dahlia, canna, cassava, etc., or in the caryopsis (see p. 91) of cereals as in the cases of wheat, barley, oats, etc.

The structure of the starch granule.—When examined by the unaided eye starch looks like a rather coarse, white powder, but under a microscope it is found to consist of a series of stratified concentric layers, the outer ones appearing denser than those near the hilum.[1] From different sources the granules differ in shape and size, and also in their behaviour towards physical tests as with polarised light, selenite plates, and the like (cf. Plates I. and II.).

The outer coating of the granule is considered to be composed of a kind of starch-cellulose, but this is by no means certain, while the interior is of starch-flour or granulose. The impervious outer cover protects the granule and prevents the action of cold water. The granulose is an intensely colloidal body (see p. 76), and though water may be absorbed by it, none of it diffuses through the outer

---

[1] The 'hilum' is the point or nucleus in a starch granule round which as an organic centre the layers are arranged.

PLATE I

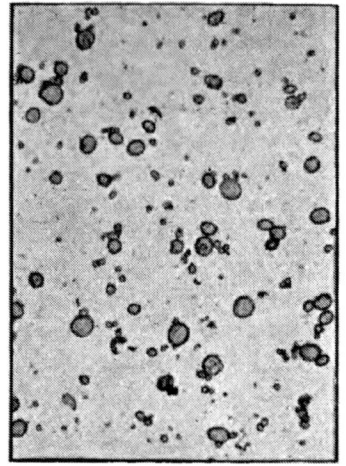
Fig. 11.

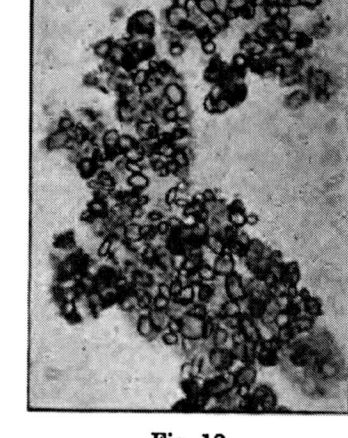
Fig. 12.

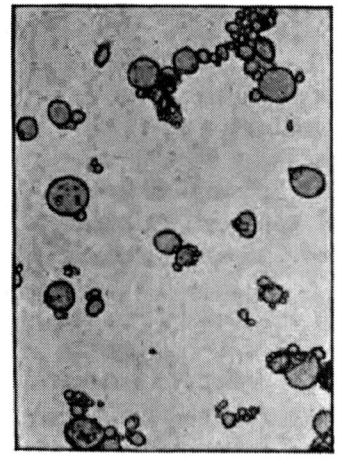
Fig. 13.

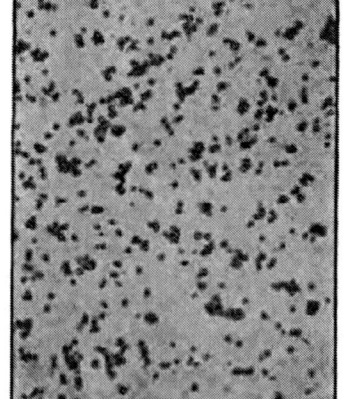
Fig. 14.

STARCHES. (Magnification × 120 diams.)

11. Wheat.   12. Barley.   13. Rye.   14. Rice.

PLATE II

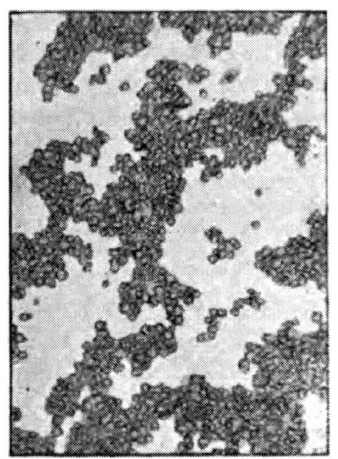

Fig. 15.

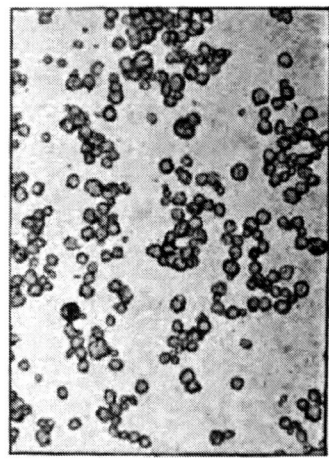

Fig. 16.

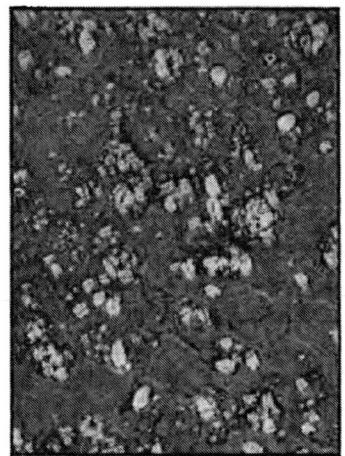

Fig. 17.

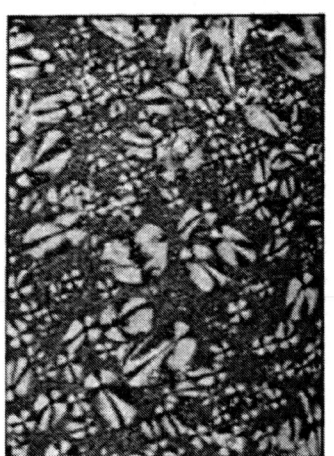

Fig. 18.

STARCHES. (Magnification × 120 diams.)

15. Oat.   16. Maize.   17. Section of potato tuber with starch granules *in situ*.   18. Potato starch (polarised).

ORGANIC CONSTITUENTS OF THE CEREALS 73

cover; hence starch is said to be insoluble in water. If, however, the cover be ruptured either by pressure or heat, the granulose may then be separated from its protecting cover. The granulose is stained blue by iodine solution, and the farinose or cover a brownish yellow.

The starch granules from different sources vary considerably in shape and size. Those from tubers are oval to almost oyster-shell-like in shape, as the potato (Fig. 17) and canna starches; cereals yield starches more or less spheroidal in form, e.g. wheat (Fig. 11), rye (Fig. 13), barley (Fig. 12), and maize (Fig. 16). Rice (Fig. 14) is an exception, being very small in size and cornered or angular in shape.

The extraction of starch from a cereal.—For this purpose the cereal such as wheat or maize should be perfectly ripe and mature. It is cleaned and separated from all other seeds, etc., by the processes described in the preparation of wheat for milling. The cereal is then steeped in water for two or three days until it is softened. The next step is grinding between burr-stones with a stream of water flowing continuously through the feed-hopper so as to carry the thin paste on to the starch-separators. The starch passes through the bolt-cloth as a milky fluid, leaving the husk, germ, and other particles behind. This residue is passed into the centrifugals to get rid of moisture, then pressed and sent out as cattle-food.

The milky fluid runs into the wooden settling vats, in which the starch falls to the bottom, and the clear water is then run off. The starch is next washed with weak alkali and thoroughly agitated with it, so as to remove nitrogenous bodies, fats, and acidity. The washing is repeated several times; finally all traces of the alkali are removed with water, and the starch dried. During the drying certain impurities come to the surface of the blocks of starch with the moisture and form a yellowish crust. This is removed, leaving the remainder as white blocks of dry starch.

Archbold shows that a bushel of cereal of fifty-six lbs. yields about half its weight of starch. Thus

Starch about 50 per cent.,	28·00 lbs.
Dry residue for cattle food,	13·70 ,,
Removed during cleansing,	0·73 ,,
Loss during extraction,	7·95 ,,
Natural moisture,	5·62 ,,
	Total 56·00 lbs.

The starch content of the different cereals is given below.

Barley	from	52 to	65	per cent.
Wheat	,,	56 ,,	69	,,
Rye	,,	51 ,,	56	,,
Maize	,,	52 ,,	56	,,
Oats	,,	52 ,,	57	,,
Rice (hulled)	,,	76 ,,	81	,,
Potatoes (tubers)	,,	15 ,,	21	,,

The properties of starch.—Starch, a white lustrous powder of specific gravity 1·55 to 1·65, is insoluble in water, alcohol, ether, and other of the usual solvents. Ordinary air-dried starch contains from 13 to 18 per cent. of water; but, when dried at 212° to 218° F. (100° to 103° C.), the whole of this is expelled leaving the starch in a very hygroscopic state. It reabsorbs from 7 to 10 per cent. of water from the air.

It may be heated to 320° F. (160° C.) without change, but above this, water of combination is driven off and chemical action ensues in which dextrins and reducing sugars are formed. The tuber starches are the most readily affected in this way, and those of the cereals, especially rice, the least. The action of hot water is progressive; the granulose absorbs water rapidly and swells until the outer covering is burst, when starch paste or gelatinised starch is formed. The starches from different sources gelatinise at different temperatures, potato and tuber starches between 149°-162° F. (65°-72° C.), and those of the cereals between 167°-185° F. (75°-85° C.).

Dilute acids convert starch into maltose, intermediate bodies, and dextrins if the action is allowed to continue for only a short time ; but, if the boiling with acid goes on for three hours, the starch is converted by hydrolysis into dextrose :

$$\underset{\text{Starch}}{C_{12}H_{20}O_{10}} + \underset{\text{Water}}{2\ H_2O} = \underset{\text{Dextrose}}{2\ C_6H_{12}O_6}$$

The action of diastase and its preparations on starch is of great importance to the baker.

Starch paste is prepared by grinding up some starch with cold water and then pouring this milky fluid into an excess of boiling water. Some of this is cooled down to 145° F. (63° C.), mixed with either diastase paste or some malt flour or saliva, and allowed to stand for about ten minutes. According to C. O'Sullivan the starch is transformed into maltose and dextrin :

$$\underset{\text{Starch}}{3\ C_{12}H_{20}O_{10}} + \underset{\text{Water}}{2\ H_2O} = \underset{\text{Maltose}}{2\ C_{12}H_{22}O_{11}} + \underset{\text{Dextrin}}{C_{12}H_{20}O_{10}}$$

At higher temperatures the proportions of maltose and dextrin differ. Diastase does not convert starch into dextrose or into any sugar lower than maltose. The maltose may be detected by boiling with Fehling's solution, in which case red cuprous oxide will be formed. Starch may be proved to be absent by cooling some of the converted liquid to the ordinary temperature and adding iodine solution. If starch is absent no blue iodide of starch can be formed. A baker's scalded flour consists chiefly of gelatinised starch, and iodine added to some of this cooled down yields an intense blue colour. If treated with diastase as above, malt sugar may easily be detected and starch proved to be absent, because the latter has been transformed into maltose, intermediate bodies and dextrin.

When starch is treated with concentrated sulphuric acid and warmed, water is abstracted and carbon set free, just as with any other carbohydrate. Ordinary pure commercial starch contains from 87 to 92 per cent. of starch, from 7 to 10 per cent. of water, with traces up to about

0·75 per cent. of nitrogenous matter, fats, reducing sugars, and mineral salts.

Owing to its colloidal nature and the difficulty of obtaining a clear solution, the molecular weight of starch has never yet been determined. According to Brown and Morris soluble starch contains one-fifth of its weight of a dextrin of formula ($C_{12}H_{20}O_{10}$) and molecular weight 6480. Therefore soluble starch is five times this or $5\{(C_{12}H_{20}O_{10})_{20}\}$ $=32,400$. This only goes to prove that granular starch is an exceedingly complex body of very high molecular weight.

This so-called soluble starch is a form prepared by treating granular starch for several days with a dilute solution of acid. The starch then loses its power of forming starch paste. It is readily acted upon by diastase.

The form obtained from rice and cassava starches makes admirable wafer paper, so largely used by the confectioner.

The Dextrins, Amylins, or Starch Gums $(C_{12}H_{20}O_{10})_n$.

The dextrins probably consist of mixtures of several or many isomeric bodies which are colloidal and uncrystallisable. The word 'isomeric' comes from the Greek *isos*, equal, and *meros*, a share or portion. Isomeric bodies are those composed of the same elements, in the same proportion, but differing in their chemical and physical properties.

Substances like sugar, salt, and nitre, which when in solution can pass through a porous membrane like vegetable parchment, are termed 'crystalloids'; whilst bodies such as starches, dextrins, gums, albumen, gluten, glue, etc., which are of a gelatinous nature, are unable to pass through vegetable parchment, and are termed 'colloids.' Enzymes are reversible colloids, because, if precipitated from their solution by alcohol, they again dissolve when shaken up with cool water.

The dextrins are soluble in water and precipitated from such solution by strong alcohol. This was the method

ORGANIC CONSTITUENTS OF THE CEREALS

adopted by C. O'Sullivan in separating maltose from the dextrins in his work on starch transformations.

Dextrins occur widely distributed in nature in plants, and to some extent in animal products. They are always associated with starch or its derived products. In starch transformations with either acid or diastase, the dextrins are by-products.

They may be prepared by heating starches alone to temperatures varying between 338° and 536° F. (170° and 280° C.), a whole range of dextrins or British gums from white to yellow and even brown shades of colour being produced.

They may also be obtained by the action of heat and dilute acids on starches; or by the action of diastase on starch paste at a high temperature. All these methods yield mixtures of dextrins, and other bodies. If continuously heated with dilute acids, the dextrins are transformed into dextrose or, more correctly, glucose.

Dextrin is prepared commercially by moistening a mixture of cheap starches with two per cent. strength of nitric acid, allowing to dry in the air, and then heating with constant stirring on an iron plate to about 230° F. (110° C.). This makes a good gum for stamps and adhesive labels.

During the baking of dough in an oven, some of the outer crust is converted into dextrins and reducing sugars. Where steam is used, this mixture of dextrins and sugars gives the glaze to the surface of the loaf.

The properties of dextrins.—The dextrins are gummy, non-crystalline powders, soluble in water; these solutions are dextro-rotatory, the specific rotation being $(a)_{D_{3\cdot 86}}=$ $+200\cdot 4$. When pure they do not reduce Fehling's solution, but most samples contain reducing sugars. They are not directly fermentable with ordinary yeast, yet a special species, the schizo-saccharomyces Pombé, contains enzymes which first hydrolyse and then ferment the dextrins. Iodine solutions colour solutions of the dextrins either violet or red, according to the constitution of the compounds themselves, whilst one of the dextrins gives no coloration with iodine solution.

The gums.—These are amorphous or non-crystalline, transparent substances widely distributed through plant life. When brought into water, they become sticky or gummy like the dextrins; some go into solution from which they may be precipitated by alcohol. These are the true gums and are distinguished from the wood gums or vegetable mucilages by the fact that the latter swell up in water, and do not give a clear solution, as they are really in a state of suspension. Both groups when boiled with dilute sulphuric acid yield reducing sugars. Gum-arabic is a true gum, while gum tragacanth or gum dragon is a vegetable mucilage.

The Celluloses, Lignoses, or Woody-fibres $(C_{12}H_{20}O_{10})_n$

The celluloses form the principal constituent of the cell-membranes of all plants, and when examined microscopically exhibit organised structure, resembling a mass of network or matted fibre. It is the skeleton form of all vegetable tissues, such as linen, cotton, flax, hemp, esparto, ramie, etc. Dragendorff in his work on plant analysis proved that cellulose from different orders of plants differs in composition, density, and other factors. Thus, the cellulose from the phanerogams or flowering plants is readily dissolved by Schweitzer's reagent, but that from the fungi is either insoluble or only slightly soluble.

Cellulose forms the framework of all parts of the wheat plant and other cereals. It is likewise the chief constituent of bran and other husky materials. As found in nature it is always associated with gums, resins, sugars, fats, colouring matter, mineral salts, etc. Swedish filter-paper is one of the purest forms of cellulose found in commerce. Raw cotton is probably the purest form of natural cellulose, and from this source it is usually prepared in the pure state.

It is a white, semi-transparent compound of 1·462 specific gravity, and is insoluble in all the common reagents.

Concentrated sulphuric acid in the cold slowly dissolves it with much swelling up. If rapidly diluted and boiled, reducing sugars are then formed.

When unglazed paper is passed through a bath of strong sulphuric acid several times, then washed thoroughly and dried, vegetable parchment is obtained. Caustic alkalies like those of soda and potash modify its structure and mercerise it. Oxidising agents convert it into oxycellulose which readily dyes. If treated in the cold with a mixture of concentrated nitric and sulphuric acids, nitrate of cellulose — gun-cotton, a high explosive — is formed. Collodion is tri-nitro-cellulose dissolved in ether-alcohol mixture.

Nitro-cellulose and camphor yield a hard gummy mass known as celluloid, a highly inflammable preparation used in the manufacture of combs, buttons, and other useful articles.

Organic Acids

A limited number of organic acids occur in the bakery materials and products. The more important of these are acetic, butyric, lactic, succinic, and tartaric acids. Organic acids are classified according to the number of carboxylic groups they contain. Thus acetic, butyric, and lactic each contain one of the groups and are therefore termed mono-carboxylic acids; whilst succinic, malic and tartaric contain two and are di-carboxylic acids. Citric is the best known tri-carboxylic acid. The word carboxylic is a contraction of carbonyl and hydroxyl and the distinctive group occurring in the formula of this series of acids is —COOH.

Acetic or the acid of vinegar, and butyric, the acid of butter fat, both belong to the fatty acids. Lactic is a member of the oxyfatty acids, and is frequently spoken of as the 'fixed acidity' of food-stuffs in which it occurs, because unlike acetic it is non-volatile in steam.

Acetic acid ($CH_3.COOH$).—Acetic acid is prepared by two processes:—by the destructive distillation of wood, and by the action of acetic bacteria on dilute solutions of alcohol, especially in low-strength alcoholic beverages such as clarets, Burgundy, Rhine and Moselle wines (all of which contain less than twelve per cent. of spirit), ales and beer, cider and perry, etc.

The alcohol produced in dough by fermentation is oxidised to acetic acid, the smell of which may be recognised in the steam that issues from the oven during the baking of bread.

The malt vinegar industry depends on the power of the various acetic acid groups of bacteria to oxidise alcohol to acetic acid. The reaction is somewhat complicated, but may be represented by the equations:

$$\underset{\text{Alcohol}}{CH_3.CH_2OH} + \underset{\text{Oxygen}}{O} = \underset{\text{Acetaldehyde}}{CH_3.CHO} + \underset{\text{Water}}{H_2O}$$

and $\underset{\text{Acetaldehyde}}{CH_3.CHO} + \underset{\text{Oxygen}}{O} = \underset{\text{Acetic acid}}{CH_3.COOH}$

The purest and strongest form is the glacial acetic acid, a very pungent, acrid-smelling liquid, which produces white blisters if allowed to touch the skin. The liquid boils at 244·4° F. (118° C.) and has a sp. gr. of 1·080. It readily mixes with water, alcohol, and ether in all proportions. This strong liquid forms a good solvent for many substances that are insoluble in water. The ordinary acid of commerce contains about thirty-three per cent. of acetic acid. Such an acid is used in making royal icing, acetic acid flavouring essences, and for many other purposes. The amount of this acid in vinegars rarely exceeds six or seven per cent., which is the strength prepared in the various vinegar processes.

The salts of the acid are the acetates, and these are of considerable importance in a number of industries. Verdigris, a basic copper acetate, is formed by allowing thin copper sheets to stand in vinegar, or when copper vessels used in jam-making or for sugar-boiling are allowed to remain dirty after use in contact with air and moisture. The verdigris forms as a greenish or greenish-blue deposit on the copper or brass vessels. This copper salt is a strong poison and therefore ought not to be allowed to come into contact with foods.

Butyric acids ($C_4H_8O_2$).—The more important of the two butyric acids is the ordinary or normal butyric ($C_3H_7.COOH$) which occurs in the free and combined state in nature. Thus, wherever organic nitrogenous matter and filth are allowed to collect, bacterial fermentation takes place resulting in the formation of butyric acid. This is the case especially during moist, hot weather in dirty, untidily kept bakeries, and it leads to the presence of string mould and other diseases in bread.

Butyric acid in combination with glycerin is the important volatile fat in butter. When from any cause this glyceride decomposes, the butter is said to have become rancid, because of the nauseous odour of the free acid. This same acid exists in clothing used in bakeries and left unwashed for a few days. Stale perspiration on the person smells equally disagreeably owing to the formation of butyric acid.

The free acid is a thick liquid, of nauseous odour, which boils at about 325° F. (162·8° C.). The liquid mixes readily with water and confers on the mixture its unpleasant smell. Its salts are the butyrates, the ethereal salts or esters being used as essences.

Lactic acids ($C_3H_6O_3$).—The 'fixed acidity' or lactic acid of food-stuffs ($CH_3.CHOH.COOH$), is formed by the action of the many different groups of lactic ferments on carbohydrates in the presence of nitrogenous matter; hence it exists in all carbohydrate food-stuffs and beverages, and in milk. In the free state, it is a thick, sticky, sour-smelling liquid usually of a brownish colour, although when pure it is colourless. If dough has been allowed to over-ferment, and also over-prove, the characteristic odour of this acid may be observed. It is a common smell in bakeries where the place and utensils are not kept scrupulously clean. The organisms which give rise to lactic acid can be seen if milk is kept for a day or two in a warm place and then a drop of the watery liquid examin[ed] under a microscope.

The lactic acid is spoken of as 'fixed acidity' since, distilled with steam, it is not volatile but begins to deco[m]pose, whereas acetic acid or 'volatile acidity' readi[ly] passes over quite unchanged with the steam. The sa[lts] of lactic acid are the lactates, of which the best know[n] are the lactates of lime and zinc.

Succinic acid, $\begin{array}{l}CH_2.COOH \\ | \\ CH_2.COOH\end{array}$.—This is the third member [of] the series of di-carboxylic acids. Its chief interest to t[he] baker lies in the fact that it is formed by the action of yea[st] in the dough during fermentation. It is a white solid bod[y] obtained by distilling amber. The salts are the succinate[s].

Malic acid, $\begin{array}{l}CH_2.COOH \\ | \\ CHOH.COOH\end{array}$.—Malic is an important frui[t] acid, which exists in the free state, and also as its potassiu[m] acid salt in unripe, sharp-tasting, sweet fruits like th[e] apple (Latin *malum*, from which it takes its name), rowa[n] or mountain ash berries, gooseberries, raspberries, blackberries, grapes, bananas, pineapples, etc., where it i[s] frequently associated with both citric and tartaric acids.

The free acid is a pleasant tasting compound crystallising in white, deliquescent, nodular lumps or needles which easily dissolve in water. Its salts are the malates; with the exception of the potassium acid compound they are of little importance.

Tartaric acid, $\begin{array}{l}CHOH.COOH \\ | \\ CHOH.COOH\end{array}$.—Tartaric acid occurs very widely distributed in the vegetable kingdom both in the free state and as its acid salts—the tartrates—being generally associated with malic and citric acids. Its chief source, however, is the deposit of argol that takes place in the fermentation of grape-juice or must. The argol is purified and decolorised, yielding the cream of tartar of

ORGANIC CONSTITUENTS OF THE CEREALS

commerce. From this the lime tartrate is obtained by precipitating the solution with a soluble lime salt. The lime tartrate is now decomposed with sulphuric acid, the calcium sulphate separated out, and the clear liquors evaporated to crystallising point. As the work is carried out in lead-lined vessels, the crystals of tartaric acid always contain traces of lead. When required for food purposes, the crystals must be purified and freed from lead. The crystals are monoclinic prisms which melt at 275° F. (135° C.). When heated strongly they decompose, forming a number of different compounds, and smell not unlike burnt sugar at the charring stage.

They possess a very strong acid taste and are somewhat poisonous when taken in quantity. The acid is readily soluble in hot and cold water, yielding solutions which possess optical properties and turn the plane of polarisation to the right hand.

Tartaric acid is used in calico printing and dyeing, in medicine, and in the preparation of self-raising powders and effervescing drinks. Its most important salt is the bitartrate of potassium or cream of tartar. This when pure forms hard rhombic crystals, which are only moderately soluble in water. The best form for aeration purposes is the powder, the highest quality of which contains ninety-eight per cent. of real cream of tartar. When brought into contact with bicarbonate of soda and water, Rochelle salt and carbon dioxide are formed. The proportions are approximately two parts by weight of cream of tartar to one of bicarbonate of soda.

$$\begin{array}{c} CH.OH.COOH \\ | \\ CHOH.COOK \end{array} + NaHCO_3 = \begin{array}{c} CHOH.COONa \\ | \\ CHOH.COOK \end{array} + CO_2 + H_2O$$

Cream of Tartar   Bicarbonate of Soda   Rochelle Salt   Carbon dioxide   Water

Citric acid, $\begin{array}{c} CH_2.COOH \\ | \\ CHOH.COOH \\ | \\ CH_2.COOH \end{array}$ or $C_6H_8O_7$.—Citric acid is a good example of a tricarboxylic body, yielding three serie[s] of salts somewhat like ordinary phosphoric acid. Citri[c] occurs widely distributed in nature associated with mali[c] and tartaric acids and their potassium acid salts. It i[s] prepared by processes very similar to those used for tartari[c] acid. The starting point is the juice from lemons, which is heated to boiling with chalk and the lime citrate decomposed, etc. The acid crystallises with one molecule of water in hard rhombic prisms. These readily dissolve in water and alcohol.

The solution possesses a pleasant acid taste not so harsh as tartaric, and moreover it is not liable to give convulsions in the stomach as is tartaric when taken internally in quantity. It is therefore much more suitable for the preparation of aerated beverages. Its salts are the citrates.

THE FATS

The oils or fats, which are so widely distributed through the vegetable and animal kingdoms, are organic salts composed of the base glycerin combined with a fatty acid. They are of two different classes : the *volatile* fats which confer flavour and smell on the substances in which they exist, as, for example, butyrin, one of the chief volatile constituents of butter ; and the *fixed* fats which are either white to yellowish liquids, semifluids, or solids. These latter possess neither flavour nor aroma except to a very limited extent, as in the case of the three common fats that are found in all the cereal oils, lard and margarine, viz., olein, a yellowish oily liquid, the chief constituent of olive oil ; palmitin, a white pasty solid found in palm oil and human fat, and stearin, a white hard solid forming the bulk of kitchen grease or tallow.

Glycerin is a trihydric alcohol of the composition

$$\begin{array}{c} CH_2.OH \\ | \\ CH.OH \\ | \\ CH_2.OH \end{array}$$

ORGANIC CONSTITUENTS OF THE CEREALS

When strongly heated it loses two molecules of water and forms acrolein, an aldehyde characterised by possessing the odour of burnt fat:

$$CH_2OH.CHOH.CH_2OH - 2\ H_2O = CH_2 : CH.CHO$$
Glycerin   Water   Acrolein

A similar reaction takes place in the cooking of flesh-meats, puff-paste goods, etc., if the temperature of the oven is too high. Acrolein has an exceedingly pungent and disagreeable odour.

The more important common fats are butyrin, lauristin, myristin, olein, palmitin, and stearin. These are compounds or glycerides composed of the trihydric or tri-acid base glycerin and the fatty acid that gives its name to the salt; thus butyrin, the chief volatile glyceride in butter, is composed of glycerin combined with three molecules of butyric acid ($C_3H_7.COOH$).

$$\begin{matrix} CH_2.OH \\ | \\ CH.OH \\ | \\ CH_2.OH \end{matrix} + \begin{cases} C_3H_7.COOH \\ C_3H_7.COOH \\ C_3H_7.COOH \end{cases} = \begin{matrix} CH_2.O.CO.C_3H_7 \\ | \\ CH.O.CO.C_3H_7 \\ | \\ CH_2.O.CO.C_3H_7 \end{matrix} + 3\ H_2O$$

Glycerin   Butyric acid   Tributyrin   Water

The other triglycerides are similarly composed. If these or any other triglycerides are heated with water at a pressure, *i.e.* really superheated steam—they are decomposed into glycerin and the corresponding free fatty acid. Example, of palmitin or tripalmitin—

$$\begin{matrix} CH_2.O.CO.C_{15}H_{31} \\ | \\ CH.O.CO.C_{15}H_{31} \\ | \\ CH_2.O.CO.C_{15}H_{31} \end{matrix} + \begin{cases} H.OH \\ H.OH \\ H.OH \end{cases} = \begin{matrix} CH_2.OH \\ | \\ CH.OH \\ | \\ CH_2.OH \end{matrix} + 3\ C_{15}H_{31}.COOH$$

Tripalmitin   Water   Glycerin   Palmitic acid

Similar decompositions may be obtained by boiling with water and a small quantity of sulphuric acid.

When any of these natural fats are boiled with caustic alkalies like caustic soda or potash, or lead hydrate, the glycerides are broken up into glycerin and the corresponding salt of the fatty acids; these latter being known as soaps. The ordinary hard or soda soaps are manufactured by boiling mixtures of molten fats first with weak and then with stronger solutions of caustic soda or soda-lye. Let X stand for fatty acid, then the reaction may be expressed by the equation—

$$\begin{matrix} CH_2.X \\ | \\ CH.X \\ | \\ CH_2.X \end{matrix} + \begin{cases} NaOH \\ NaOH \\ NaOH \end{cases} = \begin{matrix} CH_2.OH \\ | \\ CH.OH \\ | \\ CH_2.OH \end{matrix} + 3NaX$$

Triglyceride Caustic soda Glycerine Soda soap

From this it will be seen that the soaps are metallic salts of the higher fatty acids.

It has already been pointed out that the three glycerides, olein, palmitin, and stearin, are common to both vegetable and animal fats; these occur then in the fats used for food purposes such as butter, lard, nut or vegetable butter, margarine, neutral or cotton-seed oil preparations, and others. The chief point of difference between vegetable and animal fats is that all vegetable fats contain small quantities of the solid alcohol phytosterol, while animal fats contain cholesterol. These may be detected by preparing their acetates and examining the crystals by the help of a microscope.

Fats are used in breadmaking as an improver. A small quantity, two to three ozs. per fourteen lbs. of flour, improves the flavour and texture, makes the crust short, and helps to keep the crumb of the loaf moist. If too large quantities be employed, it tends to spoil both colour and flavour, whilst at the same time increasing the cost.

The natural fat or oil in the cereals exists for the most part in the germ, to which it gives a yellowish buttery appearance; it also saves the germ from being broken up in the milling process. Wheat oil contains a small quantity of volatile fat, which readily decomposes and tends to give the flour a rancid flavour. This is one of the reasons why millers take out the germ. The chief part of wheat fat,

ORGANIC CONSTITUENTS OF THE CEREALS

however, consists of the fixed non-volatile glycerides—olein, palmitin, myristin, stearin, and minute quantities of others.

The oil itself when refined is a dark yellowish liquid possessing the characteristic flavour and smell of the cereal oils. The quantity in wheat varies somewhat with the different sources; thus different wheats contain from 0·90 to 2·71 per cent., English averaging about 1·65. Whole meal contains from 1·52 to 1·87 per cent.; standard meal about 2·03, and patent flours from 0·61 to 1·48 per cent. Wheat germs contain from 6·56 to 10·31 per cent. of fat. It is scarcely necessary to point out that the mineral oils and fats are for the most part hydrocarbons and not glycerides, therefore they will not saponify, *i.e.* yield soap and glycerin when boiled up with a caustic alkali.

THE NITROGENOUS CONSTITUENTS OF WHEAT AND FLOUR

These form one of the most difficult subjects of study, as, unfortunately, very little of a definite character is known of these bodies. Most of them, especially the proteids and gluten, are of unknown composition and constitution. They are of a colloidal nature, readily coagulated by heat or very dilute acid; they combine with resins and tannins forming compounds, which are somewhat soluble in sugar solutions but easily thrown out of solution.

The majority of them, in fact all except the nucleins, are composed of the elements carbon, hydrogen, nitrogen, oxygen, and sulphur.

The nucleins contain the five before-mentioned elements and, in addition, phosphorus and iron.

The nitrogenous bodies may be divided into:—the *proteids* or *albuminoids*, including the special proteid or mixture of proteids known as gluten, which occurs only in wheat and rye, rendering the meals from these two cereals fit for breadmaking; the *nucleins*, very highly complex bodies generally found in the nuclei of plants and animals;

and the *soluble ferments* or *enzymes*. These latter bodies will be considered in their proper place in connection with fermentation.

The **proteids** are a group of nitrogenous compounds or mixtures of compounds which are very widely distributed in plant life, and which when absorbed and assimilated by animals, act as flesh-forming constituents. They are or form one of the proximate food principles.

Their mode of formation by plants is to a very large extent a matter of conjecture. They may be produced by the combination of either carbohydrate or fatty compounds, or even the higher alcohols, with simple forms of nitrogenous compounds absorbed from the soil or air by the plants.

When formed the proteids are stored away, often with the starches as in the case of the cereals, to act as reserve food supplies for the embryo during the early stages of germination. At the proper time, they are degraded by the action of the proteolytic enzymes into compounds of a comparatively simple constitution which are soluble, crystallisable, and diffusible; hence they may pass by the processes of osmosis (see p. 125) through the cell-like structure of the cotyledon into the growing embryo.

The more important proteins of wheat are :—leucosin, an albumin, two or more insoluble proteins, a globulin, gluten, and possibly proteoses, which latter are decomposition products.

In the case of the wheat berry, a considerable amount of the nitrogenous content is found in the aleurone cells. These form a covering, a single cell in thickness, next to the starch-containing cells all over the berry, with the exception of the space occupied by the embryo. This helps to account for the well-known fact that the lower grades of flour, which are taken from the wheat berry near to the bran, contain rather more nitrogen than the patents. The gluten, or matter which goes to form it, is distributed throughout the whole of the endosperm probably in the spaces between the starch-containing cells. If a fine section of a wheat endosperm be stained first with iodine

ORGANIC CONSTITUENTS OF THE CEREALS

solution to colour the starch granules blue, and then with haematoxylin solution, the spaces between the starch-containing cells will be of a dark pink shade, showing the presence of nitrogenous matter, and as all flours contain gluten in fairly regular proportions from the same wheats, the inference is that the pink to red colour is due to gluten.

At the present time gluten is considered to be a mixture of two proteids, viz., glutenin and gliadin.

The glutenin is the constituent which gives strength and toughness to gluten; therefore a flour that contains a gluten in which there is a high proportion of glutenin to gliadin is a strong flour capable of yielding a loaf of large volume with little or no flavour.

Gliadin is vegetable gelatin, a soft sticky body which tones down the strong, harsh glutenin. Flours made from English wheats contain only a small quantity of gluten, but this has a relatively high proportion of gliadin; hence the small volume of loaf obtained from English wheaten flours. Such a flour is suitable for blending with a strong spring wheaten flour, or for cake-making. Both glutenin and gliadin are looked upon as being composed of a proteid and an amino-acid.

As far back as 1859, Kühne, Meissner, and others of the same school of thought showed that the proteids may be broken down by a series of steps into compounds becoming less complex at each step, and that the process closely resembles that of the hydrolysis of starch; that dilute acids behaved very much like pepsin or papäin in that the proteids were hydrolysed by these to peptones, and that the action of alkalies resembled that of trypsin, in which the proteids were degraded much lower, even to the form of amides. In more recent times, Osborne, Chittenden, and other American workers have carried out a large number of researches on the subject of the cereal proteids and their derived products.

The amides as a group are soluble, crystallisable, and diffusible compounds which contain the amino group $-CH.NH_2$. The most interesting of these is asparagin, which may be obtained as large, colourless crystals containing one molecule of water,

$$\begin{array}{c} CH.NH_2.COOH \\ | \\ CH_2.CO.NH_2 \end{array}.H_2O$$

Asparagin exists in asparagus sprouts and in cereal rootlets. It forms an excellent nitrogenous yeast food. Most of the proteids and their derived products have a percentage composition varying between—

	Carbon	Hydrogen	Nitrogen	Oxygen	Sulphur
	49·0	6·6	14·9	20·8	0·3
and	55·2	7·4	18·5	25·3	2·3

The nucleins are much more complex than any of the proteids, and are mixtures of nitrogenous bodies containing, amongst other things, phosphorised fat. Their hydrolytic products form excellent food for plants and animals.

CHAPTER VII

THE CEREALS AND THEIR COMPOSITION

THE cereals or grain-producing plants belong to the great sub-class *Glumaceae* of the Monocotyledons. This sub-class takes its name from the fact that its members have their flowers arranged inside scaly bracts or 'glumes,' kinds of husks which protect these minute and delicate blooms.

The sub-class is further divided into a number of natural orders or families, and each of these into a genus. The natural order of the *Gramineae* or grasses is characterised by possessing hollow stems, ligules and split leaf-sheaths. The chief members of this order of plants are :—the giant bamboo, sugar cane, sorghum cane, the cereals including wheat, barley, maize, oats, rye, and rice, and all the meadow and wayside grasses. All of these members possess a number of points in common with one another. The chief parts of a grass plant are (Fig. 19) :—

The tufted roots from which spring a number of hollow stems, clothed with split leaf-sheaths that are bound to the stems with a strap or ligule ; the stems divided into sections by contractions or nodes, and at the head of the stem a spindle on which is developed first the flower and finally the ear of corn (Fig. 20). Each little berry is botanically known as a *caryopsis*—a dry, one-sided fruit in which the 'pericarp' and 'testa' are fused together into one membrane, the bran. The seed is also albuminous.

The family name for the wheat plant is *Triticum*, and if the plants of this genus be examined they will be found to possess all the parts of a grass. Again if a wheat flower be carefully observed with a strong pocket lens, the resemblance to the flowers of other grasses is very close

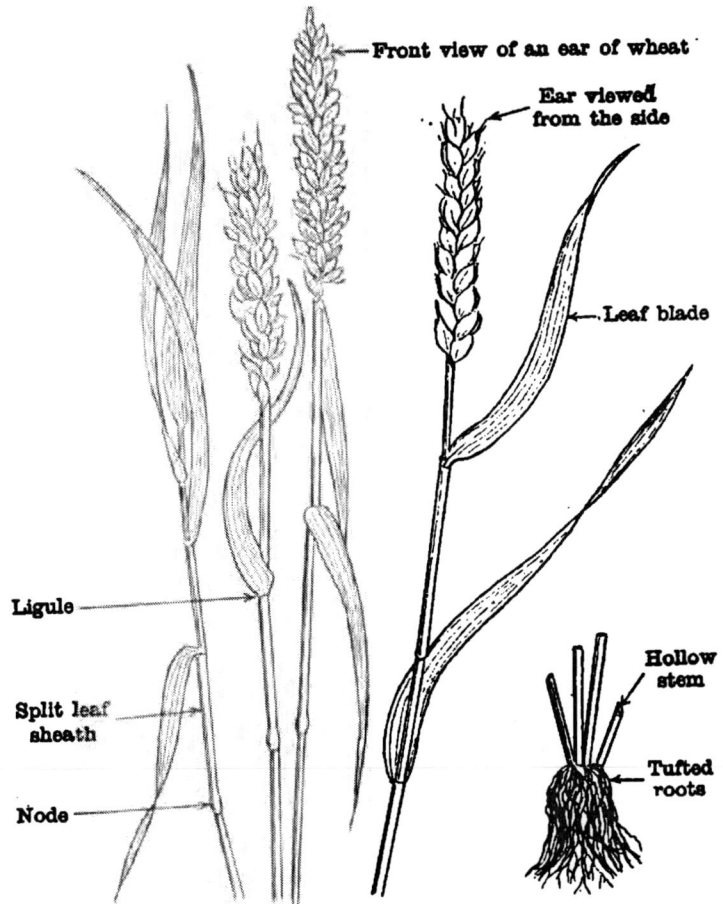

Fig. 19.—Drawing of a Wheat Plant to illustrate the Morphology of Cereals.

(Fig. 21). Both the male and female parts are arranged in one flower which consists of three stamens growing from

PLATE III

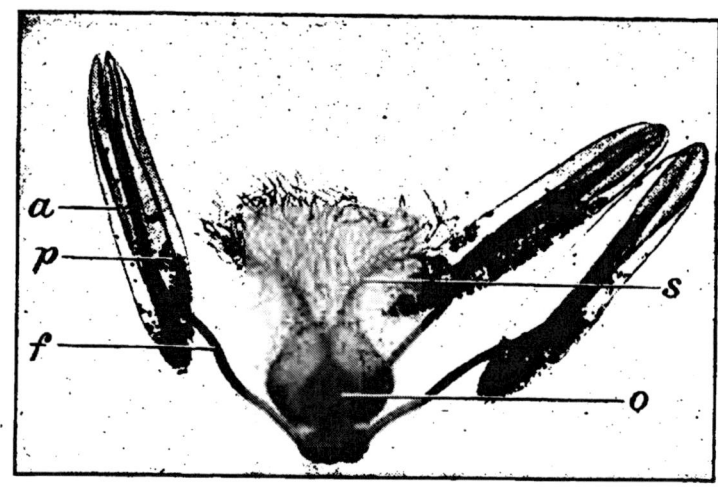

Fig. 21. WHEAT FLOWER (highly magnified).

Male parts—*a*, anther ; *p*, pollen grains ; *f*, filament.
Female parts—*s*, feathery stigma ; *o*, ovary.

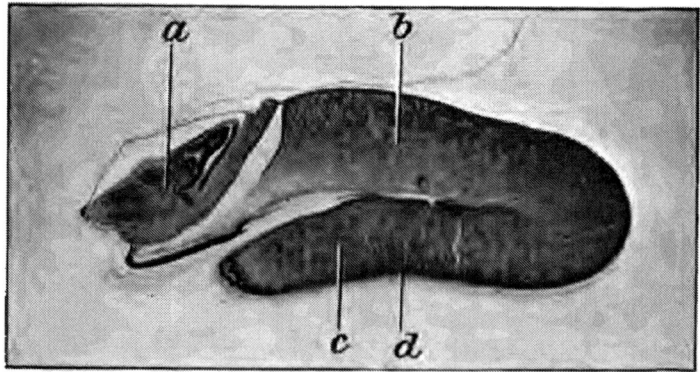

Fig. 22.—WHEAT BERRY. Longitudinal section (× 8 diams.)

a, Embryo or germ. *b*, Endosperm or albumen.
c, Starch. *d*, Bran.

THE CEREALS AND THEIR COMPOSITION 93

below the base of the ovary, hence the flower is *hypogenous*. These stamens or male organs are built up of a long hollow membrane or filament on the top of which is the anther or hollow box containing the pollen grains. The female parts

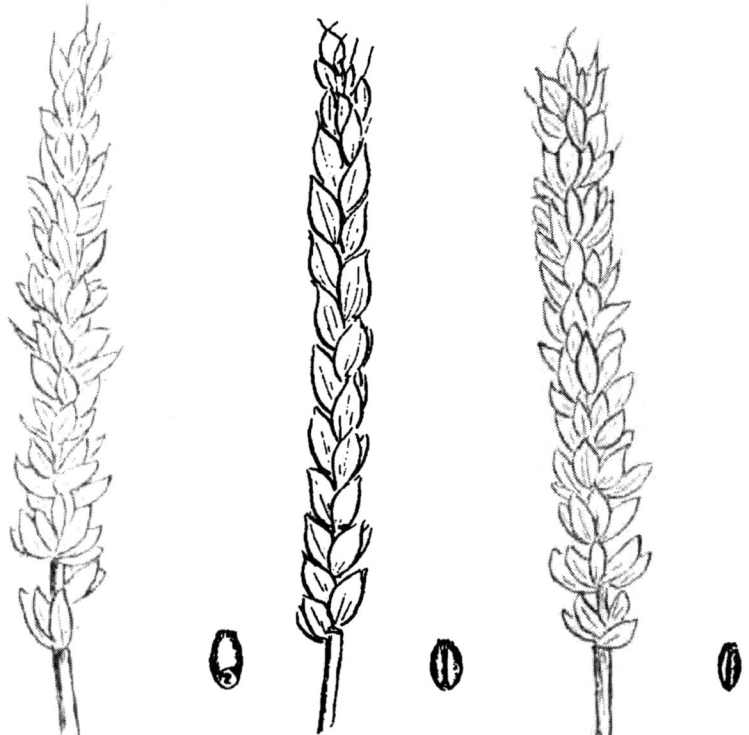

Fig. 20.—Ears and Grains of three Varieties of Wheat.

are composed of an ovary, the upper portion of which forms the pistil, this latter being developed into two feathery stigmas which collect the pollen grains to fertilise the ovary. The whole of the flower is enveloped inside the protecting scaly bracts or glumes. A wheat flower in England may best be examined in June and July as in September the harvest begins.

Classification of wheats.—Perhaps the best recent classification of wheats is that of Professor Dr. Otto Stapf, who read a very interesting paper on the 'History of Wheats' at the Winnipeg meeting of the British Association in 1909. A summary of this paper is given in an article on wheats by Dr. Edward J. Russell in No. 18 of *Science Progress*, from which the following excerpts are taken.

Wheats are divided into four groups :—

(1) Einkorn (*Triticum monococcum*); this has one grain very compact and bearded on each spikelet. It is the oldest known wheat and was recently found by Schliemann in the ruins of Troy; also in neolithic remains in Switzerland and Hungary, and it was known to the Greeks. It is exceptionally resistant to 'rust,' and is still grown in Spain, France, Switzerland, Germany, and the Balkan States. Stapf found it in Syria and Upper Mesopotamia, and points out that the only obvious change between it and *Tr. oegilopioides*, a wild form, is the much fewer long white hairs of the spindle as compared with their number in the wild forms. Other domestic wheats have altered in the same way.

(2) The second group comprises four classes that are now very distinct :—

    (*a*) The hard or macaroni wheats (*Tr. durum*).
    (*b*) Emmer (*Tr. dicoccum*).
    (*c*) The English or Rivet wheats (*Tr. turgidum*).
    (*d*) Polish wheats (*Tr. polonicum*).

Macaroni wheat has three or four flowers per spikelet, long bearded ears and hard pointed grains. It is grown in most of the European countries round the Mediterranean Sea. Its chief uses are for the manufacture of macaroni, and for blending with softer wheats in milling.

Emmer is a bearded wheat with two grains per spikelet. It is cultivated in South Germany, Spain, Italy,

THE CEREALS AND THEIR COMPOSITION 95

Servia, Switzerland, India, Abyssinia, Canada, and the United States of America.

The English or Rivet wheat is another of the cereals of ancient Egypt. The grains are large in size and plump, and there may be as many as five per spikelet. Although of poor quality it yields good crops and is the commonest bearded wheat in England.

Polish wheat possesses large outer glumes with grains very long and hard. It is a mutation from *Tr. durum*. It gives a poor yield and is grown only in a few districts other than Italy, Spain, and Abyssinia.

(3) The third group is economically of great importance, including as it does all the common ordinary wheats, bearded and otherwise, grown for breadmaking. All these are grouped under the term *Tr. vulgare*. The bearded varieties usually grow best in hot, dry countries, and the beardless ones in cooler climates.

(4) The fourth group consists of the Spelt wheats. As in the case of Einkorn, the grains do not readily detach themselves from the chaff, and hence do not thresh out like *Tr. vulgare*. On the northern shores of the Black Sea there still flourishes a species, *Tr. cylindricum*, which seems to have been the original form of the Spelts.

Many of the above classified species and varieties of wheats are cultivated in the more temperate zones of the earth, but in England the *Triticum turgidum* is perhaps the commonest grown, whilst some *Tr. durum* or hard macaroni wheat for mixing purposes, and the varied mutations known as *Tr. vulgare*, which include the red and white Fife wheats and some of the newer and stronger varieties of the improved French wheats, are also grown.

The strong spring wheats are little grown in England, as the yields of grain and straw are poor compared with the *turgidum* variety, which is a soft one containing a low proportion of a weak gluten. This latter variety yields plenty of straw for farm use, whilst the flour from it gives bread of good flavour.

Both spring and winter-sown wheats are largely grown

on the American continent. Other wheats are the *Triticum muticum*, also known as Bohemian, Italian, or white wheat, and *Tr. spelta*, or the ordinary thin Spelt wheat of France, South Germany, etc. *Tr. durum* or hard wheat is largely grown in Italy owing to the quantity of gluten it contains —approximately 17·0 per cent.—and its suitability for making macaroni, a favourite Italian food. The chief wheat-growing countries of the world include England, South and South-West Russia, India, Persia, Hungary, and parts of Austria, Canada, the United States of America, Argentina, the southern or cooler portions of Australia, and New Zealand.

Spring wheats of the Minnesota type yield strong flours containing much gluten of a tough, elastic kind. Russian, Indian, and Persian wheats are very hard and dry, with a fair proportion of gluten. Winter-sown wheats are generally soft with not too much gluten; Argentina and the southern hemisphere wheats belong to this class.

English wheats are about a quarter of an inch long and one-half that length in diameter. A bushel varies between 58 and 63 lbs. in weight with an average of 60 lbs. Other wheats than English vary much more in weight; thus the heaviest and best European reaches 67 lbs. per bushel and the lightest 55 lbs. Hungarian wheats for export, by government regulation, must not fall below 60·75 lbs.

The structure of the wheat berry.—If examined externally the following points may be noticed (Fig. 23). The berry is somewhat barrel-shaped; at the top is a tuft of hairs—the beard; at the lower end or point of attachment to the spindle on the dorsal or outer side is a small peculiar-shaped protuberance which indicates the position of the germ beneath the bran; on the opposite, inner, or ventral side is a deep furrow running the whole length of the grain. This is the crease which harbours a quantity of dust and micro-organisms, giving rise to difficulties in the cleaning preparatory to milling the wheat.

In continuance of the examination a section is cut across

THE CEREALS AND THEIR COMPOSITION

the grain, viz. a transverse section, so as to permit of an internal examination of the berry. Beginning from the outside inwards, if the eye is assisted by a strong pocket-lens or reading glass, the following parts may be seen:— the outer skins—pericarp and testa—forming the bran; a single layer of rectangular cells full of minute grains of nitrogenous matter; these are the *aleurone* or cereallin cells, the function of which is to supply the young growing

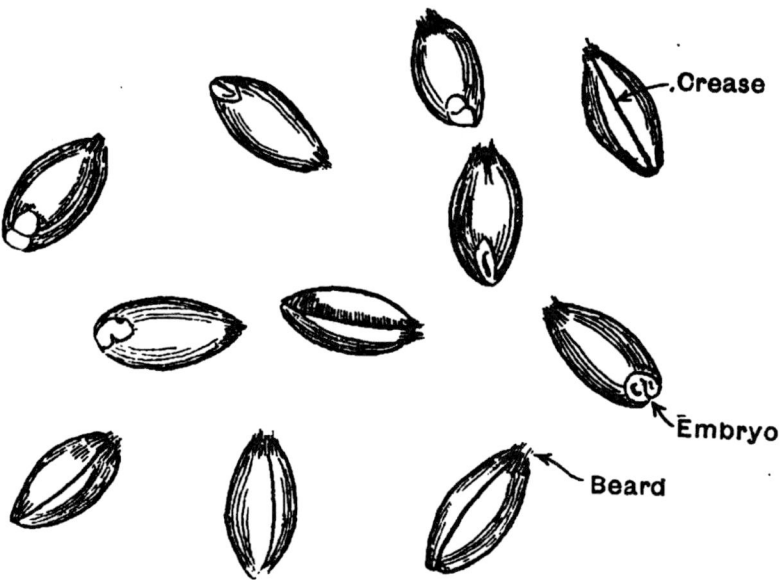

Fig. 23.—Wheat Berries (magnified).

embryo with its proper nitrogenous food; and the starch-containing cells packed full of starch granules of varying size. The spaces between the cell-walls are probably filled with the substance known as 'gluten.'

If a longitudinal section (Figs. 22, 24, and 25), that is one cut from the top to the bottom of the berry through the embryo and crease, be examined, the following will be seen:—

the interior of the berry consists of two uneven parts—the major portion or *endosperm* or albumen, and the small part at one side near the bottom, which is the *germ* or embryo. The germ is protected from injury by a covering of light wood cells—the *scutellum*; lying between this and the endosperm is a row of deep rectangular cells—the absorptive epithelial layer (Fig. 26). In these will be found the enzymes, which afterwards during germination act on the constituents of the endosperm, converting them into foods suitable for the embryonic plant, until it is able to obtain its sustenance from the air and soil.

In Fig. 24, *a* are the aleurone cells, *b* the testa, and *c* the pericarp; the empty starch cells are shown at *d*, while at *e* are a few starch granules that still remain. In Fig. 25 the lower part shows the aleurone cells highly magnified.

In Fig. 26, *a* is the acrospire, *b* the plumule, *c*, *d*, and *e* the root-sheath, rootlet, and root-cap respectively. At *f* are starch granules, *g* are the absorptive epithelial cells, *h* the cotyledon, and *i* the scutellum.

If sections be cut off other cereals, the general arrangement will be seen to conform to that of the wheat berry as above described. There are, however, sundry points of difference. For example, wheat and rye have a single row of aleurone granules, barley has usually three though occasionally only two. Wheat possesses a number of fine hairs at the top of the berry, barley has none, but in most cases the outer husk or dorsal pale is prolonged into an awn. When the cereals are ground between hard French burr-stones into meals, these will be found to contain particles of the endosperm or starchy matter, mixed up with hairs, bits of bran, aleurone granules, germ, epidermal cells, etc.

The chemical composition of the cereals.—The cereals contain the chief proximate principles of food-stuffs, viz. carbohydrates, fats, proteins, and mineral salts with water, but not in the proportions to form a perfect food. This is not of much importance, as they are not relied on

PLATE IV

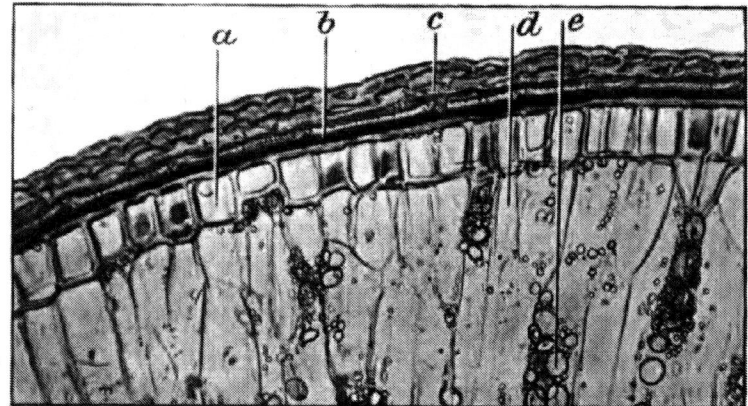

Fig. 24.—Part longitudinal section of a wheat endosperm with most of the starch granules removed.

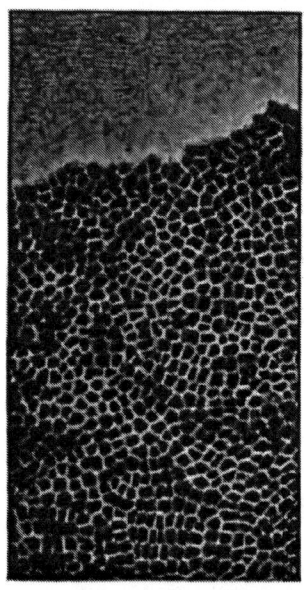

Fig. 25.—Highly magnified section through aleurone cells, showing the granules.

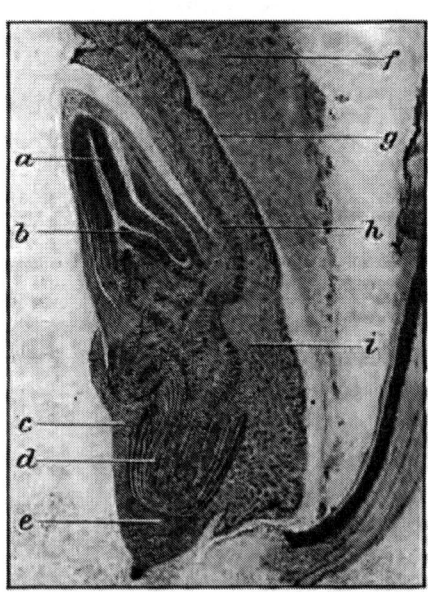

Fig. 26.—Section of wheat germ.

THE CEREALS AND THEIR COMPOSITION

alone as foods but are always eaten with other food. Bread is generally taken as bread and butter; rice with milk; oatmeals in various forms with both sugars and milk; hence the deficiency in certain of these proximate principles is made up by the addition of others. As a matter of fact, the Biblical statement is absolutely true : 'Man does not live by bread alone.'

If wheat and other cereals are chemically examined, their composition, although generally similar, differs considerably in the quantities in which the constituents are present. But the same cereals, for example the wheats, differ also very considerably among themselves. Thus two important constituents, the proteins and carbohydrates, vary enormously. Dammer in his composition of flour-wheats as distinct from those used in feeding cattle and fowls, gives the following figures :—

Constituents.	Minimum.	Maximum.	Average.
Water,	5·33 %	19·10 %	13·56 %
Proteins,	8·19 ,,	24·16 ,,	12·42 ,,
Fats,	1·00 ,,	2·65 ,,	1·70 ,,
Mineral Salts,	0·95 ,,	2·59 ,,	1·71 ,,
Cellulose	1·23 ,,	6·42 ,,	2·66 ,,
Starch, sugar, etc.	61·28 ,,	77·32 ,,	67·89 ,,

The author in his experience has also found large variations not only in wheat and barley, but in other cereals.

The composition of wheats from various sources.

Constituents.	English.	English.	Russian.	Canadian.	Argentina.
Water,	10·74 %	13·56 %	12·77 %	13·97 %	12·29 %
Proteins,	11·98 ,,	12·42 ,,	17·26 ,,	12·48 ,,	13·12 ,,
Fats,	1·29 ,,	1·73 ,,	1·59 ,,	1·57 ,,	1·43 ,,
Mineral Salts,	1·37 ,,	1·84 ,,	1·71 ,,	1·73 ,,	1·58 ,,
Cellulose,	2·26 ,,	2·38 ,,	2·13 ,,	2·88 ,,	2·73 ,,
Starch, sugars, dextrins, gums,	72·15 ,,	67·69 ,,	64·38 ,,	67·17 ,,	68·60 ,,
Undetermined,	0·21 ,,	0·37 ,,	0·16 ,,	0·20 ,,	0·24 ,,

The amount of sugars as sucrose in wheats varies between 0·82 and 2·75 per cent.

The composition of cereals other than wheats.

Constituents.	Goldthorpe Barley.	Chevalier Barley.	Rye.	Maize.	Oats.	Huskless Rice.
Water,	13·15 %	12·91 %	14·43 %	12·89 %	13·28 %	12·11 %
Proteins,	11·47 ,,	12·69 ,,	10·37 ,,	9·67 ,,	14·81 ,,	7·62 ,,
Fats,	1·97 ,,	2·47 ,,	2·15 ,,	4·71 ,,	4·36 ,,	0·22 ,,
Mineral Salts,	2·48 ,,	2·58 ,,	1·86 ,,	1·60 ,,	2·71 ,,	0·31 ,,
Cellulose,	7·93 ,,	10·51 ,,	2·18 ,,	2·39 ,,	11·82 ,,	0·20 ,,
Starch,	59·28 ,,	55·68 ,,	63·03 ,,	62·80 ,,	49·12 ,,	77·25 ,,
Sugars (sucroses),	1·63 ,,	1·34 ,,	1·67 ,,	2·63 ,,	1·92 ,,	0·33 ,,
Dextrins, gums,	1·68 ,,	1·52 ,,	4·03 ,,	2·91 ,,	1·78 ,,	1·52 ,,
Undetermined,	0·41 ,,	0·30 ,,	0·28 ,,	0·40 ,,	0·20 ,,	0·44 ,,

The chemical constituents of the mineral salts.—The constituents of the ash or mineral salts of wheat differ considerably with the varieties and the soils on which they are grown. The chief salts are the primary phosphates of potassium, magnesium, and calcium, there being little more than traces of other substances. The subjoined analyses of wheat and barley ash give the student an idea of their composition :—

Constituents.	Wheat.	Barley.
Oxide of potassium (K_2O),	31·47 %	21·26 %
Oxide of sodium (Na_2O),	0·49 ,,	2·45 ,,
Oxide of calcium (CaO),	2·61 ,,	2·63 ,,
Oxide of magnesium (MgO),	9·57 ,,	8·74 ,,
Oxides of iron and aluminium (Fe_2O_3 and Al_2O_3),	0·68 ,,	0·98 ,,
Phosphoric anhydride (P_2O_5),	53·83 ,,	34·79 ,,
Sulphuric anhydride (SO_3),	0·67 ,,	1·65 ,,
Chlorine (Cl.),	0·04 ,,	0·88 ,,
Silica (SiO_2),	0·63 ,,	26·59 ,,

The natural acidity of the wheat berry is due chiefly to the primary phosphates of the type KH_2PO_4. It is

THE CEREALS AND THEIR COMPOSITION

also in some measure due to the presence of organic acids, especially lactic acid, $CH_3 \cdot CHOH \cdot COOH$.

The germ or embryo of the wheat berry.—The germ (Fig. 26), as previously pointed out, forms a kind of swelling or excrescence at the lower end of the dorsal or outer side of the wheat berry. With care it may be excised from its position, brought on to flannel over a bowl of water, so arranged that the flannel is kept moist by touching the water. Given light and warmth the little embryo, which occupies about a sixtieth of the whole wheat berry, begins to grow. If examined frequently at the early stages of growth, much information may be obtained of the germ. It is somewhat triangular in shape and of a yellowish buttery appearance. The germ is rich in nitrogenous matter, fats, and mineral salts, especially phosphates of potash. Several groups of enzymes are closely associated with the germ, the object of these being to prepare the proper foods for the little plant when germination begins.

Analyses by the author of wheat germs taken from mixed grists.

Constituents.	No. 1.	No. 2.	No. 3.	Uncooked Hovis germ.	By Mr. Jago.
Water,	12·78 %	12·80 %	13·41 %	9·43 %	13·23 %
Proteins (total),	27·84 ,,	28·35 ,,	29·16 ,,	30·18 ,,	{ Soluble, 15·51 ,, { Insol., 13·73 ,,
Fats,	6·61 ,,	9·32 ,,	9·26 ,,	9·94 ,,	12·03 ,,
Mineral salts,	2·43 ,,	4·10 ,,	4·22 ,,	4·65 ,,	4·94 ,,
Cellulose,	1·97 ,,	2·42 ,,	2·77 ,,	3·28 ,,	{ Dextrin, 1·24 ,, { Maltose, 5·54 ,,
Sugars, gums, dextrins, and undetermined,	48·37 ,,	43·01 ,,	41·18 ,,	42·52 ,,	Undeterd., 33·78 ,,

CHAPTER VIII

MILLING, MEALS, FLOURS, AND MALTS

UNDER the heading 'milling' it is intended to include not only the actual process of reducing wheat to the state of finished flour, but also the very necessary and previous processes—the cleaning and conditioning of the wheats.

The *cleaning* consists in removing all kinds of foreign matters such as oats, barley, rye, chaff, large and small cockle, seeds, stones, string, straw, pieces of metal and other bodies. Still more is it important to wash or scour off the dust, beard, and micro-organisms, and the dirt or soil adhering especially to wheats from hot countries like India, Persia, the Malay Peninsula, etc.

The *conditioning* softens the dry, hard, brittle wheats and brings them into a state suitable for milling. The usual mode of procedure in a flour mill is to weigh all grain as it comes in, pass it through a preliminary screening machine or separator (Fig. 27), and elevate it into the silos or store bins of the granary. When required, the wheat is drawn off from the bottom of the silos on to an endless belt, elevated to the top story of the cleaning department, gradually passed from one set of machines to another until ultimately, at the washing and stoning stage, it has reached the ground floor. The different types of wheat are cleaned separately, so that each shall receive the proper treatment in both cleansing and conditioning.

The cleaning processes may be summarised somewhat as follows :—

The first machine, a separator, consists of a series of sieves so as to remove large and small bodies from the wheat, which are carried off in a special channel. The foreign seeds, about the same size as the wheat berry, are taken out by means of cockle cylinders. These are rotating cylinders of special construction (Figs. 28 and 29). From these the wheat passes into the scourer, which is a kind of revolving drum fitted with a beater. This by its rapid revolutions causes the grains to be beaten the one against the others, and thus hairs, beard, loose husk, soil, and dust are removed. Each of the machines is arranged with an aspirat-

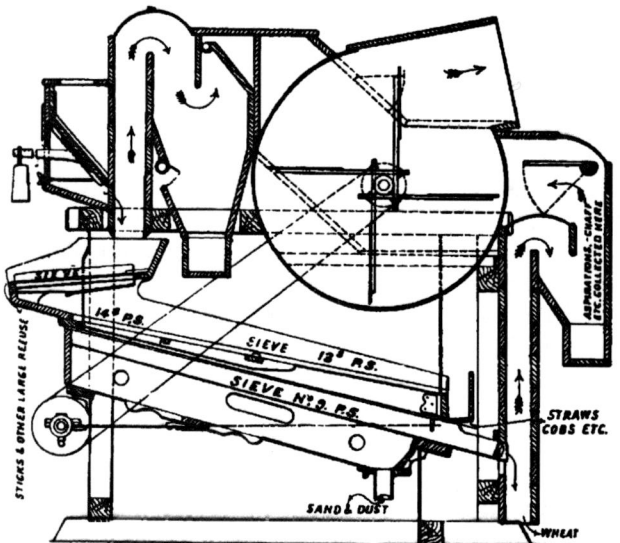

Fig. 27.—Section of Receiving or Warehouse Separator.
[*By permission of Messrs. Thos. Robinson and Son, Ltd.*]

ing current of air to carry off dust. The wheat now reaches the washers (Fig. 30), where it is further cleansed and wetted. The very hard wheats require a good deal of soaking, whilst the medium and soft ones need much less. During the washing, small stones about the size of the wheat berry are removed by making use of the difference in specific gravity between the heavy stones and the comparatively light wheat. The wheats next go to the centrifugals or whizzers, where surplus moisture is removed, then down the conditioners to be further dried, and into the store bins for cleaned wheats where the conditioning is completed. In a short time the different kinds of wheats are ready for blending to make up the particular grist of the mill. Before actually passing into the break rolls it is necessary to give a dry brushing to remove loose

Fig. 28.—Cockle, Oat and Barley Cylinders.
[*By permission of Messrs. Thos. Robinson and Son, Ltd.*]

particles and then a slight steaming. The wheat, after all this preliminary treatment, is then in a fit state to be milled.

This very complete cleansing of the wheat is an absolute necessity, not only to prevent speckled and dirty flours, but also to partially sterilise the flour and thus free it from noxious organisms. The author has shown by several researches that, in spite of all this extensive cleaning, certain classes of lightly-baked breads are liable to disease from internal sources, especially when made from low-grade flours obtained from that portion of the wheat berry near to the bran.

The plant actually employed in milling proper comprises break machines for tearing open the endosperm and liberating the starchy particles; purifiers to separate the starchy particles from the bran, germ, and offals generally; the reduction rolls which crush the starchy particles or

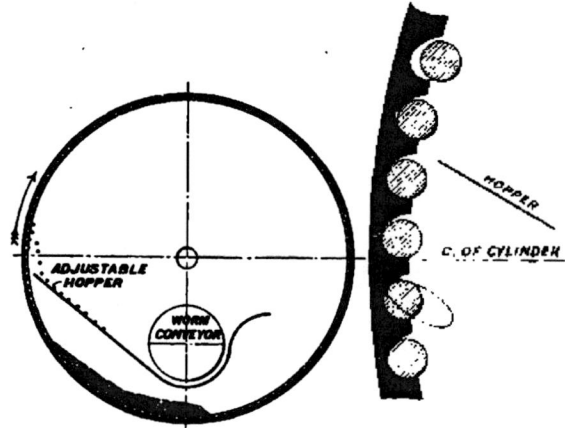

Fig. 29.—Diagram showing internal Construction of Cockle, Oat and Barley Cylinders.
[*By permission of Messrs. Thos. Robinson and Son, Ltd.*]

semolinas into flour; the silks or flour-dressing machines to grade and purify the flour; the bleaching plant; the possers for weighing and bagging the finished flour; and the various conveyors, elevators, and aspirating plants required for carrying off dust and keeping the various machines cool. Mr. A. E. Humphries, in a paper read recently before the Association of Millers, laid down the following as the necessary factors that wheats should possess in order to be suitable for milling into present-day flours:—Stability, the capacity for making a maximum quantity of bread from a given weight of flour, and for producing large fine-textured loaves, of good flavour, with a colour in both crust and crumb that should be bright in appearance.

The first set of machines in a roller mill (Fig. 31) are the *break rolls*. These carry out the operation of breaking up the endosperm of the berry by a succession of stages varying from four to seven. The rolls, which are made of steel and

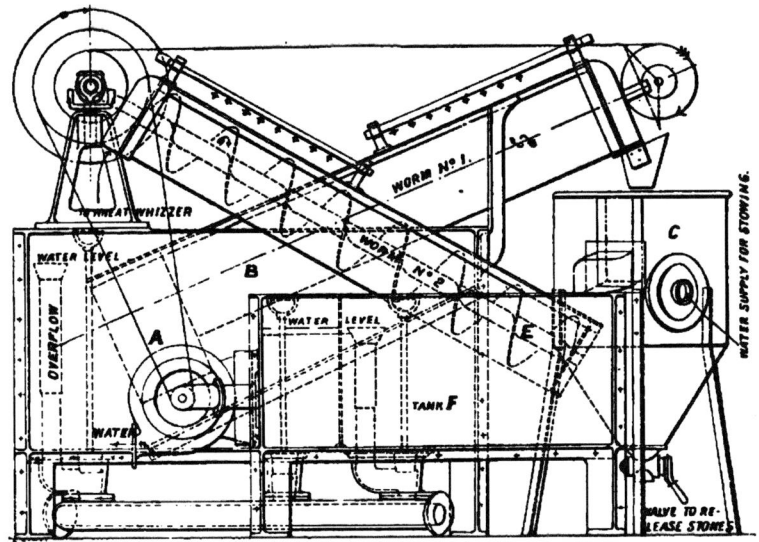

Fig. 30.—Section of Double Wheat Washer and Stoner.
[*By permission of Messrs. Thos. Robinson and Son, Ltd.*]

fluted, tear open the berry at its crease, so that in the first machine the central contents are set at liberty. The products of this first break, consisting of small angular pieces from the centre of the endosperm—the semolinas—break flour, dust, particles of husk and the remainder of the berry, are separated by adjustments in the machine, the fractions passing off in special receptacles, whilst the remnants of the berry pass into the next break machine where similar

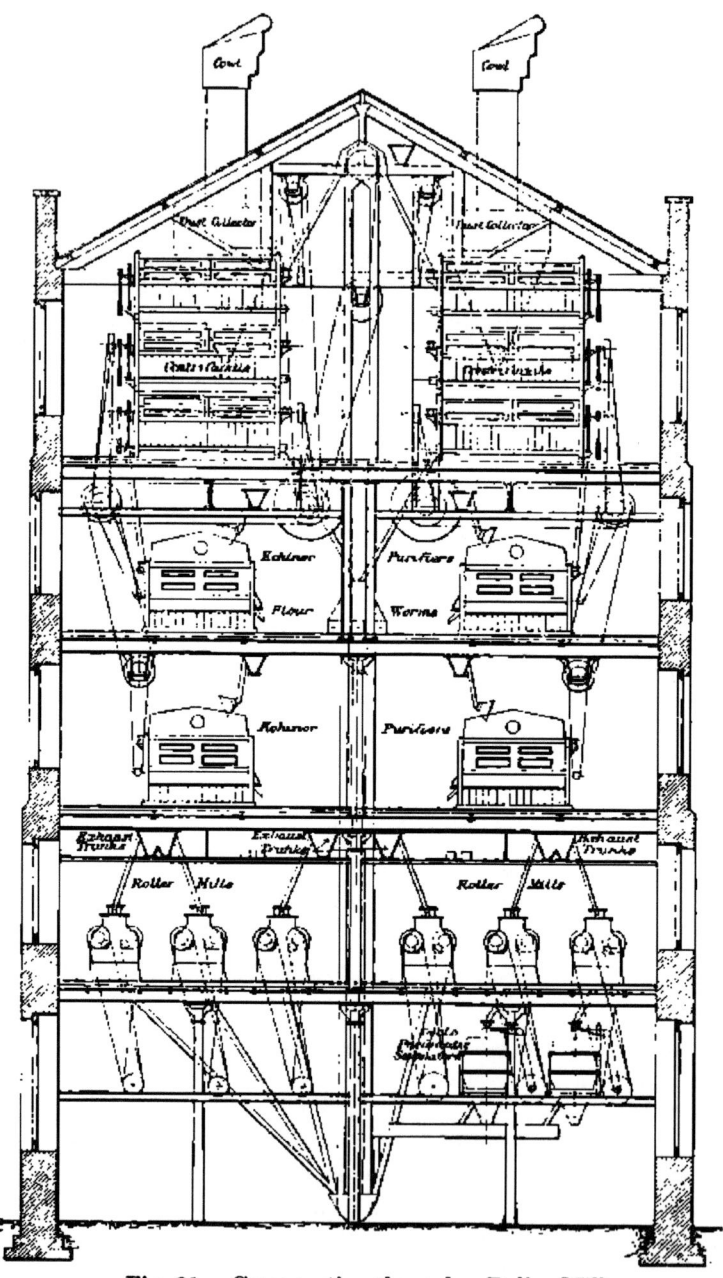

Fig. 31.—Cross-section through a Roller Mill.
[*By permission of Messrs. Thos. Robinson and Son, Ltd.*]

operations are conducted, and so on through the whole series of machines, each time getting nearer to the outside portion of the berry, until ultimately the bran is scraped almost entirely free from starchy matter. Any flour produced in the breaks is separated from the semolinas and middlings on account of the dust, mainly from the crease in the berry.

The semolinas, middlings, and dunst, containing branny particles, dust, light feathery refuse or beeswing, etc., are passed into the various *purifiers* so that, as far as possible, all particles, except the angular starchy pieces, are taken out. The purified 'throughs' are then graded into coarse and fine, and each of these is reduced into flour separately.

The *reduction* or *grinding rolls* (Fig. 32) are quite smooth and set close, thus working at a pressure. The germ at this stage becomes flattened by these rolls by reason of its content of fatty matter and so can readily be removed. The flour is then dressed by passing through the *silk sieves*, which are usually arranged in a kind of revolving cylinder. Various grades of silk are used, and any particles not passing through go through the reduction rolls again. Where no bleaching plant is employed, the finished flour, after dressing, is weighed and packed by the power *possers*, and taken to the flour stores to mature. The offals are also graded, dressed, and packed by suitable machinery.

The *bleaching plant* used in flour mills is of two types:— the chemical and the electrical. The chemical bleaching plant consists of the proper arrangement for producing oxides of nitrogen. These gases are conducted into a kind of enclosed trough through which the flour is passed by worm and other conveyors. A few seconds' treatment is sufficient for the purpose, and great care is necessary to give just the exact length of time in contact with the gas, since if the flour becomes overbleached it is practically useless. The electrical method requires even more care than the chemical, for the air which has been exposed to the 'fiery blast'

MILLING, MEALS, FLOURS, AND MALTS

contains both ozone and oxides of nitrogen. With some flours even four seconds is too long.

The bleaching of flours assists in their partial sterilising, ageing, and maturing, as well as rendering the flours a

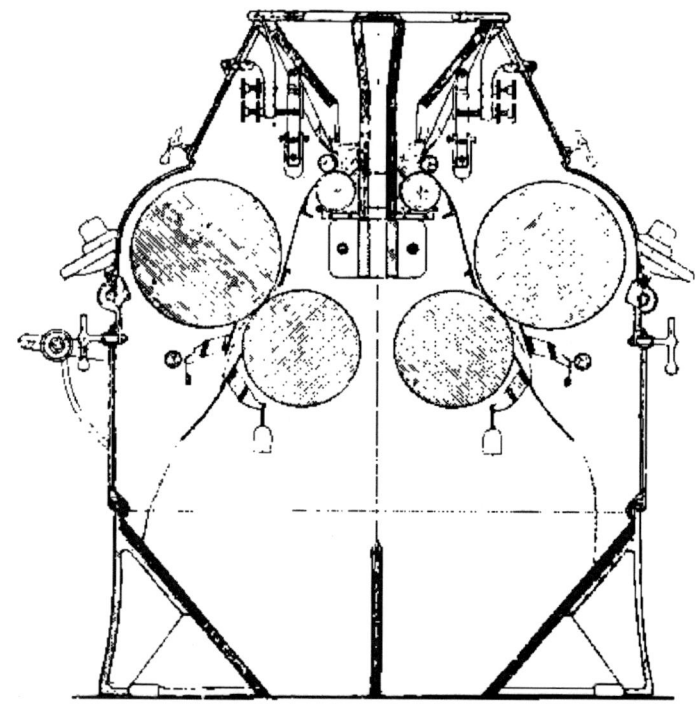

Fig. 32.—Cross-section of Reduction Roller Mill.
[*By permission of Messrs. Thos. Robinson and Son, Ltd.*]

dead white. The highest grades of flour are not improved by this treatment, and therefore are rarely bleached.

MEALS AND FLOURS

Meal is the name given to the product obtained by grinding a cereal between pairs of rolls without separating the offal from the flour. Flour, on the other hand, is the finely-dressed product in which the separation is as effective as possible. Flour so prepared is a complex mixture of chemical compounds consisting of carbohydrates, nitrogenous bodies, fats, vegetable acids, mineral salts, and water.

Meals contain all the foregoing compounds, and in addition the bran which includes much more cellulose or

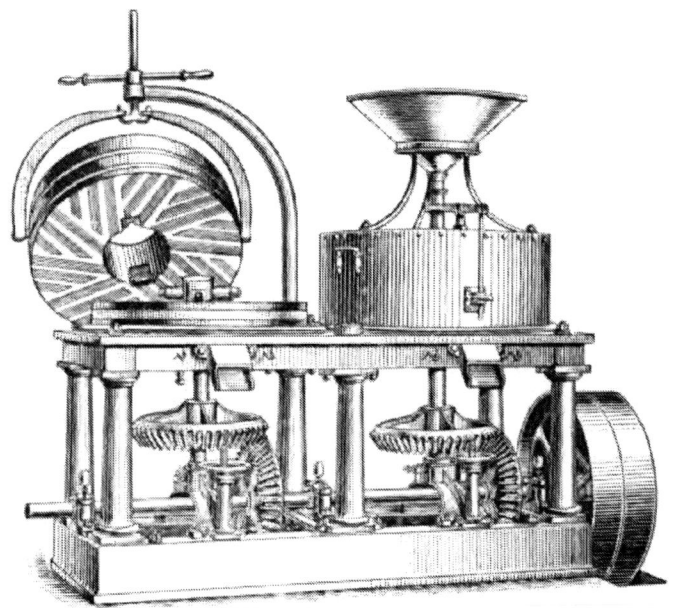

Fig. 33.—Modern French Burr-stone Mill for Wholemeals.

woody fibre, fats from the germ, mineral salts, and extractive matters.

Meals are usually classed as whole, wheat, germ, malted, and proprietary. For the preparation of the various meals, specially selected wheats are necessary, and they are best ground between French burr-stones (Fig. 33), although the cattle food meals are usually prepared by grinding between

MILLING, MEALS, FLOURS, AND MALTS

stones obtained from the mill-stone grit rocks around Hathersage in Derbyshire and other places. A genuine wholemeal contains the whole of the materials of the wheat berry; frequently, however, the coarsest bran is removed. The result then is certainly a finer meal that yields a more palatable and digestible loaf, without a serious loss of the mineral salts.

Wheat meals differ from the wholemeal in not containing the whole of the products of the wheat berry. They are prepared either by separating the germ and some of the offal, or by mixing together a low-grade white flour with a certain proportion of offal. These latter may often be distinguished by the insipid, flavourless bread they yield; such a result is largely due to the fact that they are not ground from selected, suitable wheats of the English type.

Germ meals are prepared in various ways, but one of the best, and well known in the trade, is made of 75 per cent. of a good, white flour mixed with 25 per cent. of cooked germ. The germ is intimately mixed with the proper quantity of salt for the making of the bread, and passed by means of worm conveyors through a steam-heated long cylinder, which effectually cooks and sterilises the germ. This cooking aids in the keeping properties of the meal, and at the same time prevents all enzymic action.

The malted and other meals are so numerous that it would be impossible to describe them all in the limited space of a small book. Excellent malted bread may be manufactured from a good grade of wheat meal thoroughly mixed with two to three ounces of a diastatic malt flour for every seven lbs. of wheat meal, the result being what is to all intents and purposes a malted meal.

White flours are classified differently in different parts of the country. The following classification is a common one and will be readily understood :—

    Fancy patents made from first break semolinas. Of these each miller has practically his own speciality, and it would be invidious to give names of a few of the more largely advertised, seeing that all are high-class flours.

First patents, which form the best grade of flours used in making the best bread.

Second patents and superfines, which go for the manufacture of medium qualities of bread.

XX, used for common bread alone.

Single X is a mixture of the break flour and the last scrapings from the bran. Such a flour is too woolly and dirty for breadmaking, but is largely employed in the finishing of calicoes and cotton goods generally.

The subjoined table gives the chemical composition of some flours and meals :—

Constituents.	Patent.	Superfine.	XX.	Wholemeal.	Reynolds' Wheatmeal.	Standard Flour. May 1911.
Water,	12·44 %	11·87 %	13·34 %	13·76 %	12·00 %	12·95 %
Proteins,	11·23 ,,	12·38 ,,	11·09 ,,	12·53 ,,	16·40 ,,	12·74 ,,
Fats,	0·98 ,,	1·17 ,,	1·26 ,,	1·43 ,,	2·20 ,,	2·03 ,,
Mineral Salts,	0·39 ,,	0·43 ,,	0·58 ,,	1·77 ,,	1·50 ,,	0·81 ,,
Carbohydrates,	74·67 ,,	73·79 ,,	73·29 ,,	67·63 ,,	66·70 ,,	69·86 ,,
Husky or Fibre,	0·20 ,,	0·22 ,,	0·27 ,,	2·67 ,,	1·20 ,,	1·38 ,,
Acidity as Lactic,	0·09 ,,	0·14 ,,	0·17 .,	0·21 ,,	...	0·23 ,,
Dry Gluten,	9·72 %	11·92 %	10·53 %	...	...	...

THE PROPERTIES OF FLOURS

The properties of flour, and it is here intended to apply the name flour only to the silk-dressed product so as to distinguish it from the various meals, differ very largely owing to differences in the formation of grists, the mode of preparation, and the milling. The most important point is in the formation of the grist. Each miller selects the wheats from different sources so as to form a blend or grist which will yield flours suitable for his trade.

The most important properties of flours are :—colour, strength, absorbing power, and purity.

The colour of flour is a question of the refraction and

reflection of light. Some flours are a dead white, others a greyish white, a brownish grey, a yellowish brown, or a fine creamy yellow shade of colour with a marked bloom. The latter is the typical colour of a high grade of flour which frequently has a granular feel to the hand. The different species and varieties of wheats influence colour. Starchy and weak wheats like English, and also winter sorts, yield white flours. Highly glutinous, durum, and strong wheats generally yield yellowish to dark yellow flours. The very white or dead-white flours are generally produced by the action of bleaching. This may be brought about by exposing a dull grey-looking flour to the chemical activity of oxides of nitrogen and ozone for a few seconds; but the dull appearance of the flour remains unaffected.

The colour of several flours may be compared either by means of the well-known Pékar test or by Lovibond's tintometer.

The Pékar test is carried out as follows:—A sheet of thick plate-glass or a piece of very smooth wood about four inches wide by twelve in length is required, together with an ivory or steel flour spatula. A small quantity of one of the flours is brought on to the plate, pressed tightly to exclude air-bubbles, brought to one end and the edges trimmed with the spatula. Another flour is treated similarly, then brought close to the first sample and the two carefully pressed and trimmed. Other samples may be dealt with in like manner. The colours are now compared with the help of diffused daylight, and the various shades noted. The plate containing the flours is now brought obliquely into a tank of clean water, passed through the water in a continuous sweep or curve and allowed to dry in a cool, airy place. The colours are again compared, and marked differences in the shades of colour will be noticed. With a little practice in this work a student can readily compare the colours of flours. For night-work a patent Royal Daylight electric lamp should be fitted up.

In working with a Lovibond's tintometer, the shades of colour are determined separately by comparison with glasses of standard colour, the flour being pressed tightly into small boxes specially provided for determining the colours of powders.

The strength of a flour is one of its most important properties, but up to the present time the various factors which govern strength are not altogether understood. W. B. Hardy, F.R.S., has shown that the strength of a flour is partly dependent on the presence of electrolytes such as salts, which confer cohesion on the gluten. Dilute acids and alkalies all tend to break up the gluten into fine particles; hence electrolytes confer on glutens its mechanical properties, e.g. its power of holding water; and these electrolytes similarly influence the water-holding power of any other colloid substances present. Some time ago, the author was able to show that ammonia-free water very readily disintegrates the gluten, but if alkaline salts are added the action is at once stopped. Distilled water partially dissolves gluten, while some is left in a semi-fluid and sedimentary state without tenacity. Hardy further pointed out that colloid bodies like moist gluten possess a sponge-like structure, and that solid particles decrease the strength of the network structure of gluten by internal friction, hence washed-out gluten is not quite the same as gluten in a dough.

The gluten in some flours is strong, tough, and harsh, as in the case of spring wheats, whilst in others it is weak, soft, and rather elastic, as in the typical English wheaten flours. The former type of gluten can much more readily withstand the friction produced by the starch granules, especially when the granules are rather small, and is much more resistant than that in soft wheats. The soft, weak, and rather elastic form of gluten is one of the causes of the small loaf produced by English wheaten flours. Flavour is apparently associated with the gluten, for although the loaf is small and often of a poor, greyish colour, the flavour is of the nutty character and excellent. Spring wheaten flour yields a large bold loaf, which, however, is absolutely devoid of flavour. From the foregoing it will be seen that one of the important factors influencing strength is the quality rather than the quantity of gluten.

In the section of Chap. XIII. on the nitrogenous constituents of wheat and flour it is pointed out that hot, strong alcohol dissolves out the vegetable gelatine or gliadin portion of the gluten, leaving the glutenin in a coagulated insoluble state, so that the quantity of each may be determined. If much gliadin is present it tends to make the gluten become more elastic and softer, but the relation existing between the glutenin and gliadin does not settle the question of strength. According to the Local Government Board Report of April 1911, the ' strength ' of a flour is defined as the measure of the capacity of flour for producing a bold, large-volumed, well-risen loaf. Bakers use it to indicate the amount of bread which a given amount of flour is capable of yielding.

The water-absorbing and retaining power of a flour.— These factors, which are intimately associated with the ' strength ' of a flour, are naturally dependent on the quality of the gluten, the dryness of the flour, and the nature and condition of the starch.

A strong, tough, harsh gluten is, as already stated, a good absorber, or assists in the absorption of water, but there is something over and above this. For example, many of the best, high-milled, Austrian flours possess great absorbing and retaining powers. This is not due to the harsh character of the gluten since Austrian flours possess quite a different character, yet their absorbing power is greater than that milled from a spring wheat. This is due to one of those inherent properties of such a flour which is not yet fully understood.

There is a well-known axiom amongst bakers and millers that ' a strong flour cannot be milled from a weak wheat.' What this implies is certainly not completely understood.

The dryness of a flour has an important bearing on this point. As flours are received into the bakery they contain from 11 to 14 per cent. of moisture. John Blandy's expression, 'A flour will not absorb more water than it will nor retain it,' is quite true, yet if the flour be stored for a few weeks in a dry, warm atmosphere, its absorbing and retaining powers are considerably increased. The explanation of this is that the excess of moisture is more than the flour can carry, or in other words, the quantity of water in excess of the natural moisture of the flour has been driven off. This maturing of the constituents of the flour materially assists its water-retaining power. The blending of the right flours together also acts in the same direction. It would be both useful and interesting to a baker regularly to weigh his flours when they arrive at the bakery, and also after storing for a week or two. In this way important and valuable information regarding the various 'marks' of flour would be obtained. A writer on this subject in the early years of the nineteenth century states that 'the better and older the flour, when properly stored, the more water it absorbs and retains in baking. The best flour should absorb nearly three-quarters of its weight of water, and the worst flour one-half; whilst the loss in baking should only be one-tenth.'

Stability.—Closely connected with the strength, water-absorbing, and retaining power of a flour is its stability. Flours yielding doughs that fall away quickly and drop or collapse are by no means stable.

This factor, stability, is evidently dependent partly on the gluten and partly on the material present which can be used as yeast food. Where there is much of this latter the yeast will be able to generate large volumes of carbon dioxide gas; if now the gluten is strong, tough, and elastic, so that the gas may be retained and diffused throughout the dough, there will be little fear of a falling away and collapse. Although much work has been done in this direction, very much more is required to enable the miller and baker to come to definite conclusions on the subject of strength and other factors connected with it.

There is yet another point bearing on these questions, viz. the **acidity** of a flour. When flours are not suitably stored, it has been found that the organic acidity increases. As this change progresses, the gluten and other flour constituents are degraded and the flours weakened and deteriorated, which very materially affects the baking properties of such flours.

The **purity** of a flour, that is, its freedom from adulterants of all kinds, is nowadays almost beyond suspicion. Very rarely indeed are flours found to contain any kind of foreign starch or other impurity. A few years ago some French milled flour, containing a fair percentage of talc or French chalk, was shipped from Marseilles to various ports in England, and gave rise to a mild scare for a few days. This flour belonged to the single X grade, and was to be used for making finish, size, and dextrins for the calico-printing industry. Apart from similar exceptional instances, flours to all intents and purposes are practically pure; in fact, never since the roller-milling industry became general have our flours been so white, clean, and pure as at the present time.

For baking and confectionery purposes flours are classed as weak, medium, and strong. In quick-bread processes, strong flours are blended with weak or medium ones, so as to tone down the undesirable properties of the first-named group of flours; otherwise ungainly, flavourless bread is the result. Strong flours may be used alone in the setting of sponges and ferments where the process is to be a long one, as time is required to mellow and break down the strong, tough, harsh gluten in such flours. For the doughing part, medium and soft flours are employed. In the confectionery department, strong flours are necessary in the manufacture of nearly all varieties of buns, scones, and gâteaux, for puff-paste of all kinds, tea, girdle, and barm cakes, etc. Medium flours are more suitable for intermediate types of smalls, sponge goods, cheap Madeira cakes, and the like. Soft flours are employed for the best classes of goods of all kinds, especially slab cakes, Christmas, Easter, Russian, tennis and similar cakes, short paste, short sweet paste, open and notched tarts, shortbread, and all the best soft types of biscuits, and many other high-class goods.

Malting, Malt Flour, and Extracts

In the early nineties, malt extracts were introduced into the bakery trade by the French firm, Leconte et Cie, probably on account of the more general use of American spring wheat flours in the baking industry. When barms were commonly used the baker was obliged to know something of malt, but in these days of progress it is necessary for him to understand also the process of malting and the nature of malt products.

Barley, ripe and mature, sound and sweet, is the starting-point in *malting*.

After being thoroughly cleaned by dry processes, similar to those employed in preparing wheat for milling, it is steeped in cold, hard water at temperatures about 52° F. for 54 to 72 hours, according to the condition of the barley. When steeping is complete, the softened grain is allowed to drain, after which it is thrown into long shallow heaps to become slightly heated so as to start germination. The 'couch,' as it is called, is then broken down and the grain spread out on the growing-floor to form the 'first piece.' It is turned several times to aerate and equalise both moisture and temperature. During the growing the barley is worked down the length of the floor so as to enable other pieces to be worked in regular succession down the floors. Many changes take place in the grain as it slowly germinates. The rootlets are developed to about twice the length of the barleycorn; the plumule or acrospire gradually pushes its way up the back of the corn beneath the pale or chaff which acts as a protection during the twelve or more turnings. At the same time, the various enzymes (p. 125), which exist in minute quantities in the

MILLING, MEALS, FLOURS, AND MALTS

cells adjacent to the endosperm, are developed and work their way upwards towards the opposite end of the corn, opening up and modifying the interior contents of the endosperm, or in other words converting it into malt. For bakery purposes the acrospire should be grown fully up, as this ensures a high proportion of diastase.

Growing or flooring usually occupies eight or nine days, after which the 'green malt' is thoroughly withered to check further growth and dissipate some of the excess moisture of the grain. The green malt is now loaded on to the kiln, where it is slowly and completely dried. If any of the operations are rushed, the malt suffers in a marked way and becomes unfitted for use. Kilning requires special care, and in no case is the temperature raised more than about twenty-five to thirty degrees in twenty-four hours, until all the moisture has been expelled. When this stage is reached the draughts of the kiln are closed to prevent the introduction of fresh air, and the temperature is raised to the curing point in order to render the malt friable and to give it the peculiar empyreumatic flavour and aroma.

The cured malt is thrown off the kiln, heaped up, allowed to cool, passed through the cleaning machinery to take off the dried rootlets or culms, and then stored for several weeks to mature.

Malt flour.—From such malt, malt flour or diastatic malt flour is prepared by crushing the malt between fluted rolls and passing it through sieves to take out the husky or cellulose matter. The malt being very dry, the husk breaks up into fine and coarse particles, the latter only can be removed by the sieves, hence malt flour always possesses a brownish grey shade of colour. Malt flour freshly prepared is a very hygroscopic substance, which rapidly absorbs moisture from the air and soon loses its characteristic flavour and smell. It ought to be sent out in air-tight drums instead of in the canvas bags used at present. Brewers, who are aware of these facts, are careful to keep whole malt in dry, warm stores until required for use, and only crush the malt a few hours before brewing. Bakers who stock malt flour in any quantity would be wise to follow the example of the brewers in this way, as they would then preserve the fine flavour of the malt and run less risk of the excess acidity which is so commonly present in slack malts and badly-stored malt flour.

Malt extracts and diastase pastes.—The principal point of difference between these substances is that in the malt extracts the diastase has been already used to prepare the extracts and is therefore present only in small proportions and weakened; whereas in diastase paste it is fresh, vigorous, and active. The extracts are prepared by hot-water mashing, whilst the pastes are cold-water extractives.

In the manufacture of *malt extracts* the malt is crushed between fluted rolls and then mixed with water of such a temperature that the resultant temperature of the mixture will be about 145° F., which is the point of maximum activity for diastase. Every quarter of malt (336 lbs.) requires about eleven to twelve hundred pounds weight of water. The mixture, which has a consistency of thin porridge, is allowed to stand in the mash-tub for about three hours so as to ensure the conversion of the starch of the malt into maltose and dextrins, and to modify suitably the nitrogenous bodies. This 'wort' or sugar solution is run off into a tank, and any sugars remaining in the grains are washed out by sparging. After settling for a short time the wort is passed through a filter press, and from this into another small settler adjoining the vacuum pan. From this, after some time, the thin liquors pass by suction into the pan and are boiled down to the proper consistency at a reduced pressure such that the temperature is between 132°-135° F. The thick treacly syrup is now ready to be run off into the drums in which it is sent out into commerce. The value of a malt extract depends on the quantities of malt sugar or maltose, soluble nitrogenous compounds and mineral salts present. Its chief value lies in its stimulative effect on the yeast in fermentation.

Diastase pastes, as previously stated, are cold-water extracts of malt.

The malt is crushed and made into a thin porridge with cool water, so that the temperature of the mixture is about 70° F. This mash is allowed to stand in the mash-tub for five hours, so that as much soluble matter as possible is extracted from the finely divided malt. All the liquor is run off, and both this and the grains passed through a filter-press. The liquors are settled and then boiled down in the vacuum pans as described in the preparation of malt extracts. Some slight modifications are necessary so that different strengths of diastase paste may be obtained. Cheap, low-grade pastes are prepared from inferior barleys and malts; whilst for the highest grade only the best barleys, English and foreign, after careful malting, can be employed.

Diastase pastes depend for their value not only on the carbohydrates and soluble nitrogenous constituents, but on the quantity and activity of the diastatic enzymes. Other soluble ferments or enzymes are present, but they are of less importance than the diastase. Yet even these should not be overlooked as they have considerable effect on the gluten and possibly other substances, resulting altogether in shortening the time in which the dough is ready for the oven. Diastase can only act on gelatinised or soluble starch, therefore the wheaten starch granules are unaffected by it, but as soon as they become gelatinised the starch-flour or granulose is at once acted upon and converted. Wheaten starch granules in presence of moisture burst or are said to be gelatinised at about 170° F. Diastase action is stopped in the moist state at 176° F., so that it will be seen there is little opportunity for diastatic action after the dough is in the oven. It is enough, however, to have a marked effect on the finished loaf.

Of the three malt products described, diastase pastes are the best and most useful. The quantities employed vary from a half to a pound and a half per sack of flour.

These quantities, however, may be increased with advantage to from two to three pounds per sack, especially with strong flours and short processes, without causing extra difficulties in manipulation. The author found that almost all grades of bread were very much improved by using rather higher proportions. Practically all the points of a loaf were much enhanced. The only question to be considered is the extra cost to the baker.

The advantages to be derived from the use of diastase pastes may be summed up as follows :—

Externally, the bloom, crust, volume, and the general appearance of a loaf are all improved.

Internally, the flavour—a kind of sweetness is imparted—the appearance of the crumb, and the moisture after several days' keeping, are all benefited by diastase pastes. If examined for food value, a malted loaf will be found to possess many heat-calories more than the ordinary unmalted bread ; further, such bread is much more readily digested. Malt flour, which is more easily handled, cannot be introduced in larger quantities than about a pound to a pound and a half per sack without spoiling both the external appearance and the crumb of a loaf. All three classes of malt products increase the volume and give more spring to the loaf in the oven.

A high-class, friable malt will yield about 67 per cent. of extract ; or, in other words, a quarter of malt weighing three hundredweights should give two hundredweights of extract.

This extract when used in breadmaking assists in degrading the flour, feeds the yeast, and so quickens fermentation.

In the long bread processes it is better to use a diastase paste in the earlier stages of fermentation and a malt extract in the later stages.

With strong harsh flours both are invaluable, as they mellow and tone down the gluten.

Weak flours, which contain a fair proportion of food for the yeast, do not require these extraneous aids, and, moreover, such flours will only be rendered weaker by them. If they are used the quantity should not exceed four ounces per sack of flour.

The fluid malt products must be kept in cool places, otherwise they readily ferment, lose their diastatic power and maltose, and gradually increase in acidity until they become sour.

The subjoined analytical results show the difference in chemical composition of these substances.

The composition of four of the best types of Diastase Pastes.

Constituents.	1.	2.	3.	4.
Total Solids,	75·50 %	76·60 %	78·25 %	78·40 %
Water,	24·50 ,,	23·40 ,,	21·75 ,,	21·60 ,,
Ash (Mineral Salts),	0·95 ,,	1·62 ,,	2·10 ,,	1·30 ,,
K. as Maltose,	62·60 ,,	64·09 ,,	64·40 ,,	62·30 ,,
Dextrin (calculated),	8·11 ,,	...	...	4·47 ,,
Proteins, etc.,	3·84 ,,	...	...	10·33 ,,
Specific rotatory power,	102·8°	84·85°	72·2°	95°
Diastatic capacity (Lintner),	48°	87°	113°	102°

NOTE.—Probably Nos. 2 and 3 contained added sugar.

Malt Extracts.

Constituents.	1.	2.	3.	4.
Total Solids,	77·08 %	75·12 %	78·17 %	74·97 %
Water,	22·92 ,,	24·88 ,,	21·83 ,,	25·03 ,,
Mineral Salts,	1·56 ,,	1·39 ,,	1·29 ,,	1·47 ,,
K. as Maltose,	58·44 ,,	61·26 ,,	62·97 ,,	68·22 ,,
Dextrin (calculated),	13·58 ,,	10·89 ,,	13·91 ,,	5·28 ,,
Proteins, etc.,	4·50 ,,	1·58 ,,		
Specific rotatory power,	108·1°	106·5°	97·6°	105·8°
Diastatic capacity (Lintner),	10°	11°	16°	23°

K. stands for Copper reducing power in terms of dextrose = 100.

The composition of some Malt Flours used in the baking trade.

Constituents.	Ordinary Malt Flour.	Diastase Malt Flour.	Malt from English Barley.
Total Solids, soluble in cold water,	20·81 %	61·60 %	15·54 %
Moisture,	7·03 ,,	4·81 ,,	4·49 ,,
Mineral Salts,	0·76 ,,	0·78 ,,	0·96 ,,
Maltose,	9 85 ,,	4·87 ,,	8·89 ,,
Dextrins,	9·65 ,,	} 55·95 ,,	3·15 ,,
Proteins and other bodies,	0·55 ,,		2·54 ,,
Added Sugars (Sucrose),	...		...
Opticity of cold water extract,	33·1°	58·8°	117·4°
Diastatic capacity,	25° (Lintner)	21° (Lintner)	49° (Lintner)

CHAPTER IX

FERMENTS, YEASTS, MOULDS, BACTERIA

UNTIL just recently ferments have been divided into the soluble or unorganised ferments or enzymes, and the organised ones including yeasts, moulds, and bacteria. This classification, in view of published recent research, can no longer be held, because it has been clearly demonstrated that the so-called organised ferments can only bring about fermentation by means of the enzymes contained within the cell-walls.

To understand the subject thoroughly, it is necessary to possess a knowledge of the behaviour of *crystalline* and *colloidal* substances in regard to vegetable membranes such as the cell-walls, which enclose the interior contents of any of the micro-organisms (organised ferments). As mentioned in Chap. VI. it is only the crystalline bodies like sugars, amides, and mineral salts that are soluble in water, which possess the power of readily passing through vegetable membranes. The process is known as *osmosis*, and only soluble, crystalline compounds can pass into the interior of the cell (endosmosis), or pass out from the cell (exosmosis). The foods, then, for the organised ferments must be of this character; thus the natural sugars of wheat and flour can so pass into the yeast in dough-making and bring about the phenomenon spoken of as fermentation. Starch, dextrin, and most of the proteids possess a colloidal structure and therefore cannot undergo osmosis. This accounts for the yeast being unable to attack and break up the starch of the flour in bread-making. The very intense colloid, starch, must first be gelatinised to form starch paste (scalded flour), then hydrolysed by means of the enzyme diastase into maltose (malt sugar), dextrins, and other bodies. This maltose is soluble, crystalline, and diffusible. It readily undergoes endosmosis, passing into the interior of the yeast-cell where it is acted upon by the enzymes and converted into alcohol and carbon dioxide, the latter doing the work of aeration or causing the dough to rise.

The organised ferments or micro-organisms belong to the great sub-kingdom known as the *Cryptogamia*. The members of this division of plants do not reproduce by the flowering process, hence the name, which means literally 'hidden marriage.' The cryptogams, comprising all non-flowering plants, are divided into three chief sections and seven classes. Of these, only the *Thallophyta*, particularly class I., need be considered here. The thallous plants are devoid of all the parts of a true plant, viz. leaves, stems, roots, and vascular bundles. Class I. of the thallous plants includes the microscopic fungi, *i.e.* the micro-organisms or organised ferments. These are devoid also of the green or brown colouring matter of plants, the chlorophyll granules.

The micro-organisms for purposes of study may be divided into the branching fungi and the fission fungi or bacteria.

The former, designated the *Eumycetes*, include moulds, mucors, mildews (oidium), yeasts, torula, and mycoderms; whilst the latter group, comprising the whole of the bacteria, is known as the *Schizomycetes*.

Bacteria are the smallest of all known living things. They are unicellular, the cell-wall being composed of fungi-cellulose—a form insoluble in Schweitzer's [1] reagent—which encloses a mass of fluid protoplasm.

Three shapes of bacteria are recognised:—

(a) Spherical or billiard-ball shape—*e.g.* a *coccus*.
(b) Rod or ruler-shaped—*e.g.* a *bacillus* such as *subtilis*.
(c) Spiral or corkscrew-shaped—*e.g.* a *spirillum*.

Under favourable circumstances all bacteria reproduce by fission or splitting off, the two parts either separating,

---

[1] Schweitzer's reagent is an ammoniacal solution of copper hydrate.

or hanging together in chains or clusters. The spherical forms are the only bacteria capable of splitting up in more than one direction.

A considerable number form spores inside the parent cell—endogenous spores—which possess great refractive properties and hence they glisten brightly when viewed under a high-power microscope. Bacilli frequently spore, but cocci forms do so only very rarely. Another mode of reproduction is by the continuous development of the rod lengths, after which fission ensues.

Chemically, bacteria are composed of a covering or cell-wall of fungi cellulose and internally of an aqueous solution of a very complex body or mixture of compounds known as 'protoplasm' or 'plasma.' According to Von Mohl (1844) protoplasm is a viscous, tough, elastic, transparent, and frequently granular, highly active nitrogenous body built up of carbon, hydrogen, oxygen, nitrogen, and sulphur. It is probably the most primitive organic substance known, forming the animate and, so far as can be ascertained, the ultimate basis or unit of all organic life ; it was defined by the late Professor T. H. Huxley, F.R.S., as 'the physical basis of life.'

Cellulose, on the other hand, is what is termed a carbohydrate containing carbon and the elements of water. It is closely related to cotton and other fibres, paper and similar substances, but in a number of cases the cell-wall contains very little true cellulose. Many of the groups of bacteria either contain or generate a colouring matter, the pigment Bacterio-purpurin. They exist very frequently in the many food-stuffs and hence are of considerable interest to every one taking part in the manufacture of our daily food.

Some groups possess the power of locomotion, as may be seen by carefully observing a slide made from almost any distillery yeast, when as little points of light they may be seen moving rapidly across the field of view. This motion of the Bacteria is brought about by means of extremely fine hairs or whip-like organs termed 'flagella'; so fine are these flagella that they can only be detected when suitably stained. The cocci or spherical forms as a rule are non-mobile.

Irregular forms occur commonly in old cultures, and render it difficult to recognise the different bacteria by appearance alone. This irregularity is caused by the deterioration of the cells : such are the involution forms. In size bacteria vary enormously, but all are microscopic. Those occurring in the food-stuffs range between 0·15 μ and 6 μ in diameter. The symbol μ (the Greek letter 'mu'), used as the standard of measurement in the study of micro-organisms, is a thousandth ($\frac{1}{1000}$) of a millimetre and is known as a micron.

One metre = 39·37079 English inches.
One millimetre = 0·0393708 ,,
One micron = 0·000039371 ,,
Or $\mu = \frac{1}{25,400}$ of an inch.

As the number of bacteria in nature is practically infinite, it is necessary for the purposes of study to have some kind of classification other than their shape or form, which is not by any means an unchanging factor.

A simple and useful classification is that based on the bacterial action or products formed by their life action :—

(1) The Pathogenic or disease-producing—Example, *B. typhosus*, the *Comma bacillus*, etc.
(2) The Septic or putrefactive—Example, *B. subtilis*, *termo*, *proteus* groups, etc.
(3) The Zymogenic or fermentative—Example, Acetic, Butyric, Lactic, and other acid-forming groups, *B. Viscosus*, etc.
(4) The Chromogenic or pigment-forming—Example, *B. Violaceus*, which causes blue watery milk, *B. micrococcus*, *B. prodigiosus*, etc.

The members of these various groups all occur in our ordinary food supplies. For example, water and milk are carriers of many forms of disease-producing bacteria, as witness the cholera epidemic in Hamburg nearly twenty years ago. This was traced to the town's water-supply taken from the River Elbe contaminated by an encampment of gipsies on its banks. The outbreak of typhoid in the city of Lincoln quite recently was also traced to the water supply. Numerous cases of epidemics may likewise be traced to a contaminated milk supply.

Putrefactive bacteria occur wherever there is filth in warm moist places, especially in bakeries which are both badly arranged and kept in a dirty state. The Zymogenic bacteria are always present in raw cereal and other foods, in which they set up acid fermentation.

Suitable media or foods for bacterial growth.—The most suitable nitrogenous foods are soluble proteid degradation products as peptones, amides, amino-compounds and other organic bodies, ammonium salts and nitrates of other bases, whilst in some few cases bacteria are capable of extracting their nitrogen from the air.

The more available sources of carbon are:—carbohydrates generally, glycerine, fatty acids and the alkaline salts of many vegetable acids such as malic, tartaric, citric, and other organic acids.

The mineral foods requisite include the bases:—potash, soda, lime, magnesia, and iron, combined with phosphoric, sulphuric, silicic, and hydrochloric acids. Of all these combinations the phosphates are necessary in quantity; of the remainder scarcely more than traces are required, but all must be in a dilute aqueous solution.

Bacteria are either aerobic, anaerobic, or transition forms. Aerobic bacteria are those which develop and thrive best in the presence of air; anaerobic groups flourish in the absence of air and also of light. The latter are among the organisms of the septic tank in sewage purification. The transition forms develop during one portion of their existence in air, and during another portion in the absence of air. Acids as a rule act injuriously, and either kill or check the development of bacteria. *B. typhosus*, the organism which is the cause of enteric or typhoid fever, is an exception to this, since it is capable of converting acid into alkaline media. On the other hand, alkalies and a... compounds in weak solution act as stimulants to many bacterial groups.

Light has a similar action to that of acids, and a powerful effect in killing or checking bacteria, especially the pathogenic varieties.

The members of the *Schizomycetes* group of organisms require a much higher temperature for their well-being, and to enable them to carry on their life functions, than do the members of the *Eumycetes*. These latter can flourish at temperatures nearly down to the freezing-point of water, but bacteria can rarely develop when the temperature is much below 50° F.; hence if milk and such other fluids as sugar syrups, preserves, etc., are kept cool, they will remain fit for consumption for considerable periods.

Most of the bakery bacteria develop between 60° and 85° F. Many of the pathogenic germs thrive exceedingly well about blood-heat, 98·4° F.

The temperatures suitable for spore formation vary considerably with the different species, and moreover, many bacteria require a plentiful supply of oxygen during the sporulation period.

Electricity and pressure apparently affect the *Schizomycetes* only very slightly, if at all. A great variety of products is formed during the life action of these organisms. Amongst them are hydrogen, nitrogen, carbonic acid, marsh gas, sulphuretted hydrogen, arsine, alcohols, acids, alkalies, and such deadly nitrogenous bases as the ptomaines. The processes by which these products are formed vary greatly; some are the result of fermentation and others of hydrolytic reactions, whilst some are re-combination bodies.

In order to distinguish between bacteria the following details should be carefully observed :—

(a) The most suitable media or food supplies.

(b) The stages of development and appearance at each stage.

(c) The products of decomposition.

(d) Their behaviour towards free oxygen.

...NTS, BACTERIA, MOULDS, YEASTS

modes and rapidity of multiplication.
(e) The influence of light and temperature.
(f) The action of antiseptics and other re-agents.
Their motility or non-motility.

Bacteria, when grown on the surface of fluid media, frequently become united, forming a tough gelatinous mass. In this, the outer mucilaginous coatings of the organisms become much swollen and ultimately fuse together, the bacteria being retained in the mass in quite a regular manner. Such a condition is known as a *Zoogloea* or the Zoogloeal state.

All the bacteria found in a bakery must be looked upon as harmful and disease-producing, and of all none are so dangerous as the septic or filth groups. Every measure should be adopted to keep them in check, otherwise serious consequences may ensue.

The very best means to ensure this freedom is to keep every part of the bakehouse scrupulously clean. Plenty of boiling water or steam in all cracks or other places where organisms may be harboured will, under ordinary circumstances, be effectual. In the summer time, or when there is a damp moist heat, the boiling water may be supplemented by the addition of an antiseptic such as bi-sulphite of lime, or 'Lustril' which also acts as a cleansing agent. These remedies may be still further improved by using a good system of ventilation. Let all parts of the bakery as far as possible be light and airy.

For additional information on this subject the following books may be consulted: *Bacteria*, by Conn; *Our Secret Friends and Foes*, by Professor Percy Frankland, F.R.S.; and the works of Pasteur, Schützenberger, Dr. Sims Woodhead, Professor Franz Lafar, and other writers.

THE HYPHOMYCETES

Hyphomycetes is the name given to a very numerous group of somewhat highly organised fungi of a parasitic character that infect and attack both living and dead bodies. They may be conveniently studied under the media. On the other hand, alkalies and alkaline compounds in weak solution act as stimulants to many bacterial groups.

Light has a similar action to that of acids, and has a powerful effect in killing or checking bacteria, especially the pathogenic varieties.

The members of the *Schizomycetes* group of organisms require a much higher temperature for their well-being and to enable them to carry on their life functions, than do the members of the *Eumycetes*. These latter can flourish at temperatures nearly down to the freezing-point of water, but bacteria can rarely develop when the temperature is much below 50° F.; hence if milk and such other fluids as sugar syrups, preserves, etc., are kept cool, they will remain fit for consumption for considerable periods.

Most of the bakery bacteria develop between 60° and 85° F. Many of the pathogenic germs thrive exceedingly well about blood-heat, 98·4° F.

The temperatures suitable for spore formation vary considerably with the different species, and moreover, many bacteria require a plentiful supply of oxygen during the sporulation period.

Electricity and pressure apparently affect the *Schizomycetes* only very slightly, if at all. A great variety of products is formed during the life action of these organisms. Amongst them are hydrogen, nitrogen, carbonic acid, marsh gas, sulphuretted hydrogen, arsine, alcohols, acids, alkalies, and such deadly nitrogenous bases as the ptomaines. The processes by which these products are formed vary greatly; some are the result of fermentation and others of hydrolytic reactions, whilst some are re-combination bodies.

In order to distinguish between bacteria the following details should be carefully observed :—

(a) The most suitable media or food supplies.

(b) The stages of development and appearance at each stage.

(c) The products of decomposition.

(d) Their behaviour towards free oxygen.

(e) The modes and rapidity of multiplication.
(f) The influence of light and temperature.
(g) The action of antiseptics and other re-agents.
(h) Their motility or non-motility.

Bacteria, when grown on the surface of fluid media, frequently become united, forming a tough gelatinous mass. In this, the outer mucilaginous coatings of the organisms become much swollen and ultimately fuse together, the bacteria being retained in the mass in quite a regular manner. Such a condition is known as a *Zoogloea* or the Zoogloeal state.

All the bacteria found in a bakery must be looked upon as harmful and disease-producing, and of all none are so dangerous as the septic or filth groups. Every measure should be adopted to keep them in check, otherwise serious consequences may ensue.

The very best means to ensure this freedom is to keep every part of the bakehouse scrupulously clean. Plenty of boiling water or steam in all cracks or other places where organisms may be harboured will, under ordinary circumstances, be effectual. In the summer time, or when there is a damp moist heat, the boiling water may be supplemented by the addition of an antiseptic such as bi-sulphite of lime, or 'Lustril' which also acts as a cleansing agent. These remedies may be still further improved by using a good system of ventilation. Let all parts of the bakery as far as possible be light and airy.

For additional information on this subject the following books may be consulted: *Bacteria*, by Conn; *Our Secret Friends and Foes*, by Professor Percy Frankland, F.R.S.; and the works of Pasteur, Schützenberger, Dr. Sims Woodhead, Professor Franz Lafar, and other writers.

THE HYPHOMYCETES

Hyphomycetes is the name given to a very numerous group of somewhat highly organised fungi of a parasitic character that infect and attack both living and dead bodies. They may be conveniently studied under the divisions *oidium*, *moulds*, and *mucors*; the first-named are comparatively simple, while the last group are highly complex.

In each of these groups are smaller groups or orders, and these again are subdivided into genera, species, and varieties. One interesting order, the *Mucedines*, containing the genus *Peronospora*, which genus includes the rusts, smuts, brands, and mildews that attack most grain-bearing plants, is perhaps the best known. The mycelial or fine hair-like threads are branching, thus enabling the members of the Peronospora genus to develop and penetrate plants and other food sources in all directions. The spores are of two kinds, the one carried on the tips of the mycelial threads and the other kind, which are much larger and globular in form, borne on the creeping mycelium. The botanical name for these microscopic plants comes from a Greek word meaning mildew; thus the *Erysiphe* and *Oidium* groups are plants exceedingly troublesome to the farmer, owing to their attacks on such of his crops as the cereals, roots, and fruits.

Another group of the Hyphomycetes is the *moulds*, also a numerous group and more highly developed than the oidium. Many of the members possess the power of inducing fermentation, owing to the enzymes which they secrete, but from this point of view they are unimportant. The containing cell-wall of the mycelial threads is of fungi-cellulose which yields no coloration with iodine solution; the protoplasm that fills the cells is free from nuclei, and contains neither chlorophyll nor starch granules.

The growth takes place by elongation of the cells forming the hyphae, which latter are subdivided by transverse diaphragms of cellulose known as septa. The whole of the mycelium, aerial hyphae or spore-bearing organs and conidia give rise from a single spore to aggregations botanically designated as a 'thallus.'

Moulds can flourish on very concentrated media that would readily check the development of yeasts and bacteria; for example, preserves made with too little sugar are very

FERMENTS, BACTERIA, MOULDS, YEASTS

liable to ferment and suffer attacks from the moulds. Some of them can grow in alkaline solutions, most in neutral foods, and some few even in acid solutions. Although normally aerobic, they require only minute traces of free oxygen, the absence of which induces an alternation of generation or polymorphism. The ordinary foods containing carbohydrates, mineral salts as in the ash of cereals, and nitrogen from soluble albuminous compounds, peptones, amides, amino acids, ammonium salts, and even from nitrates, are suitable for moulds. Various workers in the study of mycology have shown that differences in food supply cause differences in the chemical composition of moulds.

The modes of reproduction :—

(a) One of the simplest is by a continuous budding and dividing off—a process closely allied to the budding of yeasts and their fission. The members of the genus *Oidium* reproduce in this way, in fact it is commonly spoken of as the oidium formation.

(b) By the formation of naked spores or conidia at the ends of the aerial hyphae or conidia bearers. The *Penicillium* group, the *Eurotiums* and subdivisions of these as the *Aspergilli*, the *Dematiums*, the *Cladosporia* and *Botrytis* groups, are all excellent examples of this mode of reproduction (Fig. 34).

The *mucors*, which are more highly organised than the moulds but which in many ways they very much resemble, reproduce in two ways : (c) by the formation of spores in a special receptacle or ' sporangium,' the walls of which burst when the spores are ripe and allow the contents to escape and be dispersed in all directions. In some of the mucors these spores are furnished with cilia or hair-like appendages which greatly assist in their distribution. The abovementioned three modes of reproduction are recognised as vegetative or asexual processes.

The mucors, however, can also reproduce (d) by sexual conjugation. Two threads or hyphae join one another (copulation) and give rise to a large spore or fruit-like body known as a 'zygospore,' from which mycelial threads grow at a later period after the zygospore has dropped from the parent mycelium.

The spores produced by any of the foregoing methods are very resistant to desiccation or drying and to large variations of temperature. They frequently remain dry for years, but if brought into a suitable food medium at once begin to develop. All the three groups are well represented by their various members on our foods or any substances that contain the necessary food principles. The four

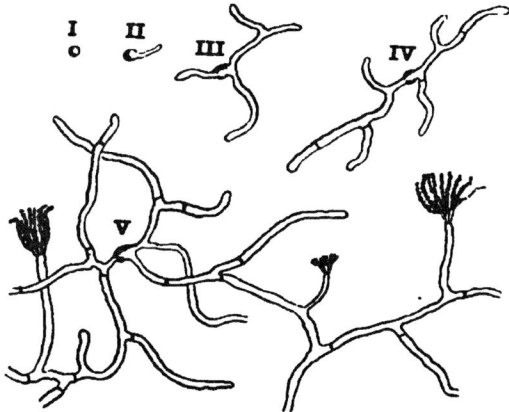

Fig. 34.—*Penicillium glaucum.* From a Microphotograph of a Mould × 105. I.-V. show the development of a complete thallus from a single spore. (From a Böttcher moist cell culture.)

commonest are :—the ordinary blue mould—*Penicillium glaucum* (Fig. 34), the sage-green mould—*Aspergillus glaucus, Mucor mucedo,* and the *Oidium lactis.* These induce in our food supplies acidity, decomposition, and mouldy or musty smells. Damp clothing under similar conditions also becomes musty and unpleasant-smelling.

Yeasts and Barms

The yeasts or *Mycomycetes* are the botanical names given to a group of saprophytic fungi—so-called because

FERMENTS, BACTERIA, MOULDS, YEASTS

they live on prepared foods—which play a very important part in all the fermentation industries, including baking, brewing, and the manufacture of wines and spirits.

The yeast plant (Fig. 35) consists of a single cell, round or oval in shape, ranging from five to eleven microns in diameter with an average of between seven and eight, or

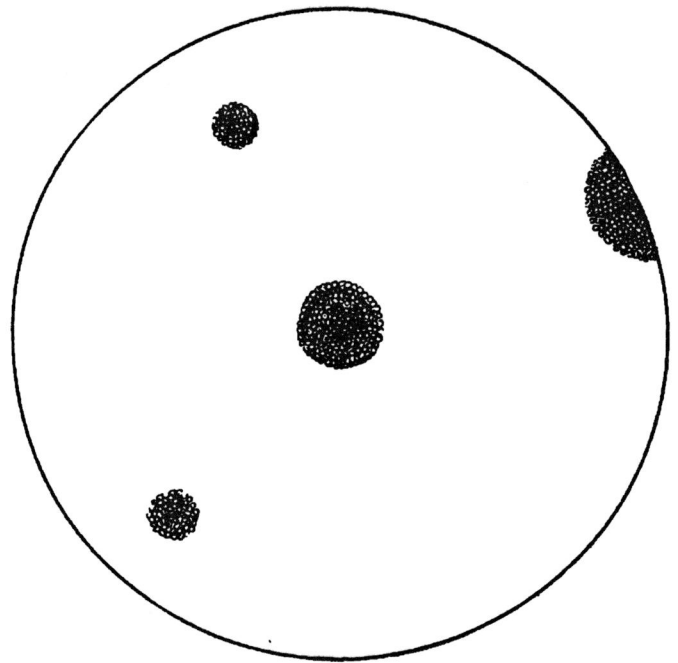

Fig. 35.—Colonies of Yeast in Wort-gelatin × 550.

from four- to three-thousandths of an inch in diameter. This may be expressed in another way : if a line be drawn exactly an inch in length, then from three to four thousand of these minute organisms could be placed on such a line.

Each cell is an individual plant surrounded by a thin transparent dual cell-wall of cellulose and filled internally with protoplasm. If a cell-wall be ruptured by pressing with a cover-glass or knife blade, the plasma can be readily stained with a weak solution of methylene blue. Live protoplasm resists staining in a high degree, but the dead mass rapidly absorbs this dye. Use is made of this reaction to detect the presence of dead cells in the yeast employed by the baker. A slide of the yeast is made in the usual way, carefully examined by the aid of a compound microscope, then a small drop of the dye solution is brought to the edge of the cover-glass. In a short time the coloured liquid becomes dispersed through the cells by the process of capillarity. This dye has a toxic effect on the yeast

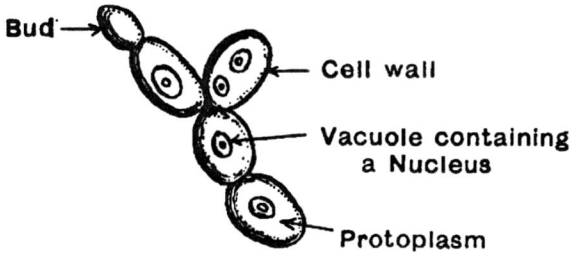

Fig. 36.—Scotch Distillery Yeast. From a Microphotograph × 1120.

cells, so that the examination for dead and weak cells must be carried out at once (see p. 150).

Most yeast cells (Fig. 36) develop vacuoles, and inside of these a nucleus containing that very complex mixture of compounds, the nucleins. The nucleus is a minute rounded body which appears to control the activities of a cell in a manner not yet fully understood. The young and vigorous cells are filled with a foamy, highly refractive form of protoplasm, whilst old cells contain dull-looking, granular protoplasm which readily separates from the cell wall. Within recent years, varieties of Saccharomycetes have been discovered that possess the power of forming true hyphae, the slender threads of which do not interlace like those of moulds, hence the yeasts are less complex than the

FERMENTS, BACTERIA, MOULDS, YEASTS

Hyphomycetes. These threads must not be confused with the film forms or pseudo-mycelia of yeasts obtained when the latter is grown on the surface of a liquid in the presence of air.

Under normal conditions the yeasts reproduce by the process of gemmation or budding. The bud is primarily formed inside the cell itself; the cell-wall is probably weakened at this point by enzyme action so that the bud is able to push its way through, after which it rapidly develops.

Janssens has shown that both in gemmation and sporula-

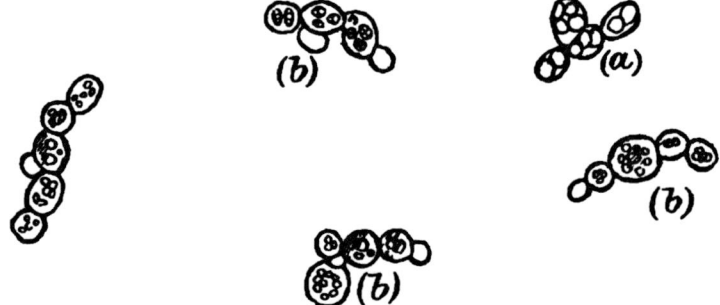

Fig. 37.—Drawing of Scotch Distillery Yeast from a Microphotograph × 560. The group of cells marked *a* show sporing. Those marked *b* show budding.

tion there is first a division of the nucleus, followed by that of the protoplasm. The bud thus formed is partially separated from the parent cell by a cellulosic diaphragm through which the food supply to the young cell passes.

When the bud has become fully developed it generally separates itself, but occasionally it adheres, giving rise to a chain of yeast cells—the strepto-formation—which often happens in the case of bakery yeasts, or clusters—the staphylo-form. Some yeasts also reproduce by an abnormal or starvation process known as sporulation (Fig. 37). This may be brought about in the laboratory by growing yeasts in sterile water on a gypsum block or on a sterilised slice of potato. The spores formed in this way are highly resistant to adverse circumstances, giving the yeast a chance to tide over periods of stress ; for example, in the wine industry during the greater part of the year when there are no grapes, the yeasts exist in this state in the ground, withstanding the cold and wet of the winter and spring ; later the dry winds raise clouds of dust and so carry the yeast spores into the air to settle on the newly-formed grapes. This statement is not a fanciful one, but a truth backed up by the splendid researches of the late Professor E. C. Hansen of Copenhagen and the late Professor Louis Pasteur of Paris. The spores are enclosed within the sac or mother-cell, hence they obtain the name ascospores. Hansen made use of sporulation to differentiate true yeasts from all others.

There are large numbers of other organisms which closely resemble the yeasts, as, for example, the *torula*, organisms taking the form of groups of minute, spherical, yeast-like cells. These occur abundantly in all places where sugars, worts, and musts are prepared, and generally are the cause of disease. The *Saccharomyces apiculatus* is a lemon-shaped yeast which exists in the bloom on fruits ; *S. niger*, *S. rosaceus*, and *S. albus* were discovered by Professor P. Frankland in the atmosphere. In addition to these many other varieties exist, but as none of them sporulate they cannot be regarded as true yeasts. Sporulation may take place between the temperatures 34° and 98° F. The film formation previously mentioned is most successful between 46° and 51° F.

Suitable media for yeasts.—Yeasts can take the carbon they require from the sugars and other carbohydrates, but the solutions should not exceed 15 per cent. strength. The nitrogen is taken chiefly from organic sources as the peptones, amides, amino compounds and others, whilst ammonium compounds, with the exception of the nitrates, are also available. The mineral salts required can be ascertained on reference to an analysis of the ash. The following figures are those of Mitscherlich :—

Ash Constituents.	Top Yeasts.	Bottom Yeasts.
Potash (K_2O),	38·81 %	28·30 %
Lime (CaO),	1·08 ,,	4·20 ,,
Magnesia (MgO),	6·13 ,,	8·10 ,,
Phosphoric acid (P_2O_5),	53·91 ,,	59·40 ,,

Nitrous acid and all of its compounds, the nitrites, which are soluble in water or sugar solution, act as direct poisons to yeasts. Nitrates and albumenoid ammonia cause rapid weakening and deterioration, especially in the absence of free oxygen. Air or free oxygen is a necessity for yeasts. Most of the great authorities on the study of yeasts, viz., Hansen, Lintner, Naegeli, and Pasteur, agree that a small quantity of free oxygen with 12 per cent. strength of sugar solutions, are the best mixtures for a vigorous fermentation with maximum growth and multiplication of yeast cells. With excess air there is a greater reproduction of cells, but less fermentation work is carried out.

A trace of acidity, especially that due to organic and phosphoric acids, assists the yeast cells, and also somewhat protects them from bacterial competition. Light, except bright sunlight, electricity and pressure appear to exert but little influence on yeasts. During the fermentation of liquids as distinct from doughs, three different periods may be observed :—

(1) The period of rest, during which there is an absorption of oxygen and a development of the vegetative functions.

(2) The period of activity, during which the sugars are broken down or hydrolysed, and then fermented to alcohols and carbon dioxide, with the production of new yeast cells.

(3) The period of slackening, in which the yeast is carried to the surface of the fermented liquid.

The classification of yeasts and fermentation.—Yeasts

are classified as the culture yeasts and the wild or disease-producing ones. The culture yeasts are those employed in the bakery, brewery, distillery, and other fermentation industries. They may be distinguished from the wild yeasts by the length of time required in sporulation, by the large size of the dull-looking spores, and by the less highly refractive nature of the aqueous protoplasm of the spores. The wild yeasts are abundant in the vegetable kingdom, on the skins of the fruits, and in the atmosphere generally, during the summer and autumn. The spores of these yeasts are small and more highly refractive than those of the culture yeasts. Some of the apparatus used in connection with pure yeast culture is illustrated in Fig. 38.

Yeasts may be distinguished from one another as follows :—

(1) By shape and appearance; yet the shape of a cell is dependent on the culture medium, the temperature at which the culture is made, the age of the culture employed, and on the presence or absence of air.

(2) By differences in the mode of culture; thus colonies of yeasts in wort-gelatine are, in many cases, for the first few days, perfect spheres, but afterwards they become fringed.

(3) By differences in fermentation, in the fermentation products and in their behaviour towards media.

(4) By differences in the time and methods of sporulation and film-forming.

A very large number of different species and varieties of yeasts have been isolated, their properties, characteristics, and other factors studied, but up to the present no satisfactory classification has been drawn up.

For the purposes of our own industry they may very well be divided into the top fermentation yeasts and the bottom fermentation yeasts of the culture group. Both belong to the same genus, *Saccharomyces Cerevisiae*, but it has been found impossible to transform the one variety into the other.

The *bottom yeasts* vary considerably in size and appearance, in their behaviour towards worts and sugar solutions, and in other characteristics. They ferment worts best at low temperatures, viz., between 38° and 52° F. Their chief use is in the fermentation of decoction worts brewed for the preparation of lager beers. Such tempera-

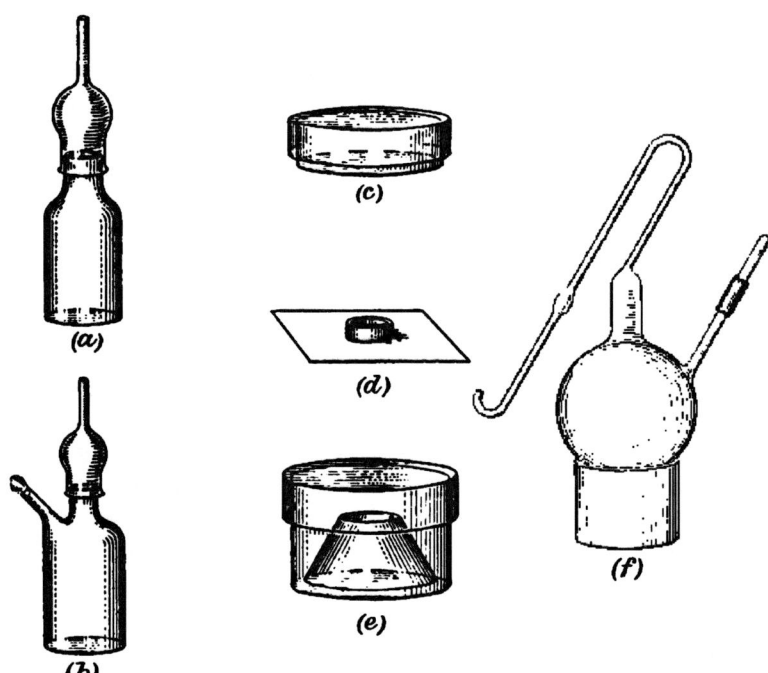

Fig. 38.—Some Apparatus required in Pure Yeast Culture:—
a. Freudenreich Flask; b. Hansen Flask; c. Petri Dish; d. Böttcher Moist Cell; e. Gypsum Block for Sporulation; f. Pasteur Flask.

tures are much too low for the yeasts to be of any great use in bakery processes.

The *top yeasts* are therefore the only ones suitable for general bakehouse work. This group belongs to *Saccharomyces Cerevisiae I*. The word 'Saccharomyces' comes from two foreign words, the first part referring to sugar or saccharine bodies, and the latter part to the fungus which ferments the sugar solutions. The word 'Cerevisiae' is derived from 'Ceres,' the goddess of corn and wine, here referring to the sources of the sugars.

A strong, healthy top yeast should possess the following characteristics :—

Uniformity of shape and size, sharpness of the cell-wall outline, presence of one or two vacuoles with the nucleus not too distinct, and the absence of foreign matters and bacteria. The name top yeast comes from the fact that during fermentation the yeasts produced are carried to the surface of the fermenting liquid; the bottom yeasts, on the other hand, sink to the bottom of the containing fermenting vessel.

Of the top yeasts, three kinds from different industries are employed in baking, viz., vinegar, brewery, and distillery yeasts. Each of these has its own particular influence on the finished loaf.

The *vinegar yeasts* always carry with them not only the aroma of vinegar but also some of the acetic and other bacteria with which they are associated. In colour, general appearance and fracture, they are satisfactory, but as regards flavour and speed of work, vinegar yeasts do not give the best of results.

Brewery yeasts carry with them their origin. The hop flavour and aroma is very persistent, even after repeated washings. The colour is much darker than that of distillery yeast, and influences the bread by rendering the crumb darker and dulling the bloom. Further, English brewery yeasts are accustomed to ferment at temperatures varying between 57° and 75° F. and at a slow speed. The finished loaf when prepared with this yeast is smaller in volume, darker in colour, faintly bitter in flavour, and with a somewhat dull bloom compared with a loaf from a good distillery yeast, but it is rarely sour.

Distillery yeasts are generally more irregular in shape and size than brewery yeasts, lighter in colour, possess a pleasant but different aroma, and are accustomed to rapid fermentation at high temperatures; they are thus in almost every way the typical yeast for the baker. The chief drawbacks to the British distillery yeasts are that they contain too high a percentage of dead cells and far too many bacteria, whilst many of them are much too variable in their characteristics and properties. These faults are mainly due to the fact that spirit is the primary object in the distillery, and yeast is only a by-product. Again, far too large a proportion of raw grain to malt is employed, thus depriving the yeast of its proper nutritious food supply. Often the production of a somewhat inferior yeast is possibly due to the lack of a suitable scientific training in many of those in charge of our large distilleries. The advantages of a good type of distiller's yeast may be summed up as follows :—

It is the best all-round type of yeast to use because it works evenly and is quick, and gives good colour, flavour, bloom, texture, and volume; whilst the two chief disadvantages are that it is rather more costly and, with careless working, there is the risk of acidity and loss of flavour.

The culture of yeast for bakery use.—Yeast for the food industries is either grown in bulk for the yield of yeast itself, or it is a kind of by-product in the production of spirit—chiefly whisky.

Abroad, one large factory produces over two hundred tons of yeast (Fig. 39) per week as its chief product, the spirit being of secondary consideration.

The writer is unable to hear of any firm in the British Isles which devotes itself to yeast manufacture as its main product. British distilleries produce spirit, while the yeast is a by-product, hence such yeast cannot hope to compete with the Continental product with any degree of real success. Moreover, British brewery yeasts occupy a similar position in this respect. Again, brewery yeasts are slow for dough fermentation, since they are accustomed to develop and work at considerably lower temperatures than those employed in a bakery.

An account of the production of yeast also involves that

144 CHEMISTRY OF BREADMAKING

of the manufacture of spirit. The proper quantities of diastatic barley malt and crushed raw grain are intimately mixed in the proportions of one part of ground malt with from three to eight parts by weight of the raw cereals, together with hot water at such a temperature that that of the mash is about 146° F. During the 'stand on' of two or more hours, the enzymes present convert the starches and other raw materials into wort constituents, such as

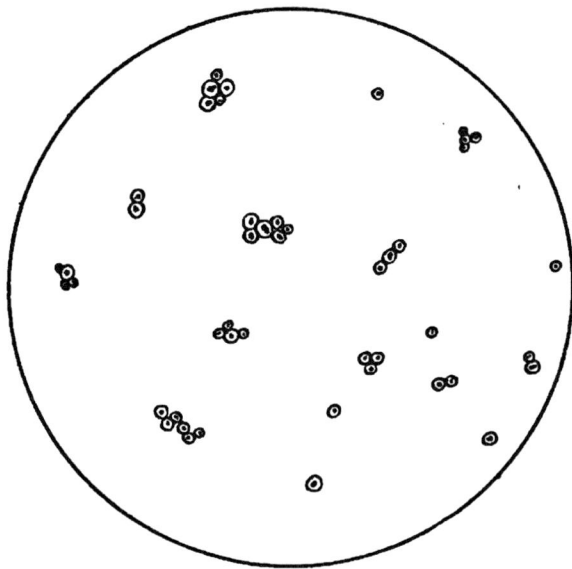

Fig. 39.—Dutch Yeast. From a Microphotograph × 365.

maltose, dextrins, peptones, amides, and the like. The sweet wort is run off from the grains; all remaining constituents are washed out by sparging; the mixture of the two is cooled to about 72° to 75° F., passed through a filter, run into the large wort becks, and pitched with yeast from a previous brew. It is very important that the pitching yeast shall be strong, fresh, vigorous, young cells free from all forms of contamination. The fermentation goes on rapidly, as shown by the increase in temperature and the

FERMENTS, BACTERIA, MOULDS, YEASTS

attenuation of the wort. In thirty-six hours the highest temperature of about 82° F. will have been attained; then, as the fermentation gradually lessens, the temperature also falls until a point lower than that of pitching is reached in, say, another thirty or more hours. During the period of active fermentation where a large yield of yeast is required, aeration must be frequent; at the same time there is a loss of spirit, hence in British distilleries aeration is not largely adopted, whilst the temperature is not allowed to go beyond 82° F. on account of the excessive evaporation of spirit.

During fermentation various heads are thrown up by the yeast; the first is known as the dirty head, since it is full of particles composed of little yeast, but much bacteria and other organisms. This head is skimmed off and rejected, while the yeast from the succeeding heads is collected, mixed, pressed, washed, and packed for the use of the baker. The alcoholic liquid from the fermentation is 'wash,' which must be filtered, settled, and got into the 'wash stills' for distillation as quickly as possible in order to prevent acetous fermentation by bacteria and consequent loss of spirit. The 'wash' has a sp. gr. of about 1002 from a 1042 wort, and contains from 10 to 13 per cent. of proof spirit by volume. A well-known general rule in distilleries is: Prepare thin mashes resulting in maltosic worts and ferment with quick top yeasts to the sp. gr. of water.

BARMS

Barms are of two classes, the virgin and others, which latter are variously named as Parisian, compound, etc. The active fermenting principle in all of them is yeast, but it is mixed up with countless bacteria and other bodies, most of which exert an influence on the finished bread. The effect in the case of the virgin barms is more marked than in the others, owing to the fact that in the former there are infinitely larger quantities of acid-forming bacteria in proportion to the yeast cells than in the latter. At once it can be seen that barms are suitable only for long processes.

Bread prepared by the aid of barms is generally of poor volume and colour, rather liable to be holey, with dull bloom and texture somewhat variable, but the flavour as a rule is good. Barms are suitable for working strong, harsh flours by long, slow processes. Owing to the large quantity of bacteria in barms it is customary to use considerably larger quantities of salt; thus from four to seven pounds per sack of flour are not unusual. More than four pounds can be distinctly tasted; again, as salt is both an antiseptic and germicide, too large quantities check the fermentation.

The making of barms.—The principles involved and methods used in making up barms are somewhat as follows :—

Malt is crushed or ground and mixed with a large volume of water at about 158° to 165° F. so as to give a thin mash at 145° to 150°. The object is to obtain malt sugar and the proper type of nitrogenous bodies to act as yeast foods. Whilst this is proceeding, a few ounces of hops, generally three or four per gallon of water, are infused in boiling water with stirring so as to extract the various constituents, viz., the essential oils for flavour, the resins and tannins for flavouring and antiseptic purposes, and the other bodies as yeast foods.

With many barms scalded flour is added to the mash to increase the quantity of sugars. The quantity of a soft flour is made into a fine batter with either cold water or some of the wort already prepared, and then the starch of the flour is gelatinised by pouring in boiling water or wort, gradually and with stirring. This scalded flour batter is either cooled down and added in bulk to the mash with stirring, or it is added cautiously with continuous stirring so as not to raise the temperature of the mash high enough to stop diastatic action. If not above 160° F. there is little risk. Some bakers use the hop extract for this purpose. All the ingredients are mixed together and stirred well, then left for two or three hours to enable saccharification, or the conversion of the starch into sugar, to take place. The sweet-tasting fluid mass is strained and rapidly cooled to 70° or 80° F.

In the case of a virgin barm, some salt and sugar are stirred in and the wort left in a cool place for twenty to thirty hours. In other kinds some barm from a previous brew, or some distillers' or brewers' yeast, is added to set up fermentation. During the time such barms are preparing the tubs should be protected with a loose-fitting cover. These barms are ready for use in about twenty-four hours.

There are many modifications in the preparation of the various barms, but the principles involved are the same, viz., the saccharifying of starch, the addition of hop extract, and the growing of yeast in the wort prepared. The alcoholic liquid containing the yeast is then used for setting sponges and other long processes of fermenting doughs.

According to the many authorities on this branch of breadmaking, the following is the comparative value of the different ferments :—

Twelve ounces of distillers' compressed yeast, sixteen ounces of brewers' compressed yeast, about four fluid pints of brewers' liquid yeast, twelve pounds of compound barm, twenty to twenty-four pounds of Parisian barm, or about thirty pounds of virgin barm are required for each sack of flour.

The Theory of Alcoholic Fermentation

From remote ages it has been known that when sugar solutions, such as the expressed juices of sweet fruits, were exposed to the air, the sweetness was gradually lost, and the liquid took on a spirituous flavour and properties. During this change it was observed that bubbles were produced and passed off into the air. It was not, however, until about 1680 that the cause of the bubbling or boiling up—hence the name fermentation from the Latin '*fervere*,' to boil—was discovered. At this period, Antony van Leeuwenhoek of Delft was working with one of the first-made compound microscopes and noticed that small spherical bodies were always present in liquids that 'bubbled up' when cold.

From that time onwards many theories were advanced to explain fermentation, but none were absolutely successful. The modern or *enzyme* theory took its rise in the last half of the nineteenth century from the work of M. Traube. Even yet very much remains to be done to satisfy every part of this theory. The following are the names of the theories displaced by the enzyme or soluble ferment theory:—the mechanical or dead mass theory of Stahl, Willis, and Liebig; the amorphous form or catalytic theory of Berzelius; the vitalistic theory of Cagniard de Latour, Schwann, and Kützing, and the physico-molecular theory of Naegeli.

Fermentation is the name given to the process, in which soluble ferments or enzymes play an important part, by which the carbohydrates, especially the sugars, are decomposed mainly into carbon dioxide and alcohol, with traces of higher alcohols, acids, and other substances. Although Cavendish and Lavoisier were the first to attempt an explanation of fermentation, M. Gay-Lussac was the first to express the reaction by an equation:

$$C_{12}H_{24}O_{12} = 4\ C_2H_5.OH + 4\ CO_2$$
Sugars　　Alcohol (51·11 %)　Carbon dioxide (48·89 %)

In this equation no account is taken of the higher alcohols or fusel oils, glycerine, succinic acid, and traces of other bodies. Yeasts are said to produce alcoholic fermentation whilst bacteria produce the acid fermentation of carbohydrates, with the formation of such acids as acetic, propionic, butyric, lactic, and others.

Putrefaction is the decomposition of nitrogenous matter by bacterial agency accompanied by the production of noxious gases such as ammonia, sulphuretted hydrogen, etc.

Decay is the slow process by which dry, and also moist, organic substances are gradually decomposed by the agency of micro-organisms growing and feeding upon them.

Recent research goes to prove that all the processes of decomposition may be referred to the action of enzymes, and that they are much more complex than was originally surmised; for example, the equation of Gay-Lussac was considered, until within the last few years, to represent approximately what actually took place during fermentation; but when Edward Buchner in 1897-8 published his researches on yeast-juice and the discovery of the enzyme *zymase*, all the previous ideas regarding fermentation were shown to be wrong. Still later research, dating to May in the present year (1911), carries the work of the brothers Buchner much farther. Zymase itself is not sufficient to induce fermentation of sugar solutions. Dr. Arthur Harden in his monograph on *Alcoholic Fermentation* (1911) conclusively proves that another enzyme, spoken of as a co-enzyme, and alkaline phosphates are absolutely essential.

The following reactions take place when a sugar is fermented normally by yeast :—

The sugar, if a biose as sucrose or maltose, is hydrolysed by enzyme action into monoses. These during decomposition by zymase and its co-enzyme form alcohol, carbon dioxide, water, other bodies, and a sugar phosphate to which the name hexose-phosphate has been given. This compound is hydrolysed by an enzyme hexose-phosphatase yielding sugar, which is at once fermented. The alkaline phosphate is then ready once again to re-form hexose-phosphate, and so the cycle of reactions goes on so long as any sugar remains in solution.

In accordance with the enzyme theory of alcoholic fermentation, all decompositions and recombinations are performed inside the yeast cell itself by the various enzymes; therefore all substances passing into the cell are necessarily of a crystalline and soluble nature, otherwise they could not diffuse through the vegetable membrane that forms the cell-wall. The same is true also for all the excretory products of the yeasts' metabolism. By ' metabolism ' is understood the power that the protoplasm of the yeast cell possesses of changing the constituents of its food into other bodies; whilst the products of this metabolism are said to be excretory.

During the hot season, both the yeast merchant and the baker experience difficulty in keeping yeast for any length of time owing to the auto- or self-fermentation of the yeast.

From the work on yeast juice carried out at the Lister Institute, it would appear that in addition to the substances before mentioned, the protoplasm also contains a glycogen, similar to the animal starch found in the liver of animals, diastase, and proteolytic enzymes. When yeast is exposed to high temperatures without suitable or sufficient food, the liquefaction and breaking up of the constituents of the cell take place, resulting in the annihilation of the yeast.

Yeast may be stored for a considerable period without deterioration provided that the atmosphere is a dry, cool one, with a temperature, however, not so low as to freeze the cells. Recently, a form of desiccated yeast has been placed on the market in sealed tins for carriage into and for use in hot climates.

The examination of yeast for bakery purposes.—A general examination of the yeast is first made to ascertain its colour, taste, smell, appearance, moisture, and the fracture when broken across.

It is now subjected to a microscopic examination and the following points noted :—the general condition of the yeast cells as regards regularity in size, a clear strong cell-wall, whether in a granular state internally, the deterioration or otherwise of the vacuoles, whether in the budding stage and the presence or absence of foreign organisms. For the purpose of this work a small quantity of the yeast is brought into a small clean bottle, shaken up with sterile water, a drop withdrawn and put on a micro-slip, then covered with a very thin cover-glass and examined as above. Several fields on each of two or three slips should be carefully observed and notes made on each. General conclusions may then be drawn from them.

The presence of dead and very weak cells can be detected by bringing a small drop of the dye methylene blue to the edge of the cover-glass, allowing it to work in for a few

FERMENTS, BACTERIA, MOULDS, YEASTS

moments and then counting all the cells per field. Next note all those that are completely stained blue, which are the dead cells; then those that are slightly or more stained, these are the weak cells in which the protoplasm is granular and the cells shrunken in size.

The *gas-evolving power* is next determined in the following way :—Five grams of the sample of yeast in as finely divided a state as possible are accurately weighed, brought into a glass flask of about two hundred and fifty c.c. capacity, and ten grams of good cane sugar added; when all the fittings are ready, add one hundred c.c. of water at about blood-heat, 98·4° F., insert the cork through which passes a bent glass tube, the opposite end dipping under a graduated glass tube, which is suspended with its lower end just under water contained in a suitable vessel as shown in the illustration (Fig. 40). The number of minutes taken for the yeast to begin the evolution of carbon dioxide gas is noted, after which readings of the number of c.c. evolved are taken for four or five consecutive half-hours. The apparatus used for this determination is a double one, so that a fair average of the gas-evolving power of the yeast can be obtained.

This determination is usually verified by making a fine batter with weighed quantities of flour, yeast, and water, which, of course, will vary according to the size of the containing vessel employed. The time at which the batter is set, the length of time taken to come to the highest point, and the length of time before dropping, are all noted and comparisons made.

It should be remembered, that if yeast is old and granular in appearance, if it contains many dead cells and is badly contaminated with motile and non-motile bacteria, then it takes longer to begin its vegetative functions, the volume of gas evolved is low and its evolution slow. Such a yeast is not fitted for the quick dough processes now in general use, especially in the towns. Where long-sponge or ferment methods are still in use, a yeast of the type described may be much improved by the addition of a pound to two pounds per sack of a good diastase paste or malt extract. For the quick processes, a very weak yeast would not recover in time to be of any effective use.

Fig. 40.—Apparatus for Measuring the Gas-evolving Power of Yeast.

CHAPTER X

BREADMAKING PROCESSES AND BREADS

THE earliest of all the breadmaking processes was that in which *leaven* was employed; the leaven itself may be looked upon as a primeval form of virgin barm, since the active constituents of this were derived in the first instance from the atmosphere, like those of the virgin barm. The bread obtained by the help of leaven was a dark-coloured kind of cake possessing the usual sweetish-sour taste.

In the present day, two methods of aerating doughs are in common use: the ordinary process in which one of the many varieties of yeast forms the active agent, and the other in which chemical compounds are employed to generate the carbon dioxide that aerates the dough. Of these latter compounds one is a metallic carbonate, usually the bicarbonate of soda—an alkaline body—although the normal carbonate, the sesqui, and crystal carbonates all find use in this direction; the other compound is either an acid or hydrogen salt of phosphoric acid, or of some organic acid like tartaric and citric, or the free acids themselves; *e.g.* cream of tartar or bitartrate of potassium, or the potassium acid citrate, or the superphosphate of lime. The powder most generally used consists of two parts by weight of cream of tartar mixed with one of bicarbonate of soda.

When powders are made up in quantity so as to save time, it is advisable to mix in with them a proportion of rice or some similar starch, as otherwise the mixture tends to cake into a hard mass, which gradually gives off its gas and becomes useless. As an alternative, patent or soda flour may be made up by thoroughly mixing two ounces of cream of tartar (98 per cent. strength) with one ounce of pure bicarbonate of soda, the two quantities being enough to aerate four pounds of a strong flour. Brown and certain special white breads are manufactured on a small scale with powder. The meal or other flour is rubbed with a small quantity of fat to shorten and enrich the finished product, then made into a bay on the working table; a smaller proportion of salt than when using yeast, well crushed to avoid lumps, is distributed over the meal, and the proper quantity of milk or water at the ordinary temperature, say 70° F., is brought into the bay, and the whole worked up into a dough of suitable consistency. After clearing, the dough is scaled off at the desired weight, moulded, and allowed to stand for a time to give the powder a chance to work.

When ready, the goods are baked in a moderately sharp oven. If the oven is too slow, the goods are dried off rather than baked; on the other hand, the oven must not be too hot, since the generation of gas should be slow and regular, otherwise the goods are not evenly aerated.

The reaction of the chemicals may be expressed by the equation :

$$\begin{array}{c} CHOH.COOH \\ | \\ CHOH.COOK \end{array} + NaHCO_3 = \begin{array}{c} CHOH.COONa \\ | \\ CHOH.COOK \end{array} + CO_2 + H_2O$$

Cream of tartar + Bicarbonate of soda = Rochelle salt + gas + water

A smaller quantity of salt is taken than with yeast because of the Rochelle salt left in the bread. This salt has a mild purgative action on the human system. If the alkaline sodium salt is used in excess, the goods are marked with yellowish-brown streaks and taste of soda. When cream of tartar is in excess, there is an unpleasant acid flavour prevalent in the finished goods. All goods made with powder are very liable to become dry, even when carefully stored.

A number of mechanical processes have from time to time been devised and patented for the purpose of aerating dough with carbonic acid gas, CO_2. Amongst these, that of Dr. Dauglish was the only one to achieve more than a slight success; yet, even that survived only for a short time.

BREADMAKING BY AERATION WITH CARBONIC ACID GAS PRODUCED BY THE ACTION OF YEAST

There are many different methods of aerating or fermenting dough, but in reality only about three of them are in common use. They are the *straight-dough* or 'offhand' process, the *ferment and dough* and the *sponge and dough* methods.

In country districts in England and Wales, and in most parts of Scotland except one or two of the larger towns, 'sponge and dough' processes of long duration are still the order of the day; but wherever good compressed yeast can be regularly obtained, straight-dough processes are becoming more and more prevalent.

Again, in many districts it is still quite common to find the potato ferment, in spite of its dirt, a usual process of preparing dough. A potato ferment can be made as follows:—Eight to ten pounds of potatoes of a mealy character are first well cleaned, then boiled, and, after standing to dry for a few minutes, pressed through a brass-wire sieve, mashed with about two gallons of water, and cooled down to 85° F. Three or four pounds of flour and eight ounces of yeast are broken up and stirred into the mash. After standing to ferment for six or eight hours, it is in a suitable condition for setting a sponge or for making up by the straight-dough process.

In the Midlands and some parts of the south of England, a ferment process is employed. This consists in making a kind of thin batter in the following way:—

From one to one and a half pounds of compressed yeast are well broken up in a gallon of water at 90° F. or at any temperature up to 98° F. as may be necessary (it should be noted that yeast is an organism and therefore cannot be dissolved), and four pounds of flour gradually stirred in to make a fine batter. This ferment should be covered and put into a warm place until ready, say in about twenty-five to thirty minutes, when it may be used for a two hours' sponge process, or for a straight-dough method to be made into bread in about four hours.

There is also another common way of preparing a ferment by means of scalded flour and malt, as follows :—

Crush or grind ten pounds of malt and mash with three gallons of water at 160° F. In the meantime infuse three ounces of hops with a gallon of boiling water for a short period and cool down the infusion to 145° F. After the malt infusion or mash has stood for two hours both this and the hop one are strained together into a barm tub, pressing out as much of the liquor as possible. Next, stir in enough strong flour with the strained liquor to form a thick paste or batter and allow to stand for twelve hours. Boiling water is now poured cautiously with continuous stirring into the batter so as to gelatinise the starch. The malt soon liquefies the scalded flour, as may be observed by the gradual thinning down of the batter.

Half a gallon of the thin batter is used per sack of two hundred and eighty pounds of flour, for making a sponge (one-third water), which is to stand for eight or ten hours. Generally, from eight to twelve ounces of good distillery yeast will be required with such a batter.

The sponge and dough bread process.—The sponge process is still the prevalent one, though it is fast being superseded by the straight or offhand method. A sponge and dough process is in reality an operation to make dough in two stages, viz., the setting of the sponge and the doughing up. Several different sponges are used, the quarter, the third, the half, and the three-quarter ; whilst the length of time may range from two to twelve or more hours. Anomalous though it may appear, there is less risk of acidity in the finished bread with a long than with a short sponge. In long-period sponges, the temperatures are kept fairly low and a proportion of salt is used, both conditions being inimical to lactic and other bacteria; hence long sponge-made bread—other conditions being equal—generally eats sweet. Short processes require less salt and a higher temperature, consequently the corresponding risks are greater.

One of the chief advantages of a sponge process is that the actual sponge is a thin medium containing all the chief essentials for the growth of yeast, and is of such a consistency that the yeast actually increases in quantity. This permits of the use of a rather less weight of yeast per sack of flour than is required in a straight-dough process, thereby effecting a considerable saving in the course of a year.

Sponges were stated to be quarter, third, half, and three-quarter ones. By this is meant that in setting the sponge, approximately one quarter, or a third, etc., of the water would be used in this operation, the remainder at the proper temperature being added at the doughing stage of the proceedings.

Sponges are also spoken of as 'twelve hours' sponge' or other period down to as short as a 'two hours.' The time stated is intended to include that occupied for all operations until the dough is ready to be scaled off and available for making up and proving. In bakeries where the one dough follows the others in a regular succession it is necessary that the quantities of the ingredients, their temperatures and the resulting doughs and times of each, should be accurately gauged and strictly followed throughout. Each and every operation must be carried out with the greatest punctuality and regularity. These are two out of four of the essentials in a bakery, the other two being cleanliness and the absence of wastefulness, *i.e.* economy.

To enable the baker to fix the correct times for a succession of doughs he ought to know the following points:—

(1) The temperatures of the flour, liquor (water), and the bakehouse.

(2) The characteristics of the yeast or barm to be used.

(3) The approximate composition of any yeast food or

bread improver which it is proposed to add to the yeast and flour.

(4) The character and type of flours to be employed. For example, bread improvers of the mineral sort, containing, say, gypsum or calcium sulphate, act as antiseptics and retard fermentation; fats when used in excess behave similarly; malt products, on the other hand, all act as stimulants to the yeast in addition to improving the finished loaf. There are on the market one or two of the mineral improvers based on Pasteur's method of preparing pure yeast, which, owing partly to the fact that they prevent bacterial competition and partly that they contain phosphates, are actually stimulants to the yeast in addition to being bread improvers.

The temperatures of the bakehouse and of the chief ingredients are of the utmost importance.

If the temperature of the sponge is low and that of the bakehouse also low, then for a given consistency the reactions going on in the sponge will be slow; if the temperature of the sponge be increased, then the changes will become accelerated and the time shortened.

The flour should be stored in a dry, warm atmosphere, as this condition of things causes an improvement in the flour in most cases and also prevents a chilling of the yeast whereby its vital functions are checked.

The temperature of the bakehouse can be ascertained by taking a reading of the thermometer hanging in a convenient place in the room.

The temperature of the water is not quite so readily obtained. It has been already pointed out that the sp. ht. or heat capacity of water is slightly more than twice that of flour. The temperature of the liquor to be used may be roughly calculated as follows: Double the given or fixed temperature for the dough and deduct that of the flour. Several slight corrections are necessary; for example, one for the temperature of the bakery itself, which ought not to be much lower than 70° F., also the necessary correction for the effect of the room itself.

An example will make this calculation clear.

The temperature of the dough is to be 80° F., that of the flour is 68° F. Find the temperature of the liquor.

Dough temperature=80°; then 80°×2=160°.

160°−68°=92° F., the liquor temperature.

Correction (1).

The bakehouse is very cold, therefore the proper allowance—depending on several factors—must be added. If the room is hot, then a deduction should be made.

Correction (2).

The bakehouse is draughty, or the vessels containing the sponges, doughs, etc., cause a loss of heat, then an increase must be made to allow for these conditions.

The characteristics of the yeast and its freedom or otherwise from bacteria, ought to be known to the baker. Where the characteristics of the yeast are constant, as in the case of a few of the more important British, a Dutch, and one or two other Continental yeasts, little or no trouble is occasioned; but, on the other hand, where the yeasts are being repeatedly changed or the yeasts themselves are not constant in quality, as is frequently the case, trouble is certain to ensue, unless the baker responsible tests the various yeasts day by day.

The character and constants of the flour or blends of flour should also be known. Thus if a flour is excessively moist owing to the use of an ' atomiser ' or special treatment in the milling, or if its gluten has been affected or even degraded, or if it has had the benefit of some artificial strengthening agent, these facts must be known by the baker to enable him to obtain the best possible result from his raw materials.

Strong flours should be employed for long-sponge or long-fermentation processes, so that the various agents acting may have time to mellow down and mature the undesirable constituents in such flours. In this way, spring wheat flours of the Minnesota Patents type may be rendered suitable and useful. For doughing up, winter wheat and softer flours are desirable. For example, a flour milled from soft English wheat imparts a nutty flavour and improves the colour, bloom, and general appearance of the finished loaf.

For the short processes, including straight doughs, port and country millers prepare from a suitably selected grist the flours required for the trade in their own and other districts. Flours of this kind are very useful to the baker and save him from holding large stocks of several varieties of flour, as was necessary in the days of long processes when bakers blended to a far greater extent than they do in modern times. Furthermore, the high quality of the bread may be more readily maintained.

Having considered the fundamentals, the baker may now proceed to set his sponge and carry out all the required operations.

For a long-sponge process, say, for example, one of ten hours' duration, the following quantities of materials will be necessary, assuming the bakery plant in this case to be a two-sack one :—

> Flour, two sacks or five hundred and sixty pounds.
> Yeast, fourteen to sixteen ounces.
> Salt, six and a half to seven pounds.
> Yeast food, say, malt flour, two pounds.
> Water, fifteen to sixteen gallons per sack, as determined.

The sponge is known as a 'half sponge.' For the setting of this, use :—

> Flour, two hundred and twenty to two hundred and forty pounds.
> Yeast, sixteen ounces.
> Salt, a pound to one and a half pounds according to the season.
> Water, fifteen gallons.

In many bakeries the sponge is prepared in the old-fashioned sponging machine, consisting of a tub fitted with a stirrer or beater. In more modern establishments a dough-mixer is used for a similar purpose. It will be noticed that the ratio of water to flour is roughly one

BREADMAKING PROCESSES AND BREADS

gallon to sixteen pounds. This gives a moderately stiff sponge, therefore if it is to stand for a long period the temperature must be fairly low, say about 72° F. When ready, dough up with the remaining materials.

It is important to note that the yeast must be very thoroughly broken up, or separated cell from cell. In the case of straight doughs this mixing of the yeast with water so as to leave no lumps is much more necessary than in sponging.

The salt should be dissolved completely in some of the liquor before using, as also should any sugar or malt extract which is to be used.

The temperature of the water for breaking up yeast must on no account exceed 104° F., or the fermentative properties of the yeast may be very seriously impaired. This and all other operations must be carefully checked or controlled by the use of thermometers. The fingers are not by any means sensitive enough to be employed as thermometers.

The liquor temperature for doughing depends on a number of factors, hence no statement of a hard and fast character can be given.

When once the dough has been made up it should not be exposed to rough handling, and as fermentation proceeds this becomes increasingly important. On the other hand, it should be borne in mind that the texture and other points of the loaf are brought out and improved by judicious working. Doughs ought not to be cut back too frequently as it entails too great a loss of the carbonic acid gas.

For an eight hours' sponge, about a third more yeast should be employed, at the rate of twelve ounces per sack.

For a good many years bread was prepared for our military forces by sponge processes and patent hop yeast. The barm was manufactured from three pounds of ground malt, which was mixed with soft water into a thin mash and gently heated to temperatures varying between 145° and 168° F. according to the season. The mash was then well-stirred together and left to stand for about one and a half hours. Simultaneously, two ounces of hops were infused in four gallons of water and maintained at 200° F. for the same period as the mash. The hop infusion was then cooled down to 160° F. and strained into the malt mash, the mixture being well stirred, covered, and allowed to stand for ten hours. It was now strained into a clean, well-scalded barm tub, and four ounces of sugar and half a gallon of yeast from a previous brew mixed with it. After again stirring, fermentation was continued for ten hours. The froth and dirty brown head was skimmed off and the yeast was ready for use. Three kinds of sponges were used, viz. the quarter, half, and three-quarters. The quantity of yeast employed amounted to nearly a gallon per sack of flour. After dropping twice, salt at the rate of four pounds per sack and the rest of the water were added and the whole worked up into a rather stiff dough. For two-pound loaves the dough was scaled at thirty-five and a half ounces, moulded, proved, and baked at 550° F. in side-flue ovens.

The straight dough process.—The straight dough or 'off-hand' process is one in which the whole of the ingredients are brought together and made into a dough at one operation.

This involves a number of considerations, some of which have already been discussed. For example, all types of flours are not available for use by this method; thus a strong, harsh flour would produce large, ungainly loaves more or less devoid of flavour and of poor colour. If a weak type of flour is used, then the volume and colour are poor, but the compensation for these deficiencies is an excellent flavour in the bread.

To overcome these difficulties the baker had to keep large stocks of flour for blending purposes in order to obtain the bread suitable for his trade. Perhaps the greatest difficulty was with the yeast. Until the days of quick-working, pressed, distillery yeast, the baker had to rely on barms or brewers' yeast. When doughs are made up and worked parallel as far as possible, one with brewers' and the other with distillers' yeast, all the advantages, with one exception, viz. that of risk from sourness, are on the side of the latter. Owing to the antiseptic properties of the hop constituents bacteria are very largely held in check, and this obviates the above risk where brewers' yeasts are employed.

The quantities of materials for an eight-hour straight dough would approximately be :—

Flour, a sack of two hundred and eighty pounds.
Yeast, twelve to fourteen ounces.
Yeast food, eight to ten ounces of a mixture consisting of six parts of good malt flour, four of sugar, and one of potassium phosphate.
Salt, three and a half pounds.
Water, fourteen to fifteen gallons according to the strength of the flour, and of such a temperature that the dough shall be between 73° and 74° F.

As a rule much shorter processes than eight hours are advisable for straight doughs, viz., from two to three hours in the dough, or from four to five hours from start to finish. To carry out the shortest useful process, *i.e.* four hours from flour to bread, the following modifications are necessary :—

Yeast, two and a half to three pounds per sack.
Yeast food, one pound of a diastase paste or the above mixture.
Salt, three pounds.
Water, the same volume at such a temperature that that of the resulting dough is about 83° F.

The mode of working is somewhat as follows : First thoroughly break up the yeast in a gallon of water at 90° F., then stir in with it the whole of the yeast food. Next, pass the flour, after having ascertained its temperature, through the sifter, so as to open out and get rid of lumps and foreign particles, into the dough-mixing machine, and set the arms revolving to lighten and aerate the flour. While this is proceeding dissolve the salt completely in a portion of the liquor from the attemperating tank, the temperature of the water in which has already been arranged. The required quantity of water is run into the mixer with the salt and the yeast, which latter should be in a state of active fermentation or 'krausen' by this time. The mixer (Fig. 41) is now closed, and the mixing operation carried out until the dough is thoroughly made and cleared. The time for this operation varies slightly with the different designs of machines, but eight to ten minutes is long enough in many cases.

Fig. 41.—Dough Mixer, showing the interior of the machine.
[*By permission of Messrs. Joseph Baker and Sons, Ltd.*]

The dough is turned out into a trough, covered up and allowed to ferment. The temperature of the dough should be taken as soon as it is collected in the trough and at intervals during the fermentation. These temperatures ought to be entered in a book kept for the purpose to enable the foreman to control all operations properly as in other fermentation industries. At the right time the dough should be 'cut back,' brought on to the working tables and thoroughly kneaded but not too roughly handled. In a quick process this is most important if the texture, colour, volume, and flavour are to be at their best. The handling of the dough during the fermentation stage assists the flavour and texture especially, by expelling the waste gases and incorporating fresh air in their place; this revives the vital activity of the yeast and enables it to complete its work in the dough constituents. Then if the gases (including air) are evenly distributed through the dough, the reticulation and vesiculation of the crumb of the loaf are certain to be regular and the texture good. Moreover, the handling has a toughening effect on the gluten and

BREADMAKING PROCESSES AND BREADS 165

assists its elasticity. Instead of bringing the dough on to the working tables for the purposes explained above it may be carried out, though not so effectually, in the dough troughs by systematically working from one end to the other.

According to Professor Wood of Cambridge, ' the volume of a loaf depends on the amount of carbonic acid gas evolved during the fermentation stage, and the power of the flour to hold the gas; and a quick evolution distends the dough much more than a slow evolution.' But, as already shown, the volume depends on the mechanical structure, *i.e.* its vesiculation, as well as on the strength of the little sacs of gluten which contain the mixture of gases. For commercial bread, a similar treatment is given to the dough just before it is ready for scaling; but for exhibition loaves an additional handing up will improve all the points of a loaf previously mentioned. Scaling may best be carried out by hand, for at this point any rough treatment of the dough seems to deaden it, or in the words of the baker ' to knock the life out of it.' Machines known as dividers have been designed for the purpose, but so far they are not quite free from this defect. Some are worse than others in this way, and produce with the same flour a rather smaller volume loaf.

Great care ought to be exercised before scaling off to prevent ' over-fermentation,' which is largely the cause of sourness and crumbliness in the finished loaf. When the dough is brought into the oven, it takes some time for the heat to check the yeast action near the centre of the loaf, hence the necessity of avoiding such a state of things. Overproof will also help to render bread crumbly.

After scaling, the dough is roughly moulded and placed close on the tables, to prevent chilling and the streaks it causes in the bread, and allowed to recover somewhat before making up. In all the succeeding operations after fermentation increasing care is required to prevent rough handling; very frequently, good loaves are spoiled in their appearance both externally and internally in this way. Moulding for different classes of bread is a process that differs considerably and can be better understood by actually working at the moulding than by any amount of description.

The moulded dough is now allowed 'to prove' until it is at the precise point when baking is required. The proving apparatus should be of such a form that all draughts are avoided, so that there is no risk of causing a thick skin on the surface of the dough which spoils the appearance of the finished loaf. Where skinning does occur, the surface of the dough should be lightly washed with warm water a few minutes before being brought into the oven. This treatment assists but does not altogether do away with the disfigurement.

The mode of setting bread in an oven is described in Chap. XII. on ovens. It is only necessary here to emphasise the statement already made that the dough must not be roughly treated. In setting in, loaves are often spoiled by throwing them on to the peel or oven-plate at this stage instead of lightly placing them in position. The dough should be evenly baked at the temperature most suitable for the particular class of bread. If the oven is too slow the dough is dried rather than baked, and if too hot the crust is over-caramelised before the interior or crumb is effectually cooked. In both cases also the volume of the loaf is generally smaller than it should be. In a slow oven the bread, especially cottage, is inclined to drop before the heat can fix the gluten, whereas in the scorching oven the outside crust is fixed and rendered impervious before the interior gases have properly expanded. This also very often leads to bursts in the side and to ugly loaves. Practically, whatever may be the baking temperature of the ovens, that of the interior of a loaf only slightly exceeds that of boiling water. The author in 1905 carried through a large number of experiments on this subject, using specially constructed maximum thermometers for the purpose. When the dough was being moulded, the thermometers were placed as near to the centre of the loaves as possible. Different baking tempera-

BREADMAKING PROCESSES AND BREADS

tures were employed, short and long baking periods, and different classes of breads were subjected to these tests. After cooling down the loaves containing the instruments were cut open and the thermometers read, but in no single case was 216° F. exceeded.

The changes proceeding in the dough during the baking may be summed up as follows. The surplus moisture is expelled together with the alcohol and the volatile acidity (acetic acid) formed at the expense of the alcohol. The little sacs or cells of gluten and starch gradually expand, causing the vesiculated appearance of the crumb of the loaf; after a time the gluten and certain other nitrogenous compounds are coagulated; the moistened starch of the dough is then gelatinised and becomes fit for food purposes. The yeast and bacteria are killed by the moist heat and thus the bread is sterilised. Externally, the starchy matters become somewhat caramelised, forming dextrin-like and other more complex carbohydrate compounds, while the traces of acidity convert some of these bodies into reducing sugars. Wet, naked steam, which is always present in the ovens both from the cooking dough and also when introduced either by means of small, narrow water-tanks, or by wet low-pressure steam, assists the latter changes, and also forms a larger proportion of dextrins, thus covering the crust of the loaves with a glaze. Wet steam in addition tends to counteract the fierce flash-heat of many of the modern ovens and thus partially preserves the goods from burning.

As soon as completely baked, the bread is drawn and stored in bread-racks in a suitable place for cooling down. The bread at this stage requires careful handling, or the loaves will be shaken and several of their characteristics spoiled. After cooling, the bread should be weighed, and where it is considered advisable, made up in clean paper wrappers to preserve it from dust and all contact with dirty or soiled surfaces. A strong pronouncement in favour of this procedure was made at the Plymouth Conference in July 1911 by the retiring president of the

National Association of Master Bakers. It certainly has the advantage of keeping the bread from contact with dirty clothes and hands during the distribution to customers.

As far back as the time of Pliny the Elder it was known that bread should weigh one-third more than the flour from which it is produced; a sack of good-quality flour ought to yield from three hundred and seventy to three hundred and eighty-four pounds of bread.

The loss of the dough in baking averages just slightly more than a tenth of the weight of dough from which the bread is made, but these figures are frequently exceeded, greatly to the detriment of both the bread and the baker. The short, straight dough process for making bread just described is only possible where high quality yeast and a regular supply of it can be obtained.

These short processes entail the use of higher temperatures, which tend to cause sourness, *i.e.* acidity, and poor flavour; hence there must be more skill and attention on the part of the baker, in order to produce a good-coloured crumb and a fine bloom on the crust.

Colour of the crumb depends on a number of factors, amongst which are :—the quality of the flour, the quantity of water employed, the method and thoroughness of working so that everything is kept strictly to its proper time and place, and the perfection of the aeration. Any slight deviation from these factors will more or less seriously affect the colour and other properties of the loaf.

Incidentally, the colour is also influenced by the use of improvers. For example, fat of various kinds when rubbed into the flour assists the shortness of the bread, especially the crust, and improves the flavour and keeping qualities, but if used in much larger quantities than three pounds per sack, it not only spoils the colour but makes the dough 'runny.' Other improvers act somewhat similarly.

The processes and quantities already given are those employed on a large scale, and with slight modifications are applicable to all the common classes of bread. For special breads or the fancy breads of commerce there are nearly as

BREADMAKING PROCESSES AND BREADS 169

many recipes and minor changes as varieties of breads themselves. Of these, the crusty breads are the more useful and saleable; examples, Coburgs, Brunswicks, large and small Viennas, etc.

Most of these contain fats or milk and sugar or other improver in addition to the fancy patent flour.

They may best be made by a quick straight dough process. The following quantities will be found useful for small batches of any of the above goods :—

    Flour, fancy patent, or a strong high-class blended with a proportion of Hungarian flour, sixteen pounds.
    Yeast, four to five ounces.
    Yeast food, three to four ounces.
    Salt, three ounces.
    Fats, about three ounces to keep the crust short.
    Liquor, seven pints (half milk and half water).

Temperature of the dough to be about 84° or 85° F. Hand up twice and scale off in two hours. Mould up in the desired shapes, prove for a time in steam, complete in the absence of steam. Cut batons, Coburgs and Brunswicks deeply. Wash with warm water and half bake under covers to obtain a fine glaze; take off the covers and finish. For Vienna smalls, baking trays similar to those used for *petits choux* will be found suitable.

For brown breads of all varieties it will be found that straight dough processes give the best results, and, for many, the time from flour to finished loaf should not exceed two and a quarter to two and a half hours. This does not apply to malt and certain proprietary breads for which a longer time is necessary owing to the extended baking period.

The following quantities are suitable for whole and wheat meals :—

    Meal, sixteen pounds.
    Yeast, six ounces.
    Salt, four ounces.
    Sugar, two or three ounces.
    Water, one gallon, or a portion of this replaced by milk.

The temperature of the dough to be about 82° to 83° F. Allow to ferment until ready, then hand up and scale off at weights to suit the trade of the district, but not exceeding thirty-five and a half ounces. A two-pounds brown loaf is the largest size in common use. Set in the oven slightly underproof. It is important to note that the temperature of a dough must never be allowed to drop if good results are to be secured, and this is particularly the case with all forms of brown breads.

Another note of caution may be useful in making brown bread. During the making into dough a fine texture may be secured by rubbing the batter on the table until it has been fined down, but bread prepared in this way is usually devoid of flavour and the characteristic colour of the particular bread.

The chemical composition of bread.—The composition varies somewhat with the process employed in the manufacture and with the ingredients used; thus scalded flour, potatoes, and such like bodies, yield a moister loaf. The subjoined analytical figures will enable the reader to gain some idea of the quantities of the constituents present.

Constituents.	White (tin).	White (crusty).	White (by König).	White (by Owen Simmons).
Water	39·64 %	37·24 %	38·5 %	40·0 %
Carbohydrates	52·23 ,,	52·98 ,,	52·1 ,,	50·0 ,,
Fibre or Cellulose	0·22 ,,	0·23 ,,	0·3 ,,	1·0 ,,
Proteins	6·77 ,,	7·95 ,,	6·9 ,,	7·0 ,,
Fats	0·40 ,,	0·68 ,,	0·8 ,,	1·0 ,,
Mineral Salts	0·60 ,,	0·73 ,,	1·2 ,,	1·0 ,,
Acidity (Lactic)	0·14 ,,	0·19 ,,	0·2 ,,	—

The quantities of water in Manchester tin loaves vary between 33 and 46 per cent., in brown breads (whole and wheat meals) between 38 and 45 per cent. The water in the crust of white bread varies from 17·86 to 26·54 per cent. with an average of 20·10 per cent., while the crumb contains from 22·86 to 47·35 per cent. with an average of 42·68 per cent.

Breadmaking machinery.—A well-equipped, up-to-date machinery bakery ought to contain an installation so complete as to render it unnecessary to handle the dough except to set it in the ovens. The important machines include : A hoist of the vertical or horizontal type fixed in the highest part of the building, and in such a convenient position as to be useful for all the required purposes. An automatic weighing and self-registering machine. A combined blender and sifter fixed over the hopper of the dough mixer.

The dough mixer, which should be one of an approved type, either on the Adair rotary or other principle. In close proximity to the mixer, a properly constructed attemperating tank with all the necessary fittings. Dough and flour troughs and working tables, all of some suitable wood free from resins, etc. Kneaders, dividers, and moulders, the latter adjustable for either tin or cottage doughs. A dough brake for sundry purposes. A sack-cleaning machine to recover flour from the sacks; various provers, setting and other racks, scales and sundry utensils as necessary.

Wherever possible the motive power should be electricity on account of its cleanliness, ease of manipulation, and its being always ready for use.

CHAPTER XI

ANTISEPTICS AND BAKEHOUSE HYGIENE

ANTISEPTICS, as the name denotes, are substances used for the prevention of putrefaction and decay. In a bakery or other place in which food is prepared scrupulous cleanliness must be observed in every possible way. Particles of sugar, flour, bread, and pieces of dough should never be allowed to remain on the floor to be trodden about the place, nor should they be merely swept up to a corner or side of the room where they act as breeding-places for all kinds of noxious germs. All tables, troughs, scales, machinery, and other implements must be thoroughly cleaned as soon as possible. Where boiling water can be employed it is one of the most effective agents in keeping places and articles both clean and sterile. Soda and soaps are useful detergents, but they are of little value for sterilising purposes. Many groups of bacteria are aided by the presence of very weak solutions of alkalies, hence the use of one or more of the antiseptics sold for the killing of these germs and maintaining everything as sterile as possible is desirable.

The more common antiseptics are :—sulphurous acid gas and its solution, the acid- or bi-sulphites especially those of soda and lime, borax, boric or boracic acid, salicylic acid, fluorides of the alkalies, lustril, fluosilicates, formaline, a 40 per cent. solution of formaldehyde in methyl alcohol, benzoic acid, and carbolic acid or phenol when in a strong solution. Phenol, thymol, and certain other chemical reagents are also classified as antiseptics, yet their action is somewhat restricted; for example, strong solutions of phenol hinder both fermentation and putrefaction, but a stiff solution of gelatin containing phenol is a recognised medium for the culture of certain groups of bacteria. Again, phenol interferes with and stops the peptonising action of pepsin, but it apparently does not influence diastatic action in any way. Thymol, the chief constituent of oil of thyme, prevents the work of yeast, moulds, and other ferments, especially diastase, but it has no effect on pepsin. Use is made of these different reactions of the two antiseptics in detecting the one enzyme group in the presence of the other. The three common fruit acids, viz. malic, tartaric, and citric acids, and their potassium acid salts, when in weak solution, prevent all diastatic action, but have no effect on the alcoholic fermentation, which, it should be remembered, is known to be caused by enzymes.

The difference in behaviour of antiseptics in some cases is probably due to the fact that certain of the enzymes have the protection of a cell-wall as with yeast.

The late Professor Dr. Louis Pasteur based his method for the preparation of pure yeast on the inhibitive action of the three acids mentioned, and also on that of phosphoric acid. Yeasts may be cultivated in the presence of weak solutions of the four acids, whilst the growth of most bacterial groups is absolutely prevented by them.

The action of moist heat, that is, boiling water and steam, has already been discussed.

The bactericidal action of light is of great importance. Pathogenic and septic or putrefactive bacteria are all inhibited by the action of plenty of sunlight. As far back as 1877 a paper of some interest was read before the Royal Society dealing with the preventive action of light on bacteria. A few years later Dr. Richardson explained the bactericidal action of light as a possible case of low temperature oxidation, because water vapour induces the formation of hydrogen peroxide which is undoubtedly an antiseptic. At the Paris Exhibition in 1900 the powerful effect of light was very forcefully illustrated by cultures of pathogenic bacteria in glass bottles in gelatin; portions of the bottles were covered with dark paper, the bottles incubated at suitable temperatures in bright sunlight and the contents afterwards completely sterilised. Wherever the dark paper had prevented light action, dense colonies of bacteria could be seen, whilst in the exposed parts the nutrient gelatin remained perfectly clear.

The lesson for the baker is that all parts of the bakery in which individuals are engaged and food prepared must be freely exposed to light and fresh air. It is owing to these two desiderata that the Health Authorities in towns and urban districts have to a very large extent done away with the underground and cellar bakehouse. The great Greek philosopher's statement that 'Light is God's shadow' is particularly applicable to any building in which our daily food is being prepared.

An account of the mode of preparation and properties of the antiseptics named in this chapter may be found in any good book on chemistry. As sulphurous acid and its salts, the bisulphites, are the commonest and most useful of antiseptics for a bakery, it may not be out of place to state that these compounds are prepared on a large scale for many manufacturing processes in the following way. Crude sulphur or disulphides or other sulphur ores of metals are roasted and burned in a suitable tray furnace in an excess of air. The sulphur dioxide (SO_2) formed is passed through purifiers and then into water to be absorbed, or into solutions or milks of the alkalies and earthy metals to form the bisulphites of them. For example, bisulphite of soda —a liquid—is obtained by passing the SO_2 gas into a moderately strong solution of caustic soda until the soda is saturated. The bisulphite of lime, the most useful of these antiseptics, is prepared by treating milk of lime in a similar way.

All wooden and earthenware vessels that have contained dough, sugar solutions, yeast, milk, or other substances which are suitable materials for the growth of moulds and bacteria, if not already sterile, may quickly be rendered so by washing with a weak solution of this latter antiseptic, allowing it to remain on the vessel for a short time and then washing off with boiling water.

In order to assist in keeping everything sterile, the walls of a bakery ought to be thoroughly cleaned, scraped, and lime-washed twice a year at convenient periods. Where possible, white glazed tiles or bricks should be employed in the construction of the important rooms of the bakery, because they not only make the place lighter but more readily lend themselves to cleanliness. Further, glazed surfaces prevent deposits of dust and bacteria on the walls.

VENTILATION

By ventilating is understood the exposing of something freely to the action of the atmospheric air ; thus the name of the process—ventilation—is derived from the Latin word *ventilo*, 'to toss in the air' (*ventus*=wind). The original idea of ventilation consisted in causing draughts to exist in all parts of the ventilated structure, thereby carrying out the exposure to 'little winds' and in addition creating much discomfort and even pain to the persons working in the place.

Natural ventilation depends upon two well-known phenomena : convection currents, and the diffusion of gases. All openings into a room or workshop permit of the entrance of air currents, as also to some extent do the walls, which are slightly porous. This fresh air mixes with the air in the rooms by diffusion, and when it becomes heated it rises to the highest point, thus setting up convection currents ; the polluted air escapes through any openings it may find, as, for example, by way of the chimney or the upper part of the door casement, or other opening.

In this way the air of the room is being continuously changed. The English system of heating by means of open fires, hence by radiation, though wasteful and extravagant, is healthful, as it is of considerable assistance to the natural ventilation. That the door is an aid to ventilation may readily be demonstrated by partially opening it and holding a taper or candle at three different points.

At the top the flame from the candle will be blown outwards by the outrush of the heated air; at the bottom of the door the flame will be blown inwards by the incoming currents of air. Midway between the top and bottom of the door there is neither outward nor inward current. In the winter-time and other cool periods of the year a sensitive thermometer will also show, by the variation in temperature, the same effects as does the flame, namely, that the warm air is rushing out at the top and the cooler air coming in at the bottom.

When rooms are heated with stoves one or more openings should be constructed at the upper portion of the rooms so as to assist in ventilating them; at the same time stoves are liable to render the atmosphere of the rooms excessively dry by raising the temperature too much above the dewpoint, and thus they cause much inconvenience and unpleasantness to those inhabiting the rooms. It is advisable in all such cases to keep a vessel full of water on the stove in order to prevent this dryness.

Several systems of artificial ventilation are comparatively common in large buildings in the more important towns. Up to the present none of these systems are perfect, though some are more full of imperfections than others. One of these systems, best known as the 'Plenum System,' passes the outside air through a kind of purifying and attemperating plant and then distributes, by means of channels below the floors, warm and cool purified air into rooms at will. This treated air is not by any means the same as the air from the outside, as may be perceived by its effect on different individuals. At the best it is only a system of dilution, which changes the atmosphere in rooms fairly quickly without creating too strong draughts, save in the winter-time when the outside temperature is low; the draughts from windows and other openings to the outer air are then apt to be excessive.

The necessity for ventilation.—In these days when the elements of hygiene are taught in every primary school, it is scarcely necessary to discuss this part of the subject. That ventilation is desirable is sufficiently proved by comparing vital statistics concerning bakeries of thirty years ago with those of the present day. Since the Medical Officers of Health have enforced the observance of more cleanly habits of working, of better arrangements in bakeries, of more regular living amongst the working bakers, and of better means of ventilation, the health, general conditions of life, and the length of life of the baker have all enormously improved.

There still remains much to be done to improve further the health of the worker and consequently to lessen the risks of disease being spread from this source. In order to keep in good health at least three thousand feet of air are required for every adult person even when doing nothing, hence when at work more than this will be necessary. To obtain such a quantity, the atmosphere must be frequently changed in the rooms; to do this efficiently, the dimensions of the rooms must be ample, say, not less than six hundred cubic feet of space per worker, and the ceiling never less than ten or twelve feet in height from the floor. Added to this there should be plenty of window space for the admission of light; separate rooms for feeding and resting; scrupulous cleanliness both in person, clothing, and in the rooms. Then the life of the worker would be more wholesome than it is in many cases at present.

CHAPTER XII

FUELS AND OVENS

THE name 'fuel' is given to any material that can be used to feed a fire so as to generate heat; fuels therefore may occur in each of the three states of matter—gas, liquid, and solid. Hydrogen, carbon, carbon monoxide, marsh gas, ethylene, acetylene, and benzene, when treated or combined with oxygen, all generate much heat; when the combustion takes place with air, the nitrogen present acts as a diluent and considerably lowers the resultant temperature. Hydrogen combines with oxygen to form water; carbon with oxygen to form, first, carbon monoxide and then carbon dioxide; in all these cases much heat is developed that can be put to practical use. All the other bodies mentioned contain carbon combined with hydrogen; the products of combustion with oxygen will be carbon dioxide and water. These two compounds are the ultimate products of combustion when hydrocarbons and carbohydrates are burned in oxygen or air.

It should be the aim in all cases of burning to generate heat, to burn the common fuels completely to these bodies, and care must be taken not to use an excessive quantity of air; otherwise the air acts as a diluent and causes cooling. All matter not completely burned before the chimney is reached means a loss of heat; hence all carbon in the form of soot, hydrocarbons, carbon monoxide and other unburnt bodies, points to considerable waste and loss of heat if allowed to pass into the outer atmosphere. Chimney gases ought to consist of nothing but carbon dioxide, water, nitrogen, and the small excess of air used. Instead of which very large proportions of carbon and carbon monoxide exist in all chimney gases, together with the volatile products from the impurities in the fuel, *e.g.* sulphur dioxide from sulphur bodies like brasses, ammonium compounds from the nitrogen constituents, etc.

The chief gaseous fuels in common use are :—water gas, ordinary coal gas, carburetted coal gas, oil gas, Mond gas, regenerator gas, and natural earth gases from the neighbourhood of oil wells. The chief constituents of these gases are enumerated in the list given above ; in a word, they contain the three elements, carbon, hydrogen, and oxygen ; therefore to obtain the maximum heating effect, all other conditions being equal, nothing but carbon dioxide and water with the excess air should pass into the chimney.

Liquid fuels include shale oils, petroleum oils, denatured alcohol, and some few other liquids. All liquid fuels before combustion are converted into gases and therefore act similarly to gaseous fuels. In using the shale and petroleum oils, care must be exercised in keeping the burner or carburetter clean, or else loss ensues and noxious vapours will be emitted.

The common fuels are the solid ones, and these include various classes of coals and cokes, wood, charcoal, and peat. The particular form of fuel to be used must in a measure depend on the type of oven, hot plate or other baking plant. Thus for side-flue, wagon ovens, and similar types of internally heated ovens, a fuel that gives flame is necessary ; but with hot-air and steam-pipe ovens coke is more suitable.

The effectual method of stoking is to keep the bars clean and free from clinker, and when fuel is required, to push the red-hot cinders towards the back of the furnace and spread a thin layer of fresh fuel near the front of the fire. A kind of distillation of the new fuel then takes place, in which the gases formed pass over the bright part of the fire and are burnt, giving rise to a maximum amount of

180   CHEMISTRY OF BREADMAKING

heat with a minimum loss of fuel products. Where large quantities of fuel are charged into the furnace, there is a great cooling down of the fire, and production of excess smoke, loss of time in heating the ovens and considerable waste of fuel being thereby caused. Clinker may be prevented from forming on the fire-bars by keeping a jet of steam or trough of water just below the fire-bars in the ash-pit.

Ovens

Ovens are classified in various ways, either according to their construction, methods of using, methods of heating, or the class of goods to be baked. Thus there are draw-plates, peel ovens, shelf ovens, etc.; or they are said to be either internally or externally heated ovens, or hot-air or steam-pipe ovens, side-flue ovens, wagon ovens, Vienna ovens, and the like.

Shelf ovens (Fig. 42) are generally small in size, containing two or more separate shelves or baking compartments, and suitable for a small mixed trade of bread and confectionery. All the chief oven builders supply several sizes of these ovens. They are all externally heated by coke, coal, or gas.

Fig. 42.— A Portable Shelf Oven.
[*By permission of Messrs. Joseph Baker and Sons, Ltd.*]

All the other varieties resolve themselves into either *internally* or *externally heated*.

The former are the original type, and include the old-fashioned wood-heated oven which gives so sweet a crust, and has recently been proclaimed as the only kind of oven in which 'standard bread' can be baked; also the side-flue, wagon oven, and the like. The externally heated types include hot-air ovens and steam-pipe ovens.

Side-flue ovens are generally single deckers, constructed of a flat 'sole' laid with special one-foot square tiles, upright sides, and a crowned arch at the top. At one side is built a short furnace which leads abruptly into the oven round which the flames and heated gases pass on their way out by the flue at the top near the mouth of the oven. Dampers are necessary in order to control the furnace.

The *wagon oven* is an older style than this, for it consists of the oven without the side furnace. An iron box wider at the upper parts of the sides than at the bottom is the wagon. This is piled up with fuel, lighted and brought into the centre of the oven as far back as possible. An iron pipe of suitable dimensions traversing the whole length of the oven is fixed into the wagon at the one end and passes through the door into the outer air, thus supplying the necessary oxygen for the combustion. The outlet flue is at the top near the mouth of the oven. When not in use, as during the baking period, this opening is closed by a damper.

In both cases the ovens are ready for use, or are said to have become solid, when all the carbonaceous matter has been burnt off and the walls glow with heat. Both these ovens are also designated *peel ovens*, since they are filled and drawn by means of a long-handled wooden spade known as a 'peel.' In the case of the side-flue special precautions are necessary in setting in and drawing.

The loaves slightly underproof are set in on the coolest side of the oven; if cottage loaves, just touching one another and equidistant. The loaves at proof or slightly over are set on the furnace side, but protected from the fierce heat on this side by setters or dummies and a long, narrow, open vessel full of water. The wet steam generated tempers down the fierce heat, prevents burning and glazes the bread by forming dextrins, sugars, and caramel-like bodies. The last loaves to be set in a side-flue oven are usually the first to be drawn. The chief disadvantages of these ovens are that they are wasteful of fuel, dirty, and not continuous. The advantage is that the heat is solid, and they give a sweet-eating crust. Where they are used in a

Fig. 43.—A Range of five single Draw-plate Steam-pipe Ovens.
[*By permission of Messrs. Joseph Baker and Sons, Ltd.*]

mixed trade, the bread is baked first, then smalls, and afterwards the confectionery goods.

Externally heated ovens are heated either by means of hot-air currents circulating over and around the oven (or ovens, as these are often constructed in pairs, one placed above the other), or by being built inside an enclosed heated space, or by steam-pipes. *Steam-pipe ovens* have become very common in recent years on account of the advantages they possess over the other types (Fig. 43). These are as follows :—They are cleaner, cheaper to work, as they take less fuel, are healthier, speedier, and continuous in their action. The important disadvantages may be summed up as follows :—They give a flash heat, are somewhat dangerous owing to the liability of the pipes to burst, are more costly to erect in the first case and difficult to regulate properly.

They may be built as double drawplates or a drawplate with a peel oven over the top. This latter arrangement is especially suitable for a mixed trade and where confectionery goods form a part of the business. Within the last three years, drawplate ovens with half-inch thick tiles have been devised so as to render the drawplate suitable for the baking of buns and other smalls. The furnace in steam-pipe ovens is small in size and may be arranged on one side or at the back of the block. The bottom layer of pipes which heat the bottom part of the lower oven forms the fire-bars in the furnace. The second row of pipes heats the upper part of this oven, and in many cases is immediately below the tiled sole of the top oven, the ends of these pipes coming into the furnace. The top row of pipes is in the upper portion of the baking space of this top oven, with the ends bent downwards so as to come into contact with the heat from the furnace. There are also sundry flues for heating purposes, such as sets of coils to provide boiling water for use in the bakery, dry provers, etc.; these flues all connect with the main flue which passes into the chimney. The pipes vary in length according to their size and their position in the oven. Their external diameter is usually one and five-sixteenths of an inch, and their internal diameter about five-eighths of an inch, thus forming a fairly thick-walled tube. The tube holds about three-quarters of a pint of well-boiled water, and it is said to be tested up to a pressure of three thousand pounds per square inch of surface before being sent out of the factory. Such a statement can scarcely be verified after a pipe is welded and sealed. In these ovens heat is conveyed and dispersed by the three processes—conduction, convection, and radiation.

184 CHEMISTRY OF BREADMAKING

The sizes of ovens.—Ovens vary in size from a half to two sacks capacity, that is, they are capable of holding the bread made from those quantities of flour. A half-sack oven should possess a baking chamber of 30 to 33 square feet, say 6 feet long by 5 feet in width; a three-quarter sack about 8 feet by 6 feet, or 48 square feet; a sack size 60 to 63 square feet; a sack and three-quarters, 11 feet by 9 feet, or 99 square feet; a two-sack about 12 feet by 10 feet, or 120 square feet. The usual allowance is two square feet of oven space for three cottage loaves, or a little less

Fig. 44.—Steam-pipe Oven.
[*By permission of Messrs. Joseph Baker and Sons, Ltd.*]

for tin bread. Thus an oven 11 feet by 9 feet should hold about 140 cottage loaves scaled at 71 ounces for quartern size, or 150 tin loaves scaled at 71½ ounces in the dough for four pounds or quartern size.

Vienna ovens.—These are constructed with a sole sloping from the back to the mouth (Fig. 45), the sole at the back being slightly higher than the upper part of the mouth of the oven, so that steam may always be kept in the oven during the baking of Vienna goods, as this keeps them crisp and soft and at the same time glazes them.

FUELS AND OVENS 185

Vienna ovens are heated either by side-flue or steam-pipes. The author has invariably found the best work,

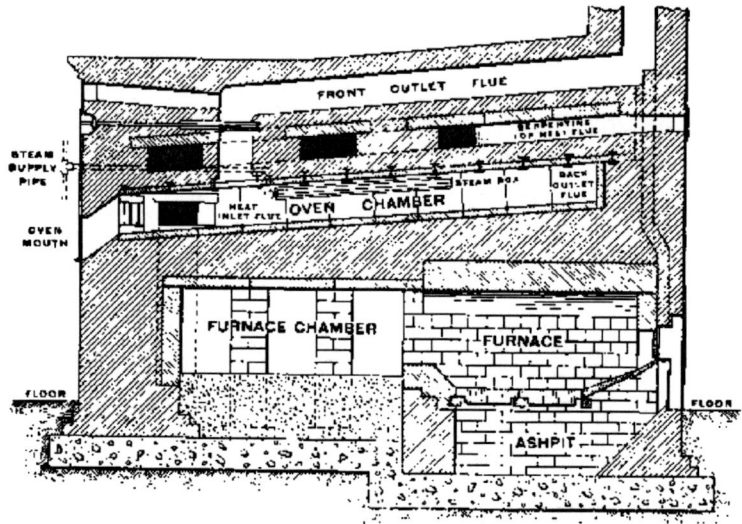

Fig. 45.—Baker's Patent Vienna Oven. Section showing a single oven fired at the back. (Note the sloping sole.)
[*By permission of Messrs. Joseph Baker and Sons, Ltd.*]

as regards the baking, turned out by the side-flue heated Vienna ovens.

The following table gives approximately the temperatures and pressures in steam-pipe ovens:—

Pressure in lbs.	Temp. of Oven.	Pressure in lbs.	Temp. of Oven.
15	250° F.	125	353° F.
20	259° ,,	150	366° ,,
25	267° ,,	165	373° ,,
30	274° ,,	230	391° ,,
40	292° ,,	235	400° ,,
50	301° ,,	415	447° ,,
100	338° ,,	420	450° ,,

CHAPTER XIII

THE ANALYSIS OF CEREAL FOODS

Water testing.—For the purposes of breadmaking a water should be free from floating particles and not too hard, whilst it must be organically pure.

The physical tests may be readily carried out as follows.

Obtain a fair sample of the water by allowing the tap to run for a minute or two, or if from a well by first pumping a few strokes to clear the pipe and then collecting the sample for the tests.

To test for colour bring some of the water into a tall, colourless glass cylinder or test glass, and place the vessel on a sheet of white paper in a position away from sunlight. If possible fill a similar vessel with pure distilled water and compare the two samples. Distilled water is devoid of colour, taste, and smell; the nearer the water sample comes to this, the better. Very often a strongly contaminated water possesses a pleasant saline taste.

After carrying out the above test bring pieces of red and blue litmus paper into the sample, allow to stand a few minutes, then note any change that may have taken place. Pure drinking water should produce no change in the litmus papers.

Too large a quantity of solids in solution may be detected by boiling down given volumes of the sample and of a known pure water on a water bath in any suitable vessel and comparing the quantities of solid matters left behind. Distilled water leaves no residue. In most cases, where there are large quantities of solids in solution, the waters will be hard or require a considerable quantity of soap to form a lather.

WATER TESTING

The hardness may be roughly tested by dissolving a small quantity of soap cut into thin shavings in a mixture of alcohol (spirits of wine) and water. A 4-oz. bottle, preferably with a glass stopper, is required. Into this measure out say two ounces of water, either a soft tap water like that of Liverpool, Glasgow, Manchester, or rainwater, and add small quantities of the soap solution, shaking very thoroughly after each addition. Note the quantity of soap solution taken to make a lather that will last four or five minutes. Clean out the bottle and repeat the operation with the sample of water to be tested. Note the quantity of the soap solution required in this case. If only a small quantity then the water is a soft one, if much it is a hard sample. If very hard it ought to be softened, by stirring in the suitable softening agent and allowing to settle, before being used for bakehouse operations.

Organic impurities of an ammoniacal character may be tested for by adding a few drops of Nessler's reagent (which may be purchased from a chemist) to some of the sample contained in the glass vessel used for noting the colour. If sewage be present the Nessler imparts to the water a reddish-brown shade of colour or even produces a brown precipitate therein, according to the quantity of impurity present. Nessler's should not give more than a faint yellow colour to a drinkable water. Other organic impurities may be detected by the aid of a solution of permanganate of potassium used in the acid condition. About half an ounce of the salt is dissolved in a quart of well-boiled cold water. A pint of the water to be tested is brought into a glass flask and a small volume of weak sulphuric acid added. The pink-coloured permanganate solution is added drop by drop with shaking until the colour of the contents of the flask remains permanently pink. The quantity used is noted. If much of the permanganate solution is required, the water is too contaminated for drinking purposes.

The only poisonous metals likely to be present are salts of lead and iron.

The lead may be tested for by the addition of a few drops of sulphuric acid solution when on standing a white precipitate is formed ; also by adding some yellow chromate of potash solution, when if lead is present a yellow precipitate settles out. Iron compounds may be detected by the addition of some ferrocyanide of potash, which causes a blue coloration or precipitate if much iron is in the water; or by adding a solution of tannin, which gives a light precipitate gradually becoming darker until at last ink is formed. Tannic acid in contact with iron salts forms tannate of iron or ink.

NOTE.—Quantities of lead and iron salts present in any water are usually so small that it is advisable always to evaporate the water to about a quarter of its bulk before carrying out these tests.

GENERAL METHODS OF ESTIMATING THE CHEMICAL CONSTITUENTS OF THE CEREALS AND OTHER FOOD-STUFFS

Moisture estimation.—The processes for this estimation vary somewhat according to the nature of the substance in which the estimation is required. Some bodies if heated above the boiling point of water 212° F. (100° C.) begin to decompose, or they may suffer oxidation and thus increase in weight. This will give a low result for the moisture.

Generally, the estimation may be carried out as follows : A wide, squat weighing-glass (Fig. 46) is accurately weighed with the lid tilted on one side so as to admit air. From five to ten grams of the substance roughly powdered or cut into thin shavings is introduced into the glass and weighed. The glass is then brought into either a water oven if the temperature must not exceed that of boiling water, or into an air bath with the temperature maintained between 212° to 218° F. (100° to 103° C.) for three

Fig. 46.—Weighing Glass.

to four hours with the lid of the glass off. Then desiccate and weigh. Repeat the heating, cooling, and weighing until constant. From the loss calculate the percentage of moisture. Note that, in weighing, the dried substance the lid of the glass must be on, since dried food-stuffs as a rule are very hygroscopic. Where other methods are necessary, they will be given in the proper place.

The estimation of the ash or mineral matter in food-stuffs.—A small platinum dish or capsule, or even a fused silica dish, is accurately weighed. Five to ten grams of the roughly powdered food-stuff, such as bread or flour, is brought into the dish and the whole weighed. The dish is now brought on to a clay triangle over a bunsen burner, and the contents gently ignited until reduced to the black or carbon state. The dish is brought into a muffle furnace and the carbon completely burned off at the lowest possible temperature. The dish then contains only a small quantity of a white to greyish-coloured ash. It is cooled in a desiccator and weighed. After the first weighing it is again ignited, desiccated and reweighed, and the operations are repeated until the weight is constant.

The weight of the empty dish is then deducted from the final weight and the percentage of ash calculated. Great care is necessary to keep the temperature down as low as possible or chlorides may be volatilised. If a muffle furnace cannot be used, the whole operation must be carried out with a bunsen or other suitable burner, taking every precaution in order to prevent loss by volatilisation.

NOTE.—The burning off of the carbon in a platinum capsule over a bunsen burner is materially assisted by bringing a piece of fine platinum gauze over the capsule. The action of this is probably of a catalytic nature.

Estimation of silica.—This is best obtained from the ash after burning off the carbonaceous and other volatile substances.

The ash, which is already in a tared platinum capsule, is accurately weighed; cover this with concentrated hydrochloric acid (HCl) and digest on a water-bath for some time. Then boil to dryness; again moisten with dilute HCl and evaporate to dryness. Take up with hot water, filter through a Swedish filter paper, wash thoroughly with boiling water, dry, ignite, desiccate, and weigh. Repeat the igniting, etc., until the weight is constant; then calculate the percentage of silica as SiO_2, usually on the weight of the ash.

The phosphates.—A fresh portion of ash is to be weighed out; digest this with moderately strong nitric acid, boil to dryness on a water-bath, take up with dilute nitric acid (HNO_3), filter off the silica and wash thoroughly. The filtrate and washings contain the whole of the phosphates. Evaporate to about fifty c.c., add a few drops of strong HNO_3 and about 20 to 30 c.c. of ammonium molybdate solution. Cover and place the beaker with its contents in a cool place for twelve hours. The phosphate will be precipitated as the yellow phospho-ammonio molybdate. Filter and wash with dilute HNO_3. Dissolve the yellow precipitate with warm ammonia, allowing to run into a clean beaker. Also dissolve the last traces of the yellow compound with ammonia, wash everything with a small quantity of fresh ammonia and then add magnesium mixture to this ammoniacal solution. Cover and again allow to stand in a cool place for twelve hours.

Filter through a special or Swedish filter paper, wash with dilute ammonia, dry, ignite, gently at first, then more strongly, desiccate and weigh. Repeat till constant in weight. From the amount of pyrophosphate of magnesium, $Mg_2P_2O_7$, calculate the phosphate to the anhydride, P_2O_5, and express as a percentage on the weight of the ash.

The fats.—Fats in food-stuffs exist either as glycerides, or as phosphorised fats, generally glycero-phosphates or lecithines. These latter bodies occur in the germ or nucleus of plants and in the yolk in animal life.

The dry ether extraction process is probably the most accurate method of estimation. In the case of liquids

THE ANALYSIS OF CEREAL FOODS 191

the sp. gr. must be ascertained, then a known volume—
5 or 10 c.c.—is used for spotting the inside of a Schleicher

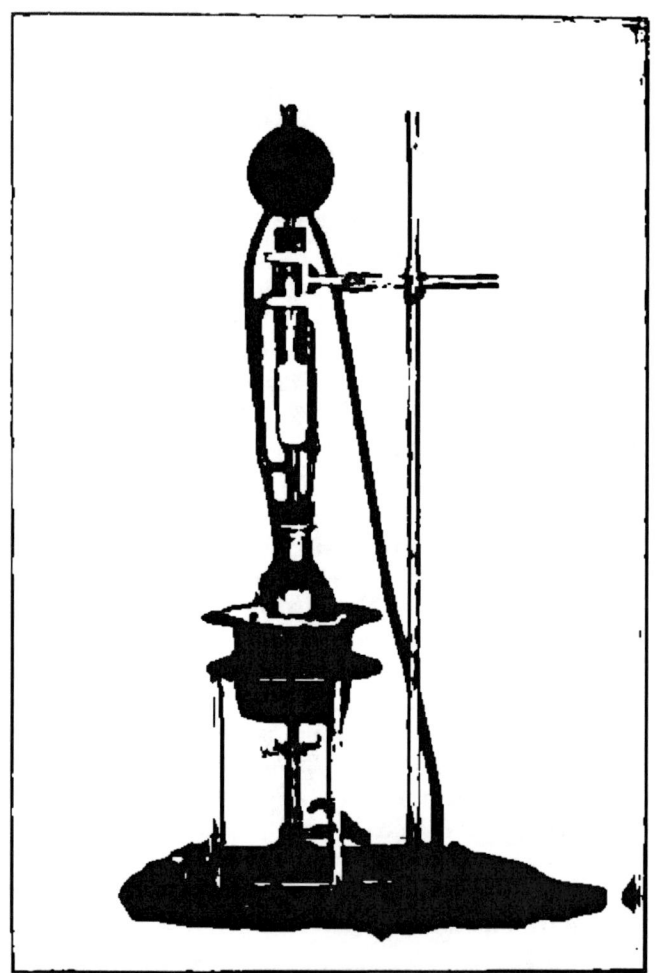

Fig. 47.—Soxhlet Fat Extractor as arranged for work.

and Schüll fat-free extraction thimble; this is air-dried
and brought into a Soxhlet extraction apparatus in which

the fat is extracted by repeated washings with dry ether (Fig. 47).

The ether is distilled off and the residue brought into a small weighed beaker together with the ether washings of the flask. The ether is allowed to evaporate by placing the beaker on to the top of an air-bath, the last traces being expelled by an air blast, then desiccated and weighed.

To extract the fat from solids, a given weight—five or ten or more grams—of the dry solid are brought into the fat-free thimble and treated as described above. With finely divided substances like flour it is better to use a double thimble of large size.

Quite recently a new nomenclature of fatty compounds has been adopted. Those fats containing nitrogen and phosphorus are termed phospholipines, while those containing nitrogen without phosphorus are named lipines.

The nitrogenous bodies.—These are of two classes, those soluble in water and those insoluble. A known weight of the solid is brought into a flask of large size and shaken for some time with a known volume of cold water. The water is allowed to remain in contact with the solid for one to three hours. The liquid is then filtered till quite bright and a given volume evaporated to dryness in a weighed porcelain dish, desiccated and weighed. From these figures the soluble extract may be calculated.

For the estimation of the soluble nitrogenous matter the residue is now treated with 10 c.c. of kjeldahl acid (kjeldahl acid is made up of equal volumes of concentrated and twenty-five per cent. fuming sulphuric acids), transferred to the small long-necked hard glass flask, one to two grams of mercury oxide added together with a piece of white paraffin wax about the size of a pea to stop frothing, and heated strongly till the whole of the residue is dissolved and the contents of the flask are quite clear but not necessarily colourless. The clear liquid is diluted with water and transferred to the distilling flask of an ammonia apparatus, the small flask carefully washed out and the washings added to the contents of the distilling flask. The apparatus is next connected together, caustic soda solution run into the acid liquid and the ammonia distilled over into a known volume of standard acid ; the excess acidity is then titrated with standard alkali and the ammonia calculated to nitrogen. $N \times 6 \cdot 3 =$ proteins.

Where the estimation is to be carried out with solids, the weighed quantity of dried solid is introduced into the hard glass flask together with either mercury oxide or fused bisulphate of potash or phosphoric anhydride (P_2O_5) and the 10 c.c. of kjeldahl acid. The process is then as already described. This latter determination gives the total quantity of nitrogenous matter in the substance, while the former gives the soluble or that which is already available for food purposes. The quantities taken for estimation vary from 5 to 10 c.c. of the soluble extract, and from one to ten grams of dry solid according to the quantity of nitrogenous matter present. Thus with a wholemeal much less would be required than with either white flour or bread.

The Examination of Wheat and other Cereals

A general external examination of the wheat berry should be made by the aid of low powers on a compound microscope. For the purpose it is better to get a complete spikelet with the husk, glumes, and berries intact; then the microscopic hairs, dust, beard, and other parts may be seen. Sections, both transverse and longitudinal, should be cut, examined, stained, and again examined. The germ ought also to be excised and examined, and the hollow from which it was removed carefully observed.

For the purpose of cutting sections the grain must be soaked in water at about blood-heat (98·4° F.) for twenty-four or thirty hours according to its condition. The sections are cut by means of a very keen razor. As soon as cut, they must be brought on to a micro-slip, a drop or two of water added, covered with a glass, and examined forthwith. The starch may be stained blue with very dilute iodine solution, the excess of iodine washed off with a spray of water, and the nitrogenous bodies (gluten) stained pink with haematoxylin solution. The pericarp and testa, which together form the bran, and the aleurone cells may easily be seen without staining. Similar sections of the little germ may also be cut and examined. Other cereals should be treated in like manner, and the points of similarity to and difference from wheat noted.

THE CHEMICAL ANALYSIS OF THE CONSTITUENTS OF CEREALS

This consists in the estimation of moisture, ash, fat, starch, cellulose, reducing and other sugars, dextrins, total nitrogenous matter and soluble extract, including that of the soluble nitrogenous content. The acidity of the soluble extract may also be determined.

For the estimation of the moisture, ash, fats, and nitrogenous matter, whole grain may be used, but it is advisable in every case to employ meal obtained by grinding up the berries in a small mill. The general processes already given are quite suitable for these determinations.

The soluble extract.—The soluble extract refers to substances soluble in water, such as gums, sugars, dextrins, certain nitrogenous compounds, and mineral salts. Ten grams of the finely divided substance are accurately weighed, placed in a flask, and covered with 200 c.c. of pure distilled water; a cork is inserted to close the flask, and the contents are repeatedly shaken at intervals during the time the mixture is allowed to stand. One hour has been found by experiment to be too short, therefore it is advisable to permit the extraction to go on for three hours. During the last half-hour refrain from disturbing the contents of the flask. Then filter till bright. Withdraw an aliquot proportion, say 50 c.c., and evaporate to dryness on a water-bath in a weighed porcelain or silica dish. Dry off in a water oven for fifteen minutes, desiccate and weigh. After the weight is constant, the contents of the dish are

THE ANALYSIS OF CEREAL FOODS

ignited, first over a bunsen burner till carbonised and then finished off in a muffle furnace. Desiccate and weigh. The result gives the amount of mineral salts extracted by cold water.

The calculations are simple. Ten grams in 200 c.c. give a five per cent. solution and mixture. Fifty c.c. are taken for evaporation, or a quarter of the whole; 50 c.c. therefore contain the amount of soluble matter from two and a half grams of the original material. By deducting the weight of the dish the amount of soluble matter in the two and a half grams is obtained. Multiply this weight by four and then by ten to give the percentage of soluble extract in the grain, flour, or bread. The weight of the ash is also multiplied by forty to give the percentage of mineral salts extracted.

An example will make this clear.

Weight of silica dish and dry extract = 73·066 grams.
Weight of silica dish = 72·952 ,,
Weight of dry extract = 0·114 ,,

Therefore $0.114 \times 4 \times 10 = 4.56$ per cent. of extract.

The acidity determination.—The acidity of cereals and cereal products is due partly to the acid phosphates present and partly to organic acids. Whatever may be the cause of it, the acidity is always calculated as lactic acid, $C_3H_6O_3$, or $CH_3\text{-}CHOH.COOH$ (molecular weight, 90).

The acidity may be quantitatively estimated in an aliquot portion of the soluble extract. The liquid, as in the previous estimation, must be filtered bright, then 25 c.c. are withdrawn by a pipette, brought into a small flask, a few drops of an indicator such as methyl orange added, and then titrated by means of a burette with centi-normal alkali, preferably caustic soda. A second portion of 25 c.c. is similarly titrated, and the mean of the two results used to calculate the acidity.

Example of an acidity calculation :—

Twenty-five c.c. of a XX flour soluble extract required (1) 2·6 c.c. and (2) 2·4 c.c. of centinormal $\left(\frac{N}{100}\right)$ caustic soda. Mean 2·5 c.c.

One c.c. of $\frac{N}{100}$ caustic soda contains 0·0004 gram of soda, therefore 2·5 c.c. contains 0·001 gram.

Now 40 parts of caustic soda = 90 parts of lactic acid.

Therefore 0·001 of caustic soda $= \frac{0·001 \times 90}{40}$

= 0·00225 lactic acid.

25 c.c. of soluble extract contain 0·00225 lactic.

100 c.c. of soluble extract contain $\frac{0·00225 \times 100}{25} = 0·009$ lactic.

100 c.c. are the extract from five grams of flour and contain 0·009 lactic. Therefore 100 grams of flour contain $\frac{0·009 \times 100}{5} = 0·18$ per cent. lactic.

Reducing and other sugars and the dextrins.—A further portion of the clear, bright soluble extract is employed for the sugars and the dextrins. This consists in determining (*a*) the opticity of the liquid; (*b*) the copper-reducing power, and calculating this to maltose; (*c*) treating with dilute acid for twenty-five minutes to hydrolyse sucrose to invert sugars and again determining the copper-reducing power.

(*a*) The *specific rotatory power* (S.R.P.) or opticity.— The S.R.P. of any optically active substance is the angle through which a beam of plane polarised light of definite degree of refrangibility is rotated on passing through a layer of the substance a thousand millimetres in thickness and containing ten grams of substance per hundred c.c. of the solution. Or, it may be defined as the amount of turning that a beam of polarised light undergoes when it passes through a metre length of a ten per cent. solution of the substance.

THE ANALYSIS OF CEREAL FOODS

In practice it is very difficult to pass a beam through a column of liquid one metre long; therefore it is usual to employ tubes of one or two decimetres in length, and to multiply the reading by ten or five as the case may be. At the same time the errors are increased in the same proportion.

The two instruments in common use for the determination of the opticity of sugars and other optically active carbohydrates are the Laurent, which is used with a sodium flame, and in which percentages of cane sugar (sucrose) may be read off directly; and the Schmidt-Haensch, a white light instrument, the readings of which may be converted into angular measure by multiplying by 0·344.

To use the Laurent polarimeter: First adjust the zero point of the instrument and note any correction. Note the temperature of the room in which the instrument is placed; the readings are accurate between 60° and 68° F. Rinse out the previously cleaned tube with a few drops of the liquid to be determined; fill the tube completely, slide on the top glass disc and affix the end. Bring into position and take the reading at once. Also take a reading with a second tube; the two readings should coincide. The calculation may be simplified by using the formula:—

$$\text{S.R.P.}, (a)_D^{3·86} = \frac{100 \times a}{l \times c}$$

where a = the angle of rotation.

l = length of tube in decimetres.

c = concentration or grams of solids per 100 c.c.

Example.—Find the percentage of cane sugar in the sample in which the length of tube used was two decimetres, the solids 9·86, and the angular rotation 12·85°.

Then $\dfrac{100 \times a}{l \times c} = \dfrac{100 \times 12·85°}{2 \times 9·86} = \dfrac{1285}{19·72} = 65·162$ S.R.P.

The S.R.P. of 100 per cent. sucrose is 66·5.

Therefore in the example, $\dfrac{65·162 \times 100}{66·5} = 98·73$ per cent. of sucrose.

To convert yellow light $(a)_D$ readings into white light $(a)_j$ readings, multiply by 1·1084, the product

$$(a)_D \times 1\cdot 1084 = (a)_j.$$

Example.—The S.R.P. of sucrose $(a)_D$ is 66·5. Find the S.R.P. for white light $(a)_j$.

$$66\cdot 5 \times 1\cdot 1084 = 73\cdot 70.$$

The following figures represent the accepted S.R.P. for the pure substances :—

Substance.	S.R.P. for $(a)_D$.	S.R.P. for $(a)_j$.
Dextrins	200·4	216·0
Maltose	138·0	150·0
Sucrose	66·5	73·8
Dextrose	52·8	58·52
Lævulose	−95·65	−105·98
Invert sugar	−21·3	−23·60
Lactose	52·53	57·22
Raffinose	104·5	115·83

Frequently, solutions which are to be examined by polarised light, although quite bright, are so darkly coloured as to prevent a beam of light passing. In such cases it is advisable to use a decolorising material. The three common ones are alumina cream, basic lead acetate, and bleaching powder solution. In every case the minimum quantity of these solutions should be employed, as they carry down sugar and introduce other errors.

For 100 c.c. of a ten per cent. solution of sugar, from $2\frac{1}{2}$ to 5 c.c. is usually sufficient. Bring 50 c.c. of the sugar solution into 100 c.c. flask, add $2\frac{1}{2}$ or more c.c. of alumina cream or other reagent, make up to the hundred mark with pure distilled water, put in the stopper, shake up, allow to settle for a few minutes, filter and take the necessary readings. Should the alumina cream not be efficient try the basic lead acetate, or both together, using the lead first. Not more than 5 c.c. of the two combined may be

THE ANALYSIS OF CEREAL FOODS

employed. Very occasionally, in ordinary practice, the bleaching powder method of decolorisation may be required, or even the boiling up with finely ground animal charcoal.

NOTE.—1° on a Laurent instrument represents 0·1619 grams of sugar (sucrose) per hundred cubic centimetres of solution.

(b) *The copper-reducing power of sugars.*—All the more common sugars, except the sucroses, possess the power of reducing, in a greater or less degree, an alkaline copper tartrate solution, commonly known as Fehling's solution, to the state of red cuprous oxide, Cu_2O. K, the copper-reducing power of a sugar, is defined to be the amount of cupric oxide, CuO, calculated to dextrose that a hundred parts will reduce. As dextrose possesses the highest reducing power, it is taken as the standard for comparison.

The values for K are as follows :—

For dextrose=100 ; for maltose=61·07.

For lævulose=92·4 ; for invert sugar=96·6.

Fehling's solution is made up as two solutions, which are not mixed until required for use.

(1) Dissolve 69·2 grams of pure recrystallised copper sulphate $CuSO_4 \cdot 5 H_2O$, in water and make up to a litre.

(2) Dissolve 346 grams of Rochelle salt and 130 grams of caustic soda (both these compounds must be pure) in water and make up to a litre. If flocculent matter settles out, the solution must be filtered through glass wool. When required, 25 c.c. of each solution are mixed together to form 50 c.c. of the clear, dark blue liquid known as Fehling's alkaline copper tartrate solution. One molecule of pure dextrose is able to reduce exactly five molecules of this copper solution ; or, 0·05 gram of pure dextrose exactly reduces 10 c.c. of standard Fehling's solution.

To use Fehling's reagent, bring 50 c.c. of the Fehling into a white glazed porcelain beaker, add 40 c.c. of distilled water, place in a water-bath and bring to the boil. Then into this, by means of a pipette, run 10 c.c. of the reducing sugar solution, cover the beaker with a clock glass and boil exactly twelve minutes. Take out of the water-bath, allow to settle for a few minutes, and filter off the red cuprous oxide through a Swedish filter paper. Wash out the beaker very thoroughly, wash all the blue copper salt out of the filter paper, dry, ignite, desiccate, and weigh as black oxide of copper, CuO. During ignition the carbon of the filter paper reduces some of the oxide of copper to the metallic state. Dissolve this with about two drops of strong nitric acid, and again ignite to convert the copper nitrate into CuO.

$$\mathrm{Cu}\!\!<\!\!{}^{NO_3}_{NO_3} = CuO + 2\,NO_2 + O.$$

Copper nitrate = Copper oxide + Dioxide of nitrogen + Oxygen.
Weight of $CuO \times 0 \cdot 7435$ = maltose.

NOTE.—It should be arranged that the 10 c.c. of reducing sugar solution contains between 0·10 and 0·15 grams of sugar.

By the process described, the reducing sugars, if any, in the cold water extract of cereals may be accurately determined. If sucroses are present these must be hydrolysed to invert sugar. Ten c.c. of the extract are brought into a small glass flask, 1 c.c. of HCl added and the liquid heated in a water-bath for twenty-five minutes at boiling point. The acid is neutralised with about 1 c.c. of caustic soda (NaOH) solution, and the copper-reducing power determined as already explained. Deduct the CuO, if any, from the reducing sugars, from the total CuO obtained in this determination and calculate the remainder to sucrose.

Weight of $CuO \times 0 \cdot 4715 \times \frac{19}{20}$ = cane sugar or sucrose.

The **dextrins** present can be determined directly by the process given, or as is usually the case indirectly from the total S.R.P. The sugars found by the copper-reducing process are calculated to their opticity (S.R.P.). This is deducted from the total S.R.P., and the remaining S.R.P. calculated to dextrins.

The dextrins, which do not reduce Fehling's solution or Knapp's mercuric cyanide solution, may be freed from

THE ANALYSIS OF CEREAL FOODS

dextrose and maltose by heating with an excess of an alkaline solution of mercuric cyanide which oxidises the two sugars without affecting the dextrins present.

Five grams of the substance containing the dextrins are dissolved in water, the solution made up to 100 c.c. at 60° F. and filtered bright if necessary; 10 c.c. of this are boiled with 10 c.c. of Knapp's reagent, filtered bright, and the S.R.P. of the solution read off in a Laurent polarimeter as already described, and the percentage of dextrins calculated. Where the mercury is found to interfere, it may be precipitated with sulphuretted hydrogen gas and the liquid filtered bright before the opticity is taken.

Estimation of starch in cereals.—The starch in cereals is usually determined by a modification of the original method devised by Maercker.

Finely crush about four grams of the wheat or other cereal, then weigh accurately three grams into a glass bottle, cover with distilled water and heat in a pressure vessel for about an hour. Cool to 150° F. Stir in 5 c.c. of malt extract, the value of which is known, and maintain at 145° or 146° F. for twenty-five minutes. Make faintly acid with tartaric acid solution, then again heat under pressure. Cool as before, treat with another 5 c.c. of malt extract for thirty minutes, then bring to the boil for five minutes. Cool to 60° F. and make up to 100 c.c. in a graduated flask. Filter till bright. Determine the copper-reducing power with 10 c.c. Also take the rotation or opticity. From the figures obtained, calculate the percentage of starch.

The estimation of starch in flour, commercial starch, etc.—This determination is based on that of Dragendorff. The starchy matter is generally mixed up with fats, proteins, sugars, colouring matter, amylans, pectins, mineral salts, etc. Three grams of the finely ground substance are mixed in a flask with 30 c.c. of a five per cent. solution of caustic potash, heated for twenty-four hours on a water-bath, filtered while hot through a weighed Swedish filter paper, and the residue on the filter paper washed with hot absolute alcohol, cold ordinary alcohol, and lastly with water; then dried at 230° F. (110° C.), desiccated and weighed.

The loss is that of the foreign substances mentioned above. The amount of the remainder, minus the weight of the filter paper, agrees approximately with that of the starch and fibre (a). The filter paper and its contents are then cut up, placed in a flask, boiled with distilled water for an hour, cooled to 150° F., treated with 5 c.c. of malt extract of known value, maintained at 146° F. for thirty minutes, brought up to the boil for five minutes, filtered hot through another weighed filter paper, washed, dried, desiccated and weighed (b). The difference between the weights of (a) and (b) gives the starch. The fibre or cellulose is the residue minus the weight of the two filter papers.

The starch may also be determined by cooling the contents of the flask after boiling to 60° F., and determining the copper-reducing power in 10 c.c. and also the opticity.

Estimation of the fibre or husky matter, or cellulose.—Weigh out approximately two and a half grams of the substance, grind, then weigh accurately two grams into a small flask. Add enough of a one per cent. solution of sulphuric acid to more than cover the material and boil for at least half an hour. Pour off as much of the acid as possible, replace with a one per cent. solution of caustic potash and again boil for half an hour. Exhaust very thoroughly with the reagents in the order given — cold water, concentrated alcohol and ether; then dry and weigh. Even after the above treatment the cellulose contains traces of wood-gums, suberin and its acid, silica, hydro-cellulose, etc.

According to Professor A. G. Green, this fibre cellulose is a colloidal aggregate of a large number of somewhat simple cellulose molecules.

THE ANALYSIS OF CEREAL FOODS

Flour Analysis

As a preliminary to the chemical analysis, all flours should be subjected to a physical examination. This includes the handling to observe the condition, *i.e.* whether granular and free or soft and woolly. If pressed tightly in the hand high-grade flours fly off in all directions, or appear to squirt from between the fingers. Inferior ones ball and clog, especially if unduly moist. Any unpleasant odour, or anything unusual in general appearance, should also be noted.

The **colour** of a flour is determined by the Pékar test, first in the dry, then in the wet and afterwards in the dried state. A known high-grade flour of the pale, creamy, bloomy appearance should be used as a standard for comparison.

The **strength** of flour is an unsettled factor, dependent largely on the quality and condition of the gluten. It can only be considered in connection with the absorbing power, the retaining power, the gluten, and the viscosity of such flour.

The **gluten** may be approximately determined as follows:—Weigh out accurately twenty-five grams of the flour into a glazed porcelain dish, size IV. or V. Make it into a clear dough with 12 or 13 c.c. of cold water. Cover the little ball of dough with cold water, and allow to stand for between thirty and sixty minutes.

Wash out the starch and soluble matters in a large excess of water, being careful not to separate the dough. Pour off the water into another dish, and note that there should be no gluten particles or pieces of dough at the bottom of the vessel. When the washings no longer become milky and the gluten contains no lumps of visible flour and is practically of one shade of colour, the excess water may be pressed out, the gluten brought on to a piece of counterpoised aluminium foil (thin sheet aluminium) and weighed in the wet state, and its percentage calculated by multiplying by four; this result divided by three gives approximately the percentage of dry gluten. The wet gluten may then be dried in an air-bath at 212° to 218° F. until the weight is constant. The figures obtained will agree very closely with those from the calculated dry gluten. Two estimations should be carried out, and the condition, colour, and other points noted before the gluten is dried; the mean of the results is taken as the percentage.

The separation of the gluten into glutenin and gliadin is effected by washing out the gluten in the ordinary way, weighing to obtain the wet gluten; then this and the aluminium foil are brought into a flask containing about 100 c.c. of strong alcohol, digested on a water-bath for some time, and filtered. The residue is washed with strong alcohol, dried and weighed to give the insoluble glutenin. The alcoholic filtrate is distilled to recover most of the alcohol, the rest containing the sticky gliadin is transferred to a small weighed beaker, the alcohol evaporated off, and the residue cooled and weighed; the later operations are repeated until the weight is constant. From the figures obtained the weight of the gliadin is calculated.

The **absorbing power** is determined by weighing out twenty-eight grams of the flour into a glazed porcelain dish and running measured volumes of water into it from a burette, then making up into a dough of the proper consistency. The number of c.c. and decimals of a c.c. gives gallons and decimals of a gallon per sack of flour (280 lbs.). This result can now be confirmed by making up a batch or dough with seven to fourteen pounds of flour and proper quantities of yeast, salt, and water, such that the consistency is the same as before. Weigh the dough as soon as properly cleared, making allowance for the yeast and salt. The figures should agree with the result obtained in the first part of the work.

The dough is then worked through into bread as usual. Immediately on drawing, the bread is weighed and the loss calculated. From this the retaining power of the flour is

THE ANALYSIS OF CEREAL FOODS

known. According to the condition and quality of the gluten, whether or not an excess quantity of water has been put into the dough, whether a sharp or slow oven has been used, according to the condition and state of the dough, etc., the figures obtained regarding the retaining power of the flour will be affected.

The **viscosity time** of a dough is also useful in assisting the worker to understand the quality of a gluten, but so many factors interfere as to render the results of two or more workers absolutely useless for comparison. Owing to this, it is not proposed to occupy space in describing the instruments or their manipulation, especially at this transition stage of our knowledge.

Foreign substances, as starches, crystals of mineral salts, particles of offal or husky matter, may best be detected by the aid of a compound microscope.

Bring a small quantity of the dry flour on to a micro-slip and examine it with low powers, say an ocular number two and an objective C. or a third of an inch. Make several dry slides and examine them. Offal, crystals, and other foreign particles may readily be observed. Next, make two or three wet slides by stirring a very small quantity of flour in water, bring one drop on to a slide, place over it a thin cover-glass and again examine, using an E. or one-sixth objective. This examination will reveal foreign starches if any, husky matter, germ and other insoluble bodies.

The chemical analysis of flour.—This consists in making the following determinations: Water, ash, fats, total proteins, soluble extract including the sugars, acidity, mineral salts and soluble nitrogenous bodies contained therein, starch and fibre or cellulose. In addition the tests for alum and bleaching should be carried out.

The whole of the foregoing determinations may be carried out by the processes already given in the description of the chemical analysis of cereals and their meals.

An example of the determination of the soluble extract, and the ash of this, in a first patent flour follows.

Twenty-five grams of flour were brought into a flask and treated as already described with 500 c.c. of water. A portion was filtered bright and 50 c.c. evaporated to dryness on a water-bath, dried, desiccated, and weighed.

Grams.
Weight of platinum dish and the dried extract = 51·8154
Weight of platinum dish alone . . . = 51·6320

Weight of soluble extract from 50 c.c. = 0·1834

Now 50 c.c. is one-tenth of the 500 c.c., and therefore contains the extract in 2·5 grams of flour, and this yields 0·1834 grams of extract.

$\therefore$ 100 grams yield $\dfrac{0·1834 \times 100}{2·5} = 7·34$ per cent. of soluble extract.

The contents of the platinum dish were then incinerated, desiccated, and weighed.

Grams.
Weight of platinum dish and the ash = 51·6418
Weight of the platinum dish alone = 51·6320

0·0098

$\therefore$ 100 grams yield $\dfrac{0·0098 \times 100}{2·5} = 0·392$ per cent. of ash in the soluble extract.

Alum may be detected in the following way :—Five grams of the flour are brought into a small porcelain dish, 10 c.c. of a ten per cent. solution of ammonium carbonate are added and the mixture stirred to form a paste; then 10 c.c. of a fresh solution of logwood extract are stirred in, the dish covered, and the whole allowed to stand for a few minutes. If alum has been used to lighten up and strengthen the flour, or if a bread improver containing the constituents of alum has been employed or added to the flour, a lilac coloration is formed all over the paste. If no alum is present, a pink to rose colour appears. In all cases

THE ANALYSIS OF CEREAL FOODS

a control test should be carried out with a flour already known to be pure.

The logwood extract is prepared by shaking up a small quantity of fluorescent logwood chips with a comparatively large quantity of methylated spirit.

The tests for bleaching.—These tests depend upon the presence of nitrites or nitrous acid in the flour, formed by the action of the oxides of nitrogen from the bleaching process. The tests generally adopted are those of Dr. Griess, carried out as follows after the preparation of a soluble extract of the flour.

(1) Bring some of the clear extract into a Nessler glass or other similar vessel; add about six drops of concentrated sulphuric acid and a few c.c. of a weak meta-phenylenediamine solution. Cover the vessel and allow to stand about fifteen minutes when the Bismarck brown coloration is formed if any nitrites are present.

(2) Bring some of the clear soluble extract into a Nessler glass, add one drop of concentrated hydrochloric acid, one c.c. of alpha-naphthylamine hydrochloride solution, stir with a clean glass rod, cover and allow to stand for from twenty to thirty minutes. If nitrites are present, a faint to bright pink coloration is developed.

NOTE.—The water used for making the soluble extract must be previously tested for nitrites in order to prevent the possibility of error from this cause.

THE EXAMINATION OF BREAD

Before undertaking an analysis of the chemical constituents of bread, a general examination of the bread, both externally and internally, should be made as if judging for exhibition purposes.

Externally, the following points may be considered:— The general appearance of the loaf or loaves, whether properly handled, moulded, and baked, the bloom if any, the colour, and the volume.

For the internal examination the loaf should be evenly and cleanly cut through the middle beginning at the top. The colour, flavour, texture, pile, and regularity of the crumb should then be examined. Occasionally, it is advisable to cut a very thin slice from off one of the sections and hold it up before the strong light from a window not facing the sun. This gives an opportunity of more critically judging the crumb and noting any irregularities. Streaks, due to the chilling of the dough during the making up, may thus be more readily traced and other faults distinguished.

The chemical analysis of bread.—The crumb or inside and the crust or external coating of the bread should be examined separately where necessary. For general analysis a slice is cut right through the bread and a fair sample containing the proper proportions of crumb and crust taken. The following determinations are made :—Moisture, fats, mineral salts, proteins, starch, cellulose, the soluble extract and in this the sugars, nitrogenous matter, acidity, alum, and total phosphates, by the processes already given. If it is necessary to test for bleaching, a thin slice of bread may be cut, a strong soluble extract made with tap-water, the liquid filtered and tested for nitrites by the methods given under flour analysis.

THE ANALYSIS OF THE GERM OF CEREALS

The germ or embryo of cereals is a somewhat triangular-looking body of a yellowish buttery appearance when picked out from new grain. If the cereal is old, however, the germ has darkened almost to a deep brown in colour, and the taste instead of being pleasant is decidedly the reverse. Wheat germs obtained from the mill are pale stone-colour to yellowish discs varying from three-sixteenths to a quarter of an inch in diameter. In a fit condition for food the germ must possess a pleasant oily smell and an agreeable greasy flavour. Germ in a decomposed state is dangerous to health, if used for foods, owing to the products of bacterial decomposition.

THE ANALYSIS OF CEREAL FOODS

The chemical analysis.—This consists in the estimation of the amounts of moisture, fats, ash, proteins, fibre or cellulose, sugars, soluble extract and the soluble nitrogenous matter, and the detection of enzymes. The whole of the above bodies may be estimated by the methods already given under the heading 'Estimation of the chemical constituents of the cereals,' see page 194.

The detection of enzymes.—The enzymes likely to be present are diastase, cytase, certain proteolytic ones, and those which emulsify and act on the fats. Diastase may be detected by bringing a small quantity of the cold water extract of the germ into a two per cent. solution of soluble starch, heating up to 145° F. and allowing to act for half an hour, then boiling and testing for maltose with Fehling's solution, when the characteristic red precipitate of cuprous oxide, Cu_2O, will be obtained if diastatic action has taken place.

Two examples of the complete analysis of wheat germs are given below :—

	Sample I.	Sample II.
Moisture	11·55%	13·70%
Fat	8·42 ,,	10·30 ,,
Ash	4·44 ,,	4·49 ,,
Insoluble nitrogenous matter	18·42 ,,	16·87 ,,
Soluble extract	40·20 ,,	37·85 ,,
Cellulose and fibre	2·35 ,,	3·87 ,,
Starch and undetermined	14·62 ,,	12·92 ,,
	100·00 ,,	100·00 ,,
Soluble extract—		
Cane sugar	18·87%	18·64%
Maltose	0·12 ,,	0·04 ,,
Soluble nitrogenous matter	13·26 ,,	12·00 ,,
Ash	2·88 ,,	2·76 ,,
Dextrins, gums, and undetermined	5·07 ,,	4·41 ,,
	40·20 ,,	37·85 ,,
Diastatic power (Lintner)	24°	22°

The Analysis of Malt Flour and Extracts

These should possess the usual appearance, odour, and taste of such bodies. There must be no traces of fermentation evident in the fluid products, whilst the flour must be in a fine state of division and free from lumps, mouldy smell, and insects. The chemical analysis includes the determination of the moisture, acidity, ash, sugars, proteins, and the diastatic capacity.

These may be carried out by the usual methods, care being taken with the moisture estimation not to allow the temperature to rise above 212° F. It is safer to carry out this determination in a water oven and so to avoid any chance of oxidation. This precaution of course applies only to the solid products, since the moisture in malt extracts is determined by a method described later.

The determination of the diastatic capacity (Lintner value).—Twenty-five grams of ground malt are extracted for three hours with half a litre of distilled water at 70° F., stirring well every half-hour and filtering bright. Three c.c. of this bright filtrate are allowed to act on 100 c.c. of a two per cent. soluble starch solution at 70° F. for one hour in a 200 c.c. flask. Ten c.c. of deci-normal solution of caustic soda are then added in order to check diastatic action, the liquid cooled to 60° F. and made up to 200 c.c. with distilled water; the contents of the flask are then well shaken and titrated against 5 c.c. portions of standard Fehling's solution, using ferrous thiocyanate as indicator.

This titration is carried out as follows: Five c.c. of Fehling's solution are accurately measured into a 150 c.c. boiling flask, and raised to boiling over a small naked bunsen flame. The converted starch solution is added from a burette in small quantities, the mixture being kept rotated and boiled after each addition until reduction of the copper solution is complete, which is ascertained by rapidly withdrawing a drop of the liquid with a glass rod, and bringing it at once into contact with a drop of the indicator on a porcelain spot plate, the end point being arrived at when no reddish-brown coloration is obtained.

The indicator is made up as follows :—Dissolve one gram each of ferrous ammonium sulphate and ammonium sulphocyanide in 10 c.c. of water at 120° F. Cool and add 5 c.c. of hydrochloric acid solution. Remove any traces of a red coloration with a small quantity of zinc dust.

The results are calculated by the help of the following formula :—

$$A = \frac{1000}{xy}$$

where A = the diastatic capacity.
  x = the number of c.c. of five per cent. malt extract contained in 100 c.c. of the fully diluted starch liquid.
  y = the number of c.c. of the same liquid required for the reduction of 5 c.c. of Fehling's solution.

Precautions :—

(1) Where a malt has a diastatic capacity of over fifty degrees Lintner, then only 2 c.c. of the cold water malt extract is used for the determination.

(2) In the case of a malt extract, use 3 c.c. of a four per cent. solution of the malt extract in cold water.

(3) With a diastase paste where the Lintner value is over 60° D.C., then 3 c.c. of a two per cent. solution of the diastase paste in cold water may be employed.

(4) The value of x in case (2) is arrived at as follows : 3 c.c. of 4 per cent. solution = $\frac{3 \times 4}{5}$ = 2·4 c.c. of a 5 per cent. solution in 200 c.c. of the liquid, *i.e.* 1·2 c.c. in 100 c.c.

Example.—With two malt extracts (3 c.c. of 4 per cent. solution used).

(a) In the first case, 5 c.c. of Fehling required 19 c.c. of the starch.

Then $A = \frac{1000}{1 \cdot 2 \times 19}$ = 43·86, or 44° Lintner.

(b) In the second case, 5 c.c. of Fehling required 17·5 c.c.

Then $A = \dfrac{1000}{1 \cdot 2 \times 17 \cdot 5} = 47 \cdot 6$, or 48° Lintner.

A malt or other substance possessing diastatic power is said to be 100° Lintner, when 0·1 c.c. of the five per cent. cold-water extract filtered bright, after being allowed to act on a two per cent. solution of soluble starch for one hour at 70° F., produces enough malt sugar to exactly reduce 5 c.c. of standard Fehling's solution.

The determinations of moisture and total solids in fluid malt products, sugars, starch transformation substances, etc.

Ten grams of the substance are accurately weighed out, dissolved in pure water and made up to the mark in 100 c.c. graduated flask at the temperature of 60° F. The contents of the flask are thoroughly shaken, and the specific gravity (sp. gr.) determined as follows :—

Thoroughly clean and weigh a 50 c.c. sp. gr. bottle, then fill with water at 60° F., dry and weigh. Turn out the water, rinse out twice with the liquid the gravity of which is required, fill completely as before, clean and weigh. From the figures obtained, the sp. gr. may be calculated as under :—

$$\text{Sp. gr.} = \dfrac{\text{Weight of bottle and substance} - \text{weight of bottle.}}{\text{Weight of bottle and water} - \text{weight of bottle.}}$$

Example.—A very stiff syrup gives the following figures :—
Weight of empty bottle . = 27·7905 grams.
Weight of bottle and substance = 79·3559 grams.
Weight of bottle and water = 77·7556 grams.

Find the sp. gr., the total solids, and the moisture.

$$\text{Sp. gr.} = \dfrac{79 \cdot 3559 - 27 \cdot 7905}{77 \cdot 7556 - 27 \cdot 7905} = \dfrac{51 \cdot 5654}{49 \cdot 9651}$$

$= 1 \cdot 03203$ taking water as 1·000, but with water as 1000 the sp. gr. = 1032·03 for a 10% solution.

The total solids are found by deducting a thousand from the sp. gr. and dividing the difference by 3·86.

Therefore
$$\dfrac{1032 \cdot 03 - 1000}{3 \cdot 86} = \dfrac{32 \cdot 03}{3 \cdot 86} = 8 \cdot 298.$$

THE ANALYSIS OF CEREAL FOODS

The total solids in ten grams equal 8·298 or 82·98 per cent. This deducted from a hundred gives the moisture.

$$100 - 82·98 = 17·02 \text{ per cent. of water.}$$

NOTE.—The factor 3·86, or the solids factor, has been arrived at by dissolving one gram of the pure substance in water, making up to 100 c.c. and determining the sp. gr. which in the case of sucrose works out to 1003·859; for malt products to 1004. For uniformity's sake the factor 3·86 has been adopted for all these bodies and mixtures of them. Too much care cannot be paid to working out all sp. gr. determinations at the temperature of 60° F., at which the apparatus is accurate.

The three required results then are :—

Specific gravity, 1032·03 (water=1000).
Total solids, . 82·98 per cent.
Moisture, . 17·02 per cent.

The analysis of sugars.—The colour, taste, smell, and general appearance of the sugar should first be noticed; then the chemical reaction towards litmus paper, and the tests for the presence of iron salts carried out.

High-class sugars when dissolved in water should not change blue litmus paper to red, nor give the following reactions for iron salts :—

(1) Bring some of the solution into a test tube, add a few drops of weak nitric acid and some ferrocyanide of potassium. A greenish-blue coloration and precipitate indicates iron salts.

(2) To a second portion of the solution add a few drops of weak nitric acid and some sulphocyanide of potassium. A pale pink to blood-red coloration indicates iron salts.

(3) To a third portion of the sugar solution add a few drops of a tannic acid solution. A light-coloured precipitate gradually darkening to black indicates iron salts.

Low-grade sugars are often whitened in appearance by the addition of a blue ultramarine. The presence of this body may be detected by making a strong solution of the sugar and allowing it to settle in a cool place, when a faint

214   CHEMISTRY OF BREADMAKING

blue sediment settles out. A further test may be made by adding a few drops of weak acid solution to some of the solid sugar in a test tube and noting the unpleasant smell of sulphuretted hydrogen. The presence of this is confirmed by bringing a filter paper moistened with silver nitrate solution over the mouth of the tube, when a darkening to an almost black colour indicates the presence of sulphides which are constituents of ultramarine. Lead acetate solution (sugar of lead) may be used in the place of silver nitrate.

The chemical estimations of sugar include the following determinations :—The moisture and total solids, by the sp. gr. method as already described, the mineral salts, total sugar, other sugars, nitrogenous bodies, the copper-reducing power, and the opticity, together with the acidity and iron if these substances have been detected in the preliminary examination. The whole of the above determinations to decide the purity of a sugar may be carried out by the methods already given.

The following factors may be of use in sugar analysis :—

$CuO \times 0\cdot7435$ = maltose.
$CuO \times 0\cdot4535$ = dextrose.
$CuO \times 0\cdot4715$ = invert sugar.
$CuO \times 0\cdot4715 \times \frac{19}{20}$ = sucrose.

The analysis of milks.—The following varieties of milk are used in the making of bread :—Whole milk, skim or separated milk, and dried milk or milk powders. Whole milk is an almost perfect or complete food, since it contains all four proximate principles of food—sugars, fats, proteids, and mineral salts with water.

All milk of cows, when allowed to stand, rapidly increases in acidity owing to the conversion of milk-sugar into lactic acid, except when kept at temperatures below 50° F., or when a powerful antiseptic like formalin, salicylic acid, or boric acid has been added.

The colour of milk is somewhat variable. This is due to the fat globules and pigments present. The presence of chromogenic bacteria readily effects changes in the colour ;

THE ANALYSIS OF CEREAL FOODS 215

thus it may be shades of blue, yellow, or even faintly red. Such organisms are generally the cause of diseases in milks.

Milk analysis consists in the determinations of the specific gravity, water, total solids, and fats.

The sp. gr. may be found by the process already given, or roughly by means of a hydrometer. The sp. gr. varies between 1027 and 1035 (water=1000). According to Professor H. Droop Richmond, the average of over six hundred thousand samples is 1032·1 at 60° F.

The water and total solids may be determined by bringing 5 or 10 c.c. into a tared platinum capsule together with a small weighed glass rod to stir the contents; a few drops of acetic acid, which is volatile, are added to coagulate the proteids and so prevent the formation of a scum on the surface which delays evaporation. The contents are evaporated to dryness on a water-bath, dried in a water-oven for a short time, desiccated and weighed. The loss is that of the water which has been driven off, whilst the total solids are the residue in the capsule; these are calculated to a percentage.

The fats are estimated by the ether extraction process, or by one of the many centrifugal methods. The analytical results are generally stated as, total solids, water, fats, and solids not fat. Analyses of English standard milk and others are given in the subjoined table :—

Constituents.	English Standard.	An Ordinary Sample (local).	A Low-grade Sample.	Dried Milk (whole).
Water,	87·50 %	86·84 %	95·63 %	8·96 %
Total Solids,	12·50 ,,	13·16 ,,	4·37 ,,	91·04 ,,
Fats,	3·50 ,,	4·04 ,,	1·27 ,,	15·56 ,,
Solids not Fats,	9·00 ,,	9·12 ,,	3·10 ,,	75·48 ,,
Mineral Salts,	0·72 ,,	0·73 ,,	0·34 ,,	5·73 ,,
Proteids,	3·53 ,,	3·57 ,,	1·03 ,,	27·15 ,,
Lactose,	4·75 ,,	4·82 ,,	1·73 ,,	42·60 ,,
Sp. Gr. at 60° F.,	1032·0	1032·2	1010·2	—

Dried milks may be analysed by the processes already given. The proteids are determined by the Kjeldahl method ($N \times 6.3 =$ proteids). The lactose in all the above cases is estimated by difference.

BIBLIOGRAPHY

Atwater, Mrs. H. W.,	*Bread and the Principles of Breadmaking.*
Bayliss, Dr. W. M.,	*The Nature of Enzyme Action.*
Blandy, John,	*Studies in Breadmaking.*
Fowler, Dr. G. J.,	*Bacteriological and Enzyme Chemistry.*
Goodfellow, Dr. John,	*The Dietetic Value of Bread.*
Hansen, Dr. E. C.	*Practical Studies in Fermentation, and Pamphlets.*
Harden, Dr. Arthur,	*Alcoholic Fermentation.*
Hutchison, Dr.,	*The Dietetic Value of Foods.*
Jago, William,	*The Principles of Breadmaking.*
Jago, William,	*The Technology of Breadmaking, etc.*
Jörgensen, A.,	*The Micro-organisms of Fermentation.*
Kirkland, Archibald,	*Studies for the Bakehouse.*
Kirkland, John,	*All about Breadmaking.*
Kirkland, John, and others,	*The Modern Baker, Confectioner, and Caterer.*
Klöcker, Dr. A.,	*Fermentation Organisms.*
Lafar, Professor Franz,	*Technical Mycology.* Vols. I. and II.
Lawes and Gilbert,	*The Wheat Grain, its Milling Products and Bread.*
Maercker, Dr.,	*Die Kohlenhydrates.*
Matthews, Charles G.,	*Manual of Alcoholic Fermentation.*
Newlands, B. E. R.,	*Sugar.*
Osborne, Dr. Thomas B.,	*The Vegetable Proteins.*
Osborne, Chittenden, and others,	*The Proteids of Wheat, etc.*
Scott, Charles and James,	*Vienna Bread.*
Sherman, H. C.,	*The Carbohydrates of Wheat.*
Simmons, Owen,	*The Book of Bread.*
Snyder, Dr. Henry,	*Studies on Bread and Breadmaking.*
Snyder, Dr. Henry,	*Digestibility and Nutritive Value of Bread.*

Stone, W. E.,	*The Carbohydrates of Wheat, other Cereals, and Bread.*
Tollens, Dr. B.,	*Handbuch der Kohlenhydrate.*
Tucker, J. H.,	*Manual of Sugar Chemistry.*
Wanklyn, Professor J. A.,	*Bread Analysis.*
Wells, Robert,	*Bread, Biscuits, Buns, and Cakes.*
Wiley, Dr. H. W.,	*Cereals and Cereal Products.*
Woods and Merrill,	*Digestibility and Nutritive Value of Bread.*

Encyclopædias.—Britannica, Chambers, Harmsworth, and Ure.

Science Progress.—Ethics of Food: Bread, April 1911; Wheat, October 1910.

Also the many trade journals published regularly.

INDEX

ABSORBING power of flours, 115, 204.
Acetic or vinegar acid, 22, 79, 80.
Acidic groups, 6.
Acidity of flours, 117, 195.
Acids, classification, definition and properties of, 22, 79.
Aeration of doughs, 153.
Alcohol a strong poison, 59.
Alcoholic fermentation, theory of, 147-150.
Alcohols, general, 56, 57.
Alkaline carbonates, 11.
—— waters, 18, 20.
Alkalies, general, 11, 22, 26.
Aleurone cells, 97, 98.
Aluminium compounds, 6.
Alums, their detection, 6, 206.
Amides, 89.
Ammonia in the air, 11, 12.
Analysis of cereal foods, 186, 188.
Antiseptics, 22-26, 131, 172-174.
Apatites, 25.
Ash of wheat, 28, 100.
—— the estimation of, 189.
Asparagin, 89, 90.
Atmosphere, 10, 11, 13, 32.
Atomic weights, list of, 5.
Atoms, theory and weight of, 4.
Auto-fermentation of yeast, 150.

BACTERIA, 9, 13, 24, 126-131.
Bakers' oven pyrometers, 32.
Bakery physics, 30.
Baking, effect of, 167.
Barley, 1, 100.
Barms, general, 145, 146.
—— for military sponges, 162.
—— the making of, 146, 147.
Barometers, 32, 33.
Basic lead acetate, 27.
—— salts, 27.

Bibliography, 217-218.
Bicarbonates of lime and magnesia, 17.
—— of soda, 4, 25, 153.
Biology in breadmaking, 8.
Biose sugars, 66-70.
Bisulphites as germicides, 25, 174.
Black of Edinburgh, 11.
Bleaching of grain, 25.
—— plant for, 108, 109.
—— tests, 207.
Bloom of bread, 24.
Blue-bag, 6.
Borax to soften waters, 17.
Boric or boracic acid, 22, 25.
Botany in breadmaking, 8.
Brackish waters, 17, 18.
Bread, composition of, 170.
—— examination, 207.
—— improvers, 29.
—— machinery for, 171.
—— processes, 153, 155.
—— pure and wholesome, 20.
—— the chemical analysis of, 208.
Break rolls, 106.
Breaking up of yeast, 161.
Brewing processes, 58.
Brine, settled, 23.
Brown breads, 169.
Buchner on fermentation, 149.
Burton waters, 17, 19.
Butter, 28, 81.
—— salt, 23.
Butyric acids, 81.
Butyrin, or tributyrin, 28, 85.

CALCAREOUS waters, 18, 19.
Calcium carbonate, 6, 12.
—— phosphate, 29.
—— sulphate or gypsum, 16, 21.
Calorimeters, 30.

Carbohydrates, 55, 59, 61.
Carbohydrate food, 8.
Carbonates of soda, 17, 153.
Carbon dioxide, 4, 5, 11-13, 22, 25, 29, 155.
Caryopsis, 91.
Caustic soda, 26.
Celluloses, 71, 78, 202.
Centigrade thermometer, 31.
Cereals, examination of, 193.
—— as grain producers, 91.
—— their chemical composition, 98, 99.
Cereal starches, 74.
Chemical affinity, 4, 7.
—— analysis of cereals, 194.
—— —— of flour, 205.
—— combination, laws of, 4.
—— composition of air, 10, 12.
—— —— of bread, 170.
—— —— of cereals, 99.
—— —— of water, 14.
—— compound, 3.
—— equation, 4.
—— reactions, 5.
Chemistry, inorganic and organic, 2.
Chili saltpetre, 24.
Citric acid, 83, 84.
Cleaning processes, for wheat, 102-105.
Clinkers, how to avoid, 179.
Colloids, their structure, 76, 114, 125.
Colour of the crumb of bread, 168.
—— of flours, 112, 113, 203.
Combustion of carbon, 12.
Conditioning of wheat, 102.
Conduction of heat, 3, 43.
Conservation of energy and matter, 4.
Convection, 44, 45.
Cooling of bread, 167.
Copper-reducing power of sugars, 64, 65, 199, 214.
Cream of tartar, 4, 28, 153.
—— powders, 25.
Cryptogamia, 9, 126.
Crystalloids, 76.
Cutting back of doughs, 161.

DALTON, Dr. John, 4.
Decay, definition of, 148.

Degree of moisture, 13.
Density, maximum, of water, 15.
—— of steam, 15.
Derbyshire water, 17.
Dextrins, 76, 77.
—— determination of, 196, 197, 200.
Dextrose, 61, 62, 199.
Diastase, 75, 209.
—— pastes, 120, 121, 123.
Diastatic capacity, determination of, 210, 211.
Dough mixer, 164, 171.
Dried milks, and their analysis, 216.
Drinking water, 14.
Droitwich brine baths, 20.
Dryness, action of, on flours, 116.
Dutch yeasts, 144.

EARTH'S crust, weathering of, 28.
Edinburgh water, 20.
Electrical pyrometer, 32.
Electrolytes, action of, 114.
Elements, 3.
—— names of, 4, 5.
Emery, in grinding, 6.
English mineral springs, 20.
Enzymes, or soluble ferments, 88, 125.
—— their detection, 209.
Enzyme theory of fermentation, 148, 149.
Epsom salts and mineral springs, 20.
Esters or compound ethers, 28.
Eumycetes, 126, 130.
Extractive properties of waters, 21.
Extract of malt, uses of, 122.

FAHRENHEIT thermometer, 31, 32.
Fancy breads, 169.
Fats as bread improvers, 86.
—— estimation of, 190-192.
—— general properties, 84, 85.
—— in the germ of cereals, 86, 87.
—— the composition of, 28.
Ferment and dough process, 155, 156.
Fermentation, definition of, 148.
Ferments, 125.